The Bitter End

How to Leave the Undesired Behind and Live the Life You Want
Donnel Delva

ABOUT THE AUTHOR

DONNEL DELVA is a writer, educator, and lifelong student of personal transformation. Born in Bridgeport, Connecticut, he developed a deep passion for self-improvement, devouring hundreds of self-help books in pursuit of wisdom that creates real, lasting change. Now, at just 24 years old, he distills those lessons into clear, actionable insights for others—just as the authors who shaped him still do.

By day, Donnel teaches high school English at a Jesuit college preparatory school, where he challenges students to think critically, express themselves powerfully, and discover their own paths to success. Rooted in the Jesuit ideals of reflection, self-discipline, and lifelong learning, he believes transformation is a continuous journey—one that begins the moment we decide to leave behind what no longer serves us.

Outside the classroom, you'll find him lifting weights, watching anime, or walking in the woods—always reflecting, always refining, always seeking the next level of growth.

His mission is simple: to make self-improvement accessible, practical, and transformative. With *The Bitter End*, he invites readers to step boldly into the lives they've always wanted.

The Bitter End

How to Leave the Undesired Behind and
Live the Life You Want
Donnel Delva

Published by Donnel Delva, Bridgeport, CT
Identifiers: ISBN 979-8-9926388-0-6 (English paperback) | ISBN 979-8-9926388-1-3 (English hardcover) | ISBN 979-8-9926388-4-4 (English ebook) | ISBN 979-8-9926388-2-0 (French paperback) | ISBN 979-8-9926388-3-7 (French hardcover) | ISBN 979-8-9926388-5-1 (French ebook)
Library of Congress Control Number: 2025903051
U.S. Copyright Registration Number: TX 9-479-181

This book is for educational and informational purposes only. While the author has made every effort to ensure accuracy, this book is not a substitute for professional advice. The author and publisher assume no responsibility for errors, omissions, or outcomes resulting from the use of this material. Readers should seek professional guidance where necessary.

Cover Design by Ian Koviak
1st Edition, 2025

Printed in the United States of America.

For Carl Delva,
I told you I'd do it!

For Lemane & Erla Delva,
who told me I'd do it.

CONTENTS

PREFACE

There comes a moment in life when you know something has to change. Maybe you feel stuck, trapped in circumstances that no longer serve you, weighed down by the same old habits, relationships, or mindsets that keep leading to the same disappointing results. You've picked up this book because, deep down, you're ready for that change. You're ready for your own *bitter end*—the moment where you finally say, *enough is enough.*

These moments inevitably show up. They're not here to harm you. They're here to guide you. But I know how they feel—how discomfort can trick you into thinking you're in danger when, in reality, you're standing at the edge of something greater. Discomfort isn't your enemy; it's the signal that you're approaching the unknown, the path beyond what has felt safe yet unfulfilling. And I ask you, *please*—be courageous enough to give this book a chance. Be brave enough to face yourself not with harshness, not with drill-sergeant meanness, but with tenderness and grace. Because that pull you feel, that whisper inside urging you forward, that deep knowing that something *more* is out there? That's you. That's your *God*. That's your inherent goodness inching you forward. And it has brought you here, to this book, to this moment, to see this through.

I've been there too. For a long time, I could feel myself growing, but something was still off. I was making progress in many areas, yet something inside me felt unaligned—like I was moving forward but never fully *in sync* with who I was or who I wanted to be. It was as if I were chasing better habits, smarter choices, and new experiences, but somehow still missing the clarity I needed. I knew there had to be a deeper sense of purpose, a way to live with more intention and meaning—but I couldn't quite figure out how to get there.

I used to feel melancholy so often, like a dull, quiet ache that never left. I used to destroy my mind and body with bad habits, numbing myself as a coping mechanism for the uncertainty of not knowing who I was or who I wanted to be—but being too afraid to commit to anything at all. I wasted time. And nothing—not ambition, not advice, not sheer willpower—could pull me out of it until I *surrendered*. Until I finally, honestly said, *enough is enough.* Until I stopped waiting for life to change on its own and gave these principles a true, honest, long-term chance.

That's when I made a shift. Instead of endlessly searching for answers, I decided to create them. I dove into every principle that had the potential to change my life—not just reading them, but making them part of my daily routine. The more I aligned myself with clear, actionable steps, the more I started to see shifts in my mindset, my habits, and my entire reality.

THE BITTER END

I started small. I was still my melancholy self at first, still doubting, still afraid. But I *tried*. And I *failed*. And I *tried again*. Until, eventually, learning and wisdom came. Until, piece by piece, I built myself up. At first, it was boring. Then, it became interesting. At first, it was lonely. Then, it became fulfilling beyond anything I had ever known. Now, I smile *even during the down times*, instead of ruining everything I've built. Now, I express myself *even when my voice shakes*. Now, I dream, I work, and I *believe*—even when I can't yet see the rewards.

And here's the truth: *you* are the one who will bring out your success. The principles in this book can guide you, but it's your actions, your dedication, and your willingness to change that will transform your life. Right now, you might feel stuck. You might feel weighed down. But that does not mean you aren't already capable. It does not mean you aren't already *equipped* for the life you want. When you succeed with what you learn here, you'll realize that the true power always resided in you.

What I'm sharing with you in this book isn't just theory—it's the exact steps I took to bring my life into focus. These principles helped me transform, and they can do the same for you. But you have to *trust* that they will work. Trust *me*—someone who has been exactly where you are and is now standing on the other side. If you can't trust for your own sake right now, then trust for something bigger than you. Find your *why*, your deeper purpose, your reason to keep moving forward—not just the force that pushes you from behind, but the vision that *pulls* you toward something greater.

Change is possible. True transformation is within your reach. But it doesn't happen by wishing—it happens through grounding yourself in deliberate, practical action. You don't have to stay stuck. You don't have to live a life that feels misaligned with who you are or who you are meant to be. The life you want is waiting for you, and the steps to get there are all here, laid out clearly, with the same love and intention that guided me to where I am today.

And this isn't just for other people. It is for *you*, too. Imagine how you'll feel when you turn the final page of this book, standing at *your* bitter end—not the end of who you are, but the end of the patterns, habits, and mindsets that have kept you from the life you were always meant to live. Imagine how wonderful that will be. Hold onto that truth.

I'll be with you every step of the way.

The shift you're looking for is closer than you think. Let's begin.

Donnel Delva
February 2025

The Bitter End

How to Leave the Undesired Behind and
Live the Life You Want
Donnel Delva

INTRODUCTION

The impression of this book has lived within me long before I set pen to paper. It revealed itself as a desire—a necessity even—rooted in the understanding that the knowledge I have gathered, the experiences I have endured, and the truths I have uncovered must be preserved, shared, and lived. This book is a declaration, a guide, and a testament to the power of transformation. It is not a command, nor a plea, but an offering—one designed to resonate with those who seek to step out of an undesired state and into the life they truly want. This is not theory, but practice. Not distant philosophy, but a reality that, when understood and embodied, can become as natural as breathing.

What you will find in these pages is not just personal insight or philosophical musings—it is grounded in research, studies, and empirical data. Every claim I make is supported by scientific evidence, psychological principles, and social research conducted by experts who have dedicated their lives to understanding human behavior, mindset shifts, and personal transformation. I draw upon psychological, social, emotional, and educational data—not just what has worked for me, but what has been tested, studied, and validated by researchers, interviews, surveys, and case studies. The goal is not just to inspire you, but to equip you with tangible, evidence-based strategies that have been proven to facilitate real, lasting change.

At its core, this book is structured into three sections: Foundation, Transformation, and Preservation. The Foundation is where the journey begins. Without a strong foundation, nothing you attempt to build will last. This is where you confront the fundamental truths about your imagination, discipline, and perception of reality—truths that, if fully embraced, will set the stage for everything that follows. You will learn why belief in your unwavering imagination is not just a comforting notion but a powerful creative force. Every great achievement, every breakthrough, every transformation in history began as an idea—an idea that someone refused to let go of. If you do not believe in your vision, no one else will. But belief alone is not enough. You must also be disciplined—not in a rigid, joyless way, but in the sense that true freedom comes only when you master yourself. Without discipline, your desires remain dreams, your goals remain wishes, and your life remains unchanged. You will also come to understand the world for what it is—a paradoxical dimension where contradictions exist side by side. Most people let this confusion stop them. But you, if you are willing, will learn to move through paradox rather than be paralyzed by it.

From there, we move into Transformation. This is the space where the real work begins, where the pieces of your newfound awareness start to take shape into something undeniable. Here, you will learn how to expand your realm of consciousness, breaking free from the narrow ways of thinking that have kept you trapped. You will come to realize that your thoughts shape your world—so it's time to think bigger, more expansively, more deliberately. Words, too, are not just idle sounds but charmed forces that shape your reality. The words you speak, the language you use to describe yourself, and the beliefs you reinforce all determine what you experience in life. If you do not master your words, they will master you.

But this journey is not just about expanding your mind; it is also about fortifying your spirit. Solitude is strength, and what you do with that solitude determines your power. The people who change the world—who change their own lives—are the ones who have learned to be alone, to sit with their thoughts, to sharpen their will in silence. This section will push you to think for yourself, to stop letting the world dictate your reality, and to recognize that most of what you've been told about who you are and what you can do is a lie. You will also come to understand that you do not have to avoid negative emotions—you simply need to learn how to overcome them. Pain, anger, and doubt are not enemies; they are teachers. If you suppress them, they will fester. If you face them, they will transform you. As you step further into transformation, you will see what was hidden in plain sight all along: the universe is an aiding force, constantly moving in your favor—if you allow it. Once you recognize this, everything changes.

But transformation alone is not enough—it must be maintained, cultivated, and protected. That is where Preservation comes in. This is where you learn to safeguard everything you have built. You will uncover the truth about excuses—how they keep you small, how they rob you of power, and how the moment you stop believing in them, your world opens up. You will learn the art of focusing solely on the desired state, cutting out the distractions, doubts, and outside noise that try to pull you back into mediocrity. And as you grow, you will also understand the delicate balance between flourishing and flaunting—why true success does not need to be broadcast to be real, and why external validation is the weakest foundation you could ever build upon. You will see the power of practicing unintentional asceticism, of simplifying your desires so that what truly matters rises to the surface. And when you reach the final pages of this book, you will not only understand these principles—you will be living them.

But knowledge alone is not enough. Action is everything. That is why at the end of every chapter, you will find a list of concrete actions—practical steps you can take immediately while you are still in the moment, still charged with insight, still ready to move forward. These are not generic tasks; they are specific, deliberate, and designed to produce dramatic results. They will help you take what you have learned and apply it in real-time, ensuring that you are not just reading about transformation, but experiencing it firsthand.

This book is not here to comfort you with empty reassurances. It is here to challenge you, to shake you awake, to hold up a mirror and demand that you take an unflinching look at yourself. If you are ready to laugh, to cry, to wrestle with hard truths, and to be confronted—sometimes even called out—by a friend, a mentor, a guide, then you are ready for what lies ahead. This is not just the beginning of a book;

THE BITTER END

it is the beginning of your own *bitter end*—the end of what no longer serves you, the end of limitations, the end of anything standing between you and the life you were meant to live. If you are truly ready to leave the undesired in the past and step into the version of yourself that has been waiting on the other side, then turn the page.

Your transformation begins now.

PART I: FOUNDATION

1

BELIEVE IN YOUR UNWAVERING IMAGINATION

"Look at the birds of the
air, for they neither sow
nor reap nor gather into
barns; yet your heavenly Father feeds them. Are you not
of more value than they?"
—Matthew 6:26

***

Do you remember how potent your imagination was when you were a child? Whatever happened to that? What has become of your imagination? What has become of you? Consider this: your childhood imagination was once bound-less, shaping entire worlds with ease. Why, then, do you now hesitate to tap into that same power?[1] The answer may lie not in the loss of imagination itself, but in the way we have been conditioned to perceive it over time.

3

Your Imagination Is God—The Creator

In the beginning, you created everything in sight and in mind. It didn't matter if you had not the slightest idea of how anything truly worked; you created, and it was good. Nothing held you back, and no one could tell you otherwise. You were omnipotent—mercilessly deciding the fates of every toy you gave life, every imaginary friend you invented, and any unlucky insect that crossed your path (that poor thing). You were omnipresent—completely and unceasingly aware of the ever-present moment. You had not a care in the world outside of yourself. But somewhere along the way, that effortless creativity was suppressed. Society, education, and external influences taught you to prioritize logic over imagination, reality over possibility. Yet, I'm here, my beloved reader, to tell you that your unwavering imagination still resides in you as the one true God.

Your limitless imagination is God, the Creator. Nothing in this material, third-dimensional world actually exists—or should I say, exists objectively. You might be wondering how this could be possible. After all, isn't reality something we all experience in the same way? But consider this: do you remember the adage, *if a tree falls in the forest and no one is around to hear it, does it make a sound?* The answer is no; it doesn't.[2] That adage, although posed as a question, provides us with an immense understanding of how our imagination works, the methods of its function, and the reasoning behind its purpose.

THE BITTER END

This idea may seem radical, but it aligns with discoveries in both philosophy and quantum mechanics. Human beings possess a shared imaginative consciousness beneath the surface of our egos. The collective human imagination generates the reality we decide to abide by.[3] Our egos receive information from our subconscious imagination and choose what is real and what is fake. So, to return to that fallen tree: if no one is around to hear it, then we should be inclined to believe that the tree hadn't fallen at all. And who even knows if a forest was there to begin with? As far as I'm concerned, everything outside of myself might as well be a simulation if I have not gone out to examine it myself. But of course, that is what Donnel, or the ego-self, believes.

At first glance, this may seem like a purely abstract concept, but in reality, it shapes the way we live every day. We can all imagine a tree falling in a forest and the sound it might produce, but the extent to which we believe that imaginative vision to be true ultimately determines our reality. In other words, what your ego decides to accept as true or false creates your reality.[4] In this way, our mind functions dualistically: as God, the Creator, and as Creation, the Perceiver.

This duality is what allows us to shape our world. Since nothing in this material, third-dimensional world exists objectively, human beings create the world around them based on what they perceive.[5] The world, on the other hand, humbly awaits your perception of it; it needs you to give it life, the same way you did with all your toys and imaginary friends. Without your observation of the world, the world is chaos, void, and without form. It is a grace you give the world by perceiving it, and a grace the world gives back to you as part of your creation. The power to shape your reality, then, is not something external—it is something deeply embedded in your very being.

And this power is limitless. The potential to imagine and create is infinite. The human imagination is composed of the collective subconscious of every human to ever exist.[6] That's right—all that information is stored inside of every person today, just waiting to be tapped into. What's even greater is that the human subconscious is the same subconscious across every brain![7] Our imaginative minds are interconnected as the one true reality—a record of all that happened, is happening, and is to come.

With all that information stored inside each and every one of us, the possibilities to imagine and subsequently create are endless. So how then does one begin to use their imagination to bring about their desired reality? The answer starts with your belief in what is possible for God and yourself (who are one and the same). And once you reclaim that belief, you will begin to see the world—not as it is told to you, but as you truly wish it to be.

You Are What You Believe God Is—And Vice Versa

All things are possible for the God I believe in, and because of that, anything can happen. However, while anything *can* happen, only one thing ultimately does. My God can do all things, meaning every potential reality exists simultaneously. Yet, depending on what my God desires, only one reality comes into being upon the fulfillment of that desired state.

My God knows all possible realities and the paths leading to each one. Every reality calls out for my God's attention, but only the paths my God deems most suitable for me receive that holy, indivisible focus.

I count myself incredibly fortunate to know that all I need to do to gain God's attention *is* desire. Even more fortunate is the fact that I cannot help *but* desire. Everyone desires—constantly—but the nature of those desires is shaped by our perception of both ourselves and God. Studies in psychology suggest that desire is an innate human trait, deeply tied to our self-concept and cognitive biases in how we perceive control and agency over our lives.[8]

You don't need me to tell you that if you were stranded on a deserted island, you would undoubtedly desire rescue. That desire would arise *naturally*. If you doubt this, let's consider an extreme scenario.

Picture yourself stranded on a deserted island with nothing but your dead, sun-stricken phone and an infected wound. There is no vegetation–just you and an expansion of white sand as far as your crusty eyes can see. The only proof that this shithole is an island is the eerie sound of waves crashing into a shoreline you've long given up on finding. To make matters worse, all your clothes have been sacrificed to fuel the fire you use at night, lest you freeze to death. It's a miracle you've survived at all, let alone this long. Truly imagine how it would feel. Feel the agony in your body, the fracturing of your mind, the erosion of your humanity.

Now, in this suffering, imagine your rescuer approaching from a distance. They finally reach you, offering food, water, and safe transport to a renowned hospital filled with compassionate caretakers. You, in your weakened state, lift your head, lock eyes with your savior, and manage to croak out, *"No thanks. I'm all set."* Absurd, right?

After this scenario, the only unrealistic element is the idea that you *wouldn't* desire to be saved. It defies reason. It is safe to say that desiring otherwise would be impossible—unless, of course, you were on the island to endure forty days and forty nights of temptation from the Devil, but that's a story for another time (Matthew 4:1-11).

Again, everyone desires, but our desires are dictated by what we believe God and ourselves to be. In the island scenario (I won't linger on this image too long), if you believed yourself to be a survivor—someone who endures and overcomes—your desire to live would be unwavering. Research on self-efficacy supports this—people who perceive themselves as capable are more likely to persist in difficult situations and maintain a hopeful outlook.[9] Your perception of God would align with your perception of yourself, and you would *feel* God's presence, urging you forward. However, if you saw yourself as a victim of circumstance, your outlook would be bleak. Research in cognitive psychology suggests that our perception of suffering often dictates our sense of agency and can lead to learned helplessness.[10] In that case, you would likely desire death, and your perception of God would be one of wrath, punishment, or abandonment.

Whether you see yourself through an optimistic or pessimistic lens is not God's concern. God focuses holy attention on whatever you focus on and grants exactly what you ask for—promptly and precisely.

What you desire is what you ask for, and what you ask for is what you desire. Many fail to realize that verbal prayer—asking, begging, pleading, compromising, sacrificing—is not necessary for God's attention. Your mind, body, and spirit naturally project your desires. Wherever your energy is most concentrated is the reality that comes to life. Neuroscientific studies on attentional focus support this, showing that what we repeatedly focus on becomes more deeply ingrained in our neural pathways, reinforcing specific behaviors and emotions.[11]

People fail to recognize this because they don't notice where their energy flows. Many profess one thing, seemingly wholeheartedly, but act in opposition. This isn't due to a lack of discipline; it's because their words *and* actions have yet to align with their true *desires*. There is nothing stronger than desire—no amount of words or actions can overpower its force.

If your words and actions align with your desires, you feel balanced—what some call being in a "flow state" or "the zone." Studies on psychological flow state suggest that individuals who are fully engaged in their pursuits experience heightened creativity and fulfillment, reinforcing their actions.[12] All the things they do and say align with what they want. However, if they don't align, you experience instability, as what you truly want is never reflected in what you do or say.

When people feel imbalanced, they often try to force their way back into alignment through sheer willpower. But, my dear reader, I assure you—that is unnecessary. Willpower has its merits, but it carries a fatal flaw: it *requires* an adversary. You may already feel your life is unbalanced, but the worst thing you can do is position yourself as your own enemy. You do not want to be your own foe!

Willpower has limits. You should exercise it when pursuing a desired state, but relying on it alone is insufficient. For instance, if you consider yourself overweight and aim for a healthier lifestyle, depending solely on willpower will be—how do I put this?—brutally difficult. And I don't mean difficult like lifting a heavy weight; I mean difficult as in soul-crushingly exhausting.

Relying exclusively on willpower is ineffective because it makes the undesired state an opponent. In doing so, you *invite* relentless struggle. Not only that, but human nature often takes success for granted once it is achieved, leading to a cycle of balance and imbalance, victory and defeat, over and over again. Who would willingly subject themselves to such torment?

I refuse to trap myself in that cycle. Instead, I consistently achieve my desired states by employing another method: my God-given imagination.[13]

Your Imagination Has Never Forsaken You

Instead of relying solely on willpower to reach your desired state, harness the power of your imagination. I will continue with the previously mentioned weight-loss example to illustrate how your imagination can guarantee the attainment of any desired state far more effectively than willpower alone. But first, it is essential to understand how you should view your imagination.

We all know there are no shortcuts to physical fitness or to achieving whatever we define as a healthy lifestyle. On your journey toward obtaining a healthier, more able-bodied physique, consider your imagination to be your best friend, counselor, and confidant. Your imagination has your best interests at heart and works tirelessly to ensure that you reach your desired state in the most efficient way possible.

Unlike willpower, your imagination does not require an adversary. This point is crucial (so if you've been speed-reading or drifting off, either put this book down now and return when you can focus, or refocus immediately): there is no one you need to compete with—no one at all. I'll say it again: you do not need to compete with anybody.

Many people, myself included, thrive on competition. However, when using your imagination, you are not engaged in competition because you have no adversaries—you are simply creating. Like Thors says in *Vinland Saga*, "No one is your enemy. You have no enemies at all." Remember, your imagination is God, the Creator; you are God, the Creator—not God, the Competitor.[14]

Eliminate any competitive outlook from your mind. A competitive mindset turns everyone, including yourself in your undesired state, into a foe. Seeing the world as your enemy strips you of all favorable opportunities. Operating from this hostile, competitive perspective will only sever your connection with your imagination. This separation occurs because, in a competitive world, you will always perceive time as running out. You will see your resources in the same way, believing that if you do not hurry and outpace the competition, they will attain what you seek first.[15] Furthermore, when separated from your imagination through competition, no amount of success or achievement will be enough to satisfy you in your ego-state. You will eventually take your attainment of the desired state for granted, throwing yourself back into the endless balance-versus-imbalance cycle. This is not what you want, and fortunately, there is a simple way to keep yourself in a creative mindset and in harmonious union with your imagination.

The simplest way to maintain this creative mindset and perfect union with your imagination is by instilling in yourself an everlasting sense of gratitude. I was once asked, *"Donnel, how are you like this?"* My response: "Deep inside me lies this perpetual feeling to throw both my hands up in the air and scream at the top of my lungs: THANK YOU, GOD!" Let's face it—you have everything to be grateful for. Regardless of how much you *dislike* your current state, the ability to desire any state *at all* is a grace beyond reason. Consider this: we, as humans, have the extraordinary capacity to desire things beyond the reasonable limits of what we observe in the material world.[16] The truest essence of grace, blessing, or gift lies in its undeserved nature. No matter how unfortunate you may feel, you have *already* been given the gift of desire and can obtain anything you want as long as you remain grateful. You owe it to your best friend, counselor, and confidant—your imagination—to be thankful not only for its presence but for its unwavering dedication to you. You will not find this level of commitment anywhere in the material world, so do not take it for granted!

THE BITTER END

How It All Works

If it hasn't been clear how your imagination can bring about any desired state, let's break it down further.

Your imagination exists in another dimension and must make its way into this one—must! Not sometimes, not when it feels up to it, and certainly not after your season three binge of *New Girl*. Whatever your imagination creates in that other dimension needs to manifest itself in this third-dimensional world. This is not a possibility; it is an inevitability, governed by the fundamental principles of perception and materialization.[17]

Your desire must manifest in this third-dimensional plane because it already exists in the dimension you've perceived it in—your imagination. However, while in that realm, your desired state exists without form and remains void without you. You live in this third dimension, separate from your desired state, which means both you and your desire must find each other.

You align with and realize your desired state when you become a vibrational match to it. In other words, you don't necessarily get what you desire just because you want it. You get what you desire when you embody and mirror the version of yourself that already has it. This principle is widely supported by research on the law of attraction and neuroplasticity, which suggests that mental rehearsal and embodied cognition play a role in shaping real-world outcomes.[18] Just as your desired state must make its way to you after being perceived, you must make your way to it—*must!*

13

You become a vibrational match to your desired state simply by being the person who would naturally possess that lifestyle. Since all it takes to attract a desired state is embodying the identity that aligns with it, that state can ultimately manifest for anyone who matches its frequency.

But just because you've perceived and imagined your desired state does not mean it will automatically be yours. The divine human imagination is not exclusive to any one person; rather, it is the collective subconscious of every human who has ever existed.[19] This is why future generations live lifestyles that their ancestors only dreamed of—our collective imagination continually evolves, shaping reality as new perceptions emerge. The desired state must transition from the other dimension into this third dimension, but it has no obligation to the person who first perceived it. It belongs only to the one who will give it the godly attention it needs to exist.

If that person is you—if you have fully embodied who you need to be to attract your desired state—then, and only then, does it become your reality.

Do not fall into the egotistical trap of believing you must now compete with others desiring the same lifestyle as you. Remember, creation is not competition. Desired states exist in abundance—in formless, chaotic abundance. They do not belong to anyone until they are claimed, nor do they have limited supply. They crave nothing more than to be perceived by *you*, the Creator, and given life.[20] Their desire to manifest is so strong that they will materialize for *anyone* who successfully attracts them.

THE BITTER END

So, the final question remains: How exactly will you use your imagination to attract your desired state? And more importantly—who will you become?

Immediate Action Steps

1. Revisit Childhood Creativity: Spend 10 minutes recalling a time when your imagination was boundless. What did you create? How did it feel? Write it down.

2. Challenge Perception vs. Reality: For one day, consciously question everything you assume to be real. Ask yourself: *"Do I believe this because I've experienced it, or because I was told to?"*

3. Daily Visualization Practice: Each morning, close your eyes for five minutes and visualize a world created entirely by you. See it vividly, immerse yourself in it, and feel its reality.

4. Write Your Own "God" Statement: Define what you believe God (or the ultimate creative force) to be. Then, rewrite it, substituting "God" with "I am." Read this daily.

5. Affirm: "I Am the Creator": Repeat this affirmation aloud every morning and night: *"I am the creator of my reality. What I imagine, I bring into existence."*

6. Observe Where Your Attention Goes: Carry a small notebook and track what you focus on throughout the day. Are you imagining your ideal reality or reinforcing limitations? Adjust accordingly.

7. Experiment with Reality Shifting: Before bed, vividly

imagine a desired experience as if it's happening now. Fall asleep in that state, believing it's real.

8. Flip Negative Thoughts into Creation Opportunities: Each time you catch yourself thinking, *"That's just how things are,"* stop and ask, *"What if it weren't?"* Then imagine an alternative reality.

9. Engage in Play: Spend at least 15 minutes a day doing something playful—storytelling, sketching, world-building, or pretending. Feel the joy of unrestricted imagination.

10. Decide What You Want and Own It: Write down one reality you deeply desire. Declare it as already true. Every time doubt creeps in, return to this declaration.

2

You Must Be Disciplined

"But let your 'Yes' be 'Yes,'
and your 'No,' 'No.' For whatever is more than these
is from the evil one."
—Matthew 5:37

***

Be honest with yourself, my beloved reader—when was the last time you accomplished something by using a haphazard, hurried, or desperate approach? Have you ever realized the full potential of your goals without a regimented and structured method? Do you believe you have the discipline to commit, persist, and persevere until you obtain your desires?

Understand The True Cost Of Your Desired State

In *Principles*, Ray Dalio shares his insight on the true costs of a successful business. He explains that most efforts worth completing excellently require one and a half times the original estimated cost and approximately one and a half times longer to achieve than initially anticipated—therefore, planning accordingly is crucial.[1]

Dalio hit the nail right on the head, but his insight is only the tip of the iceberg.

Most efforts worth completing excellently require one and a half times the original estimated *version of yourself*. This shouldn't come as a surprise since you literally want to augment your existence. Before you embark on achieving your ambitious dreams in this reality, contemplate the true costs of your desired lifestyle—not just the money and time but also the values, virtues, character dispositions, and attitudes you need to cultivate.[2] If you want to multiply yourself one and a half-fold, two-fold, three-fold, etc., then your psychological, emotional, and spiritual energy must likewise multiply.[3] There is no way around this fact; it is the linchpin and starting point of all endeavors.

Truly grasp what is required of yourself internally and what is needed from you to become the person reflective of your highest ideals so you don't end up sabotaging yourself or setting yourself up for inevitable failure.[4]

Oftentimes, people misunderstand what is required of themselves internally and falsely pursue their external desires without first knowing who they need to become before obtaining them.[5] I believe people misunderstand this because they fear becoming the person who possesses the mindsets, virtues, character dispositions, and attitudes without yet having the external desire in hand. To them, not seeing their external desire means they're a failure, a fraud, stupid, crazy, or unworthy—all of which are untrue and farthest from reality. This is likely an indication that they have yet to truly cultivate their highest ideals within themselves. When they should be rejoicing for having established their highest ideals and happily awaiting their desire, they bemoan and complain, ultimately sullying their blessings. These types of disheartened people live in the external—and as I will discuss in later chapters, those who live in the external endanger the most people.[6]

Before moving on, I'll discuss one simple example that demonstrates the right approach to understanding the true cost of your desires.

Let's say you routinely sleep in late, and it's now beginning to negatively impact uncompromisable areas of your life. As a result, you would like to wake up earlier in the morning to start your day. How would you go about changing your lifestyle?

What most people may say is: *"Easy—start going to sleep earlier so I can wake up earlier."* Wrong. That sort of thinking is a fallacy. To get to the *root* of the issue and truly understand the cost of your desire, you need to first ask yourself: *What exactly have I been* valuing *this whole time by sleeping in?* Identifying the value you've been operating by will reveal to you the type of person you currently are. This process will sound something like: *I've been valuing ease and comfort this whole time; therefore, I am lazy and weak.*

After identifying the person you are based on the values you've been operating by, the next step is to ask yourself: *What exactly is required of me psychologically, emotionally, and spiritually to obtain my desired lifestyle?* Again, your focus should be internal. The question is not *"What do I need to do to obtain my desired lifestyle?"* because what you do reflects the values, virtues, character dispositions, and attitudes you possess. The answer to this question will sound something like: *I need to value restoration and productivity while also feeling both happiness about resting and producing and disdain for all activities that impede my restoration and productivity. Finally, I need to believe that the greatest version of myself, the one who calls for the adherence to my highest ideals, will deliver me to the promised land. By doing so, I am caring and generative.*

Finally, after identifying your highest ideal, ask yourself a simple yes-or-no question: *Can I actually do it? Is it within my range of abilities to cultivate a new, healthy value in place of a toxic one?* If the answer is *no*, then close my book right now because, honestly, the remaining pages will only make you feel worse. (And it's not my place or passion to kick you while you're down.) If the answer is *yes*, then congratulations—the hard part is underway.

What I ultimately want you to remember when understanding the true cost of your desired state is this: it all boils down to *sacrifice*. Most people hear *sacrifice* and think, *But I want my cake and to eat it too!* To those in the market of meeting their dreams in this third-dimensional world, sacrifice is nothing more than currency—energy—an exchange. The same way your car needs gas and electricity or your cake needs flour and eggs is the same way your desired state requires you to vibrate at the same frequency as it—and to vibrate invariably.[7]

How You Do Anything Is How You Do Everything

During the 2023 NBA Playoffs, my friends tried to lure me into placing parlays on the games. Their coaxing was never ill-intentioned—on the contrary, they genuinely wanted me to share in their success. They had been winning parlays with a one-to-thirty return and were eager for me to partake in their spoils. Time and again, they sent me screenshots of their winnings, boasting hundreds of dollars in profit while risking only a fraction of that amount.

Each time they asked if I'd join them, my response remained unwavering: *"I don't gamble with my life—so why would I gamble now?"* The way you approach anything reflects the way you approach everything.

My decision to abstain from sports betting came naturally, shaped by my mindset, virtues, character, and attitudes. However, maintaining my stance was far more challenging. Each time I refused, my friends countered with the same phrase: *"I guess—but scared money don't make no money."* I laughed it off, allowing them the last word, but internally, I struggled against the temptation. As Howard Marks explains in *The Most Important Thing*, it is immensely difficult to resist the psychological impulse to buy into an overvalued stock, particularly when others appear to be making easy money.[8] Similarly, the Bible captures this struggle poignantly: "You have not yet resisted to bloodshed, striving against sin" (Hebrews 12:4).

It was clear that I would not compromise my values for the fleeting gains of sports betting, but my friends weren't entirely wrong—I was, in fact, afraid. However, what I feared was crucial. While they saw my reluctance as a fear of financial loss, I knew the real danger was losing touch with my desired state—the person I needed to be to sustain the life I envisioned.

Since you cannot serve two masters, if a lower way of life sabotages a higher one, you must abandon the lower. Before developing my mindset, virtues, character, and attitudes, I struggled to let my 'Yes' be 'Yes' and my 'No' be 'No.' The slightest temptation could sway me, much like the aroma of a freshly baked pie leading me to indulgence. I believed my problem stemmed from weak willpower combined with an insatiable appetite. I thought if I simply resisted hard enough, I could escape my undesired state. However, as I later realized, that belief was flawed.

All my assumptions about willpower, appetite, and resistance had been shaped by the same mindset that kept me bound to my lesser self. That very mindset led me to believe I could desire the nectar dripping from every luscious pie while also maintaining the discipline required for a higher way of life. As Albert Einstein wisely noted, "We cannot solve our problems with the same thinking we used to create th em."[9] My approach had to shift—but to what? That question lingered until, finally, the root of my struggles became clear. The solution I discovered proved invaluable, serving as a guiding principle in manifesting my desired state.

THE BITTER END

Don't Do Instant Gratification—Chip Away

On April 24, 2023, I participated (more accurately: idly watched on my phone from an Adirondack chair with brief moments of self-affirmation and self-admittance) in an over six-hour-long YouTube livestream hosted by Matthew Mc-Conaughey titled *The Art of Livin'*. In his livestream, he discussed his book *Greenlights* and welcomed guest speakers to share their wisdom with millions of viewers. Among these guest speakers was the dazzlingly charming Marie Forleo. She introduced me to a brilliantly simple concept that, when coupled with my readily edifying values, exponentially accelerated the trajectory of my inner growth. Her insight fortified the answer to my aforementioned question.

Marie recommended that those seeking to break from old habits and patterns that no longer serve their desired states should adopt the phrase: *"I don't do ____ (fill in the blank with something no longer serving you)."* To illustrate how she put this belief-busting phrase into practice, she shared the following anecdote:

One day, she returned home from a tiring day of being the remarkable go-getter she is and looked at her couch. Similar to the effect a hot and ready pie cooling on a windowsill has on me, the couch beckoned her for a well-deserved break. However, a voice in her head reminded her that she couldn't afford a break—she was a remarkable go-getter with a packed schedule. So, she pushed herself a bit more. Subsequently, she began to feel overwhelmed, and her mind became restless. Within the hurricane of overthinking, Marie finally heard the voice in the eye of the storm. It told her simply: *"Hey—I don't do overwhelm."* And just like that, the storm subsided entirely. With those simple words, Marie was free again and in her flow state.[10]

I invite you now, my beloved reader, to adopt Marie's words—the words that fortified my mental pivot—and say aloud to yourself: *I don't do____*. The word you choose to fill in the blank represents more than just a withered branch thrown into the fire; it creates your new belief, one that energizes and gives life to your mission statement. This mission statement will bring joy, authority, and account-ability into your life, much like ordering your favorite steak, eggs, or coffee brings a smile, a swagger, and a level of satisfaction—so take pride in it in a similar fashion.

The solution to the root of my problems found new life with a simple phrase: *I don't do instant gratification!* I chip away, chip away, and chip away some more until I see the end result—not the budding result after a few attempts into my project, but the ripe result bearing magnificently succulent fruit at the proper end of the harvest. Don't fool yourself into thinking that operating within the realm of delayed gratification requires significantly more willpow-er than instant gratification to resist the urge to quit, which, by the way, arises whenever starting a new pro-ject. What you need to truly understand is this: rejecting instant gratification stems from a wholehearted espousal of your new mindset, virtues, character dispositions, and attitudes. Only through this new line of thinking can re-jecting instant gratification adequately align with who you are.[11]

THE BITTER END

You shouldn't need to utilize your willpower merely to exist—surely, you don't exert willpower to breathe, blink, or make your heart beat. These functions occur unconsciously. When adopting a value of delayed gratification, your mindset, virtues, character dispositions, and attitudes should sound like the following:

- You should have a state of mind that thinks: *I don't do instant gratification; I do delayed gratification, which means I follow through with all tasks (with everything) to completion.*

- You should cultivate the virtues of patience, perseverance, and faith; since you are patient, persevering, and faithful, you will express yourself with phrases like: *I have no trouble waiting nor failing because I know that in keeping with my efforts, I will inevitably complete my goal and obtain my desired state.*

- You should possess the character dispositions of conscientiousness, integrity, and optimism; since you are conscientious, integral, and optimistic, you will express yourself with phrases like: *I will perform the necessary steps in obtaining my desired state and will not jeopardize nor sully the path of attainment by cutting corners or allowing shortcomings because I believe unselfish action indubitably yields exceptional completion.*

- Lastly, you should maintain a positive, unwavering, and grateful attitude; combining these attitudes will result in you expressing yourself with phrases like: *Isn't it wonderful?—the long-winded and methodical journey, full of bumps, crooks, and crannies, all leading me to my*

27

I'll end this section with a closing remark on rejecting instant gratification and preferring delayed gratification: If you don't practice delayed gratification for any other reason, do it simply because others *aren't*. In the words of Warren Buffett, "The less prudence with which others conduct their affairs, the greater the prudence with which we should conduct our own affairs."[12] In this generation, millions—if not billions—of people scroll for hours on social media, chasing the dopamine release that comes from being instantly gratified by the flick of their thumbs and the taps of their fingers. If you've followed me along in this chapter, then it shouldn't surprise you when I say that I deleted all social media in December 2020. More specifically, I deleted Facebook, Instagram (*insta*, as in *instant*, being literally in the name), Snapchat, and Twitter from all my devices but kept the accounts active so I could enjoy the convenience of signing into games like *Clash of Clans*—again, not shocking to see a game like this on the phone of someone as patient, faithful, conscientious, optimistic, and unwavering as me—through my social media logins.[13] The benefits I experienced after deleting them have been unequivocal—I'll say more on this in a later chapter.

Although I haven't met even one percent of the worldwide web's users, let alone the world's population, I can most assuredly guarantee that the person who practices delayed gratification will always outpace the person addicted to instant gratification—without fail. The reason I feel so confident in this fact is simple: the latter quits, while the former doesn't. I don't care whether you quit one percent into a task or ninety-nine percent into a task—if you quit, you get zero results. In other words, you only obtain results *after* you've completed the task, one hundred percent. Those who practice delayed gratification master the skill of completing tasks, while those who chase instant gratification *only* get a fleeting dopamine release. As a result, when those two archetypes compete, the victor is always the person prepared for the long haul. Additionally, the ability to persevere will almost always place someone in a leadership position because others can depend on them to stay committed to yielding results. With a significant percentage of the world scrolling their lives away, you owe it to yourself to practice a skill that some will perish for never having attempted.

Get Skilled At The Way It Should Be Done

One mistake I've found common among people starting new endeavors is their willingness to forgo the methods their goals demand and instead proceed in "their way."

Before I elaborate, don't get me wrong—I skin a cat far differently than the next girl, but that's because there are many ways to do it. However, people mistakenly approach uncompromisable ambitions "their way," often at the expense of high-quality results. I'm all for autonomy if your strategy produces victories, but if your life strategy results in consistent defeats—and you still feel good about yourself because at least you lost in "your way"—then you need to reconcile with the source of your overcompensation. If you find it hunky-dory to squander your personal legend time and time again, then be fucking for real. The reason you constantly fail while doing things "your way" is because you don't actually want to succeed. You are afraid. I have no idea why, but admit it, because that's the first step in overcoming your fear.[14]

This mistake—stubbornly doing things "your way" at the expense of success—rears its ugly head in everyday activities. I hope that presenting this concept through an analogy will shed light on how to get good at the way your ambitions demand.

Imagine you walk into a pizzeria with your covetously sexy lover. You get seated, the pizzeria serves bread, and you order a couple of drinks (preferably a Malibu Bay Breeze). Between your delightfully tipsy conversation, your server charms their way into getting your order. You order one large margherita pizza and another round of drinks. Your server promptly returns with the drinks and later brings what looks to be a heap of spaghetti topped with marinara and basil. Confused, you politely ask the server if there's been a mistake, because you did not order spaghetti—you ordered a margherita pizza. Your server apologizes profusely, takes the spaghetti away, and brings you some complimentary drinks as atonement.

Later, the server returns with another steaming plate—of spaghetti topped with marinara and basil. At this point, the alcohol and hunger start speaking for themselves, and you yell at the server to stop playing games and bring you your pizza, or else. Terribly sorry, the server removes the spaghetti and provides yet another round of drinks as atonement. Finally, the server returns, seemingly confident that the dish in hand will more than satisfy you both. However, from where you sit, drunk and hungry, you see only another pile of spaghetti topped with marinara and basil. That is the last straw. You and your lover stand up and barge into the kitchen, demanding to speak to the chef responsible. The chef presents themselves and asks what the matter is. You explain that you ordered a margherita pizza, yet thrice the server returned with spaghetti. The chef, blissfully calm, smiles like the Buddha and explains that the pizza erred not—that was simply "the way" they do it.

The chef elaborates on how their superior version of pizza came to be: they say that ever since they began cooking, they never understood why people pounded and contorted the flour until it became flat when they could pound and contort it "their way," so it becomes cord-like and cylindrical. The chef assures you both that their method has always resulted in happily fed customers. Enraged by this response, you scream at the chef, exclaiming that their so-called pizza is actually spaghetti and that they should pound the flour until it's flat, then spread the marinara on top, and finally place the basil. You watch as a lightbulb goes off in the chef's head. With a wink, the chef tells you that they can absolutely cook up a burrito—"their way." (You both face-fault.)

You can apply this silly example to nearly any activity, and it illustrates how people sacrifice proper results for "their way" of doing things. Like the chef, people often believe that "their way" not only improves the results but also question why others follow the conventional method. To reiterate my stance on autonomy, I believe that unconventional results require unconventional actions. If you want to be exceptional, then you must be the exception to conventional methods. However, if your unconventional method—your life strategy—consistently fails instead of prevails, then it will serve you immensely to get good at, master, and excel in the conventional method—the way it should be done.

Because let's face it—that's the way that actually yields high-quality results.[15] If I sought to build superior hammers but believed it would improve them to replace the head with that of a pickaxe, and while I'm at it, improve the handle by making it bigger to fit the new head, then I wouldn't be making superior hammers; I'd be making mediocre picks. Now, when someone goes to use my "hammer" to nail something in, they cannot. I fail to obtain the intended result and disserve everyone depending on me due to my hubris and overcompensation.[16]

A Jack Of All Trades Is An Ace In None

In *Walden*, Henry David Thoreau writes, "Our life is frittered away by detail. Simplify, simplify, simplify! I say, let your affairs be as two or three, and not a hundred or a thousand; instead of a million count half a dozen, and keep your accounts on your thumb-nail."[17]

We live in a world where phrases like "the more, the merrier" govern our decision-making. Stores like Costco, Sam's Club, and BJ's sell lifetime supplies of ingredients per portion. With this mindset embedded in the collective consciousness, it's no wonder that maintaining discipline and focusing on a single craft has become increasingly difficult. While having more may be beneficial when it comes to serving and blessing others, I argue that "the more, the miserable" applies when it comes to mastering necessary skills.

It takes a staggering amount of self-mastery to persevere in one discipline. Consider the earlier analogy about the chef. Now, imagine if the conditions were even more extreme—so much so that the chef, instead of serving spaghetti, served hammers, thinking it would be doubly beneficial to be both a chef and a blacksmith. This absurdity highlights an essential truth: when excellence is required (and you should always strive for excellence in what you do), less is more. By "less," I mean focusing on, mastering, and perfecting one skill or craft at a time. By "more," I mean achieving high-quality results. In other words, focusing deeply on one discipline yields superior outcomes.

It's true that some skills translate well across disciplines, but disciplines themselves do not always lend themselves to every skill. For example, strong listening skills might make someone both a good musician and a good therapist, as both require a deep ability to interpret and respond to sound and meaning.[18] However, being a good listener does not necessarily translate into being a good painter, since painting relies more on visual observation than auditory perception. Similarly, a skilled observer—someone who excels at noticing details—would thrive as a painter or a film critic, but that same observational prowess wouldn't necessarily make them a good musician, since they lack the auditory training essential to that craft.[19]

The level of self-mastery required to succeed in a single discipline can be bewildering because it forces people to confront their simultaneous strengths and limitations. Many believe that mastery of one skill equates to expertise in all crafts, which is an understandable misconception given the common saying, "The way you do anything is the way you do everything." However, what people truly develop through mastery is a refined *method*—a disciplined approach that *may* transfer across fields requiring similar skill sets, but not necessarily the skill itself.[20] Returning to the earlier examples, the way a skilled listener or skilled observer hones their craft may be applicable in multiple areas, but the core skill remains confined to its relevant domain.

Because of this, it's far more effective to master two or three skills—or better yet, become the leading authority in one—so that you can successfully apply it to something you love, whether that be a profession, hobby, or sport.[21] Avoid "spraying and praying" at all costs. Mastery is not about doing everything—it's about doing what matters most with precision.

Pragmatism Before Pointlessness

On my journey toward my desired state, I occasionally asked myself: *What's the point?* At this stage of the book, I took a rather lengthy pause to genuinely seek an answer—one that would console both you, my beloved reader, and myself. After a period of discernment, I arrived at a conclusion: this is precisely the point—pragmatism before pointlessness. Allow me to explain.

Pragmatism is an approach to dealing with situations sensibly and realistically, grounded in practical rather than theoretical considerations. Pragmatic individuals are often

characterized as stoic, rational, and emotionally intellig
ent.[22] On the other hand, pointlessness denotes a state
of having no purpose or feeling that an action is not
worth doing. Those who experience pointlessness often
describe their lives or work as frivolous, fruitless, ineffective, or empty.[23]

When I began to view my life through the lens of
pragmatism, I regained my confidence and momentum by
prioritizing it over pointlessness. What I mean by "before"
is this: I learned to place my emotional energy and godly
attention on pragmatism, especially during extended projects, positioning it *in front of* pointlessness.[24] Think of "before" as in "standing before your greatest version of yourself." This perspective became my mantra during difficult
periods: pragmatism in the presence of pointlessness.

When you place pragmatism before pointlessness,
the latter submits—it yields until it completely subsides.
Pointlessness often brings with it a sense of hopelessness
because the effort being exerted does not immediately
seem to bear fruit. But I ask you this: Is it that what you
are doing will not bear fruit, or is it simply that it will not
bear fruit *right now*? I argue that the issue lies within the
latter.[25]

Pointlessness typically arises in the midst of an endeavor
when gratification is delayed. If rewards were immediate,
pointlessness would not exist because you would instantly
feel fulfilled.[26] However, when you are diligently working
toward your vision, shaping it into reality, and pointlessness
begins to creep in as that whisper of doubt—*what's the point?*—I
urge you to counter it. Throw your hands in the air and pro-

claim, *"THANK YOU, GOD,"* at the top of your lungs. Reclaim the power of purpose and drown out the voice of doubt.

Placing pragmatism before pointlessness requires emotional intelligence.[27] Do not fall into the misconception that pragmatic individuals, because they are often described as stoic, lack emotions. That is incorrect. They, like everyone else, experience a full range of emotions. However, they have cultivated emotional mastery, integrating it into their emotional intelligence and ultimately achieving self-mastery.[28]

Consider yourself fortunate to experience and overcome pointlessness on your journey toward your desired state. By doing so, you are not only progressing toward your goal but also proving yourself worthy of it, aligning vibrationally with it.[29] Because, let's be honest—the greatest version of yourself has already mastered self-discipline. To become that version of yourself, you must embody their actions, mindset, and demeanor. Walk and talk like your highest self, and soon enough, you will have become that person.

Pointlessness will inevitably appear on your journey—perfect, just the signal you have been waiting for, because now you know you are on the right track. I once heard a phrase, though I cannot recall where: *Avoid dirtying something you are about to clean.* This phrase encapsulates the process of overcoming pointlessness. When doubt arises, do not compound the problem by worsening your mindset. Instead, elevate yourself by refining your thoughts and emotions. Only after mastering yourself can you truly master any discipline.

Quitting Before Results Yields No Results

THE BITTER END

I have to give all the credit for my discovery of this concept to Hooman Mardox, my mentor and founder of "Zero to App Academy," a hands-on app-building program that provides the priceless framework for building profitable apps from scratch. He's truly a marvel in my eyes, offering a step-by-step approach and wise guidance not only for seamless app development but also by serving as a beacon for a lifestyle that can change the way you see the world in an instant.

While attending Hooman's Academy, he shared an insight that has significantly enhanced the way I execute my projects: *"If you quit anywhere on your path before obtaining results, then you get zero results."*

As my mind does, it synthesized this information with my left brain while my right brain paraphrased it into a saying that resonates more with my own words: *It doesn't matter if you quit one percent into the project or ninety-nine percent into the project—if you quit, then you don't get results.*

I liken this concept to the Greek tragedy of Orpheus. If you're unfamiliar with the story, I'll give a brief overview as described by Bernard Evslin.

Orpheus' wife, Eurydice, died, and Orpheus ventured into the Underworld to retrieve her from Hades. Hades made a deal with him, saying:

> "You may have your wife. She will be given into your care, and you will conduct her yourself from Tartarus to the upper light. But if during your journey, you look back once, only once—if for any reason whatsoever you turn your eyes from

where you are headed and look back toward
where you were—then my leniency is revoked,
and Eurydice will be taken from you again, and
forever. Go..."

Bernard Evslin

So, Orpheus headed for the exit with Eurydice following
just steps behind him. Despite the doubts brewing from
not seeing her the whole time, he made it to the exit. Yet,
tragically, doubt stirred a frenzy in his mind, and he decided
to check if she was really there—to confirm that Hades had
not tricked him. And so, finally:

"Swiftly he turned, and looked back. She was
there. It was she. He reached his hand to take
her and draw her out into the light—but the
hand turned to smoke. The arm turned to
smoke. The body became mist, a spout of mist.
And the face melted. The last to go was the
mouth with its smile of welcome. Then it melted.
The bright vapor blew away in the fresh current
of air that blew through the crevasse from the
upper world."[30]

Bernard Evslin

Orpheus' heartbreaking tragedy mirrors the fate of
many quitters. These quitters are Orpheus; their desired
states, Eurydice; their opportunity to succeed, Hades' deal;
their failure, looking back. Like too many others, Orpheus
quit on his commitment to push forward without hesita-

tion—right at the cusp of success, ninety-nine percent into his journey. What does he have to show for journeying into the Underworld as a mortal?

Nothing.

No results.

Zero.

You have the opportunity, my beloved reader, to learn from Orpheus' mistake right now. Whether you're one percent into your journey and doubt has already crept in, or one percent away from nirvana, I beseech you and cheer you on: DO NOT LOOK BACK! YOU GOT THIS! PUSH FORWARD! You can be the hero—Orpheus, champion to his wife and all the world—for having resurrected her from the clutches of Hades' Underworld, making endless love, playing everlasting, chanting music. *You can.*

Moreover, as Hooman taught, when you finish through to success, you reprogram your subconscious mind, body, and spirit to complete tasks to desirable results. Remember: how you do anything is how you do everything. If you always complete the tasks that you begin—whether big or small—then you always finish and obtain results.

Lastly, allow me to rephrase this concept in hopes of clarifying anything puzzling: You only obtain results *after* completion. Briefly imagine a world where you never finish what you start: You reach for a drink of water from your bottle and leave the top half unscrewed; you open your laptop to write and leave it ajar; you lift your hat to your head and let it drop to the floor. What would you have to show for this type of life? Extreme thirst, a dusty keyboard, an uncovered head.

Though these three images serve as minor examples, they offer profound symbolic insights. How parched has your lack of discipline left you? What in your life has shriveled up and turned to dust because of your shortcomings? How many birds have to poop on your head for you to realize that you can only become your greatest version when you take responsibility for your self-mastery? Success—obtaining your desired state—all starts within the regimented system within yourself. Cultivating your system will bless all aspects of your life far beyond your grandest imagination. Fulfillment only takes discipline.

Immediate Action Steps

1. Audit Your Desired State: Write down your biggest life goal. List everything you believe it will cost you—not just time and money, but also the values, virtues, habits, and mindset shifts you will need to adopt.

2. Identify the Internal Cost of Change: Think about one major habit you want to change. Instead of focusing on what to *do*, ask yourself: *What have I been valuing by keeping this habit?* Identify the internal shift required—what new values, virtues, and attitudes must replace the old ones?

3. Define Your Personal Standard: Create your own "I don't do ___" statement for a habit or mindset that no longer serves you. Say it out loud. Write it down. Repeat it daily.

4. Adopt the "Chip Away" Mindset: Pick one goal you've been putting off because it feels overwhelming. Break it down into daily, bite-sized tasks. Commit to "chipping away" every day, even if only for 5 minutes.

5. Align Your Decisions With Your Identity: Each time you're faced with a choice, ask: *Does this decision reflect the person I am becoming?* If the answer is no, adjust your decision accordingly.

6. Journal Your Transformation: Track your progress

with a daily or weekly reflection: What did you do today that aligned with your new values? Where did you struggle, and what did you learn from it?

3

WE LIVE IN THE PARADOX DIMENSION

"For whoever desires to save
his life will lose it, but whoever loses his life for My sake
will find it." —Matthew 16:25

***

Have you ever stopped to notice–not just noticing in passing, but sincerely examined–the abnormalities in this world, in this dimension? How many of them do you brush off time and time again, and how many do you blindly accept?

There Are Infinite Paradoxical Truths

One day, I did something unusual and took a walk down a neighboring street. The walk was aimless. There was no particular distance I aimed to reach, nor any pace I needed to keep. I only knew there was a persistent sense of unease within me, a problem I couldn't quite define, and I felt that a clear-minded walk might reveal its nature. I was used to walking through Lake Mohegan, a beautiful nature spot I love, where I often meditated on obtaining my desired states. But this time was different. I didn't want to focus on my desired state—I wanted to identify the source of the unease. It was like catching the lingering scent of someone I had forgotten; the moment their fragrance returned, I felt compelled to stop everything and remember who they were, wishing desperately that I could follow that scent back to them.

So too was my desire to walk down this neighboring road—to find the unacknowledged issue within myself that left such a potent imprint.

Turning off my phone, I walked forward. At the time, I was in college and struggling—struggling to maintain a long-distance relationship, struggling to balance sobriety with constant intoxication, and struggling with my sense of purpose in the vast cosmos. I wanted to change the world, to leave a lasting impact. Yet, despite all my ambition, I remained in my undesired state. *How can I still be in my undesired state?* I thought. *How could I still be unhappy while I have a girlfriend?*

THE BITTER END

How come all the weed I smoke doesn't make me feel better? What's my purpose here on this planet? Why am I here?

Before I knew it, I had walked two miles. Right in front of a nursing home—a building I had never noticed despite having driven down this road countless times—I was struck by an overwhelming feeling of unconditional love. Amidst my hurricane of overthinking, I finally heard the voice within the eye of the storm. It stopped me in my tracks and whispered: *You're not going to change the world—you've already changed it. Be who you want to be, and you'll be free.* In that instant, I burst into tears—the dam within me had finally burst. (Looking back now, I wonder if passersby thought I was grieving outside of a nursing home.)

The realization made perfect sense. I wasn't *going* to change the world because the world was *already* changing—with or without me. As Ray Dalio put it, "The only thing consistent is change."[1] The pressure I had placed upon myself, the weight of an imagined obligation to *transform* the world, was lifted. In that moment, I was free. I understood, synchronously, the nature of paradoxical truths—truths that define this dimension. Because I had no *preordained* purpose on this planet, I was entitled to nothing. And that, paradoxically, meant I was free to choose anything. The feeling of entitlement had been the root of my unease—this false belief that I was *supposed* to change the world had trapped me in a cycle of inevitable disappointment. I had shackled myself to an impossible expectation, and the weight of constantly falling short had been crushing me. But now, I saw the truth clearly:

Strength does not come from the things we carry, but from the things we let go.

With this newfound understanding, I walked back home—renewed, alive, and free. And as my mind synthesized this revelation, it illuminated countless other paradoxical truths.

I often turn to Mother Nature as my guide in uncovering hidden truths. Through her, I have realized how abnormal this dimension is—or perhaps, how *perfectly* normal it is. Consider the food chain: worms eat leaves, birds eat worms, and in some places (such as the nightmarish land of Australia), spiders eat birds.[2] *How unfair*, I used to think, *that every living creature clings to life only to inevitably be consumed by another*. But then I questioned myself: *Is it really unfair?* People lament that life is unfair—but if life is unfair for *everyone*, does that not make it *fair*? If the sea is rough for all who sail, then are we not all in the same boat?

People place too much emphasis on external differences—status, wealth, power—believing that some have an advantage over others. But to me, it doesn't matter if someone sails on a yacht while another sails on a raft; the ocean can overturn them both in an instant. It is the nature of this dimension: the more you grasp at control, the more you lose it. Just as plant life thrives when pruned, or hair grows back thicker when cut, so too does strength emerge through surrender.[3] Gentlemen, if you want a thick beard—trim it. Ladies, if you don't—then leave it alone. Again, the paradox reveals itself.

I liken this paradox to the story of the man from Song, as described by Mengzi in *The Essential Mengzi*:

"One must work at it, but do not aim at it directly. Let the heart not forget, but do not help it grow. Do not be like the man from Song. Among the people of the state of Song, there was one who, concerned lest his grain not grow, pulled on it. Wearily, he returned home and said to his family, 'Today I am worn out. I helped the grain to grow.' His son rushed out and looked at it. The grain was withered. Those in the world who do not help the grain to grow are few. Those who abandon it, thinking it will not help, are those who do not weed their grain. Those who help it grow are those who pull on the grain. Not only does this not help, but it even harms it."[4]

Mengzi

My Friend, too, spoke of this paradox in *John 15:2* and *Matthew 20:16*, respectively:

"Every branch in Me that does not bear fruit He takes away; and every branch that bears fruit He prunes, that it may bear more fruit."
"So the last will be first, and the first last. For many are called, but few chosen."

Both my Friend and Mengzi understood the counterintuitive nature of this world. And I, too, would come to understand it—not through intellect, but through experience. That experience? Learning how to swim.

The Power Of Surrender

While growing up, my parents decreed that all water activities were forbidden; as a result, no one in my family swims. Being the fearless and limitless son, I took it upon myself to learn. First, I walked into the ocean from shore and waited to see if any instincts would kick in. They didn't. I failed miserably and almost drowned.

So, I tried a different approach: I asked my friend if I could practice in her pool to get down some basics. She agreed, and I was over more times than I felt was appropriate—about a week's worth—before heading off to be a camp counselor at a sleepaway camp on Shelter Island, NY. There, all counselors and campers were required to pass a swim test. Despite my lack of ability, I waded out into the ocean and, embarrassingly, found myself rescued by lifeguards. That experience surely bruised my confidence, but as the coolest counselor there, I used it to teach my campers—especially those who had also failed—that even the "cool kids" stumble sometimes. And that's nothing to be ashamed of. My time as a counselor marked my last attempt at swimming; that was the summer of 2021.

But being resilient, I tried again in 2023. This time, I approached it differently. I returned to the ocean with a fresh perspective, one that integrated my active nature with my passive nature. As I was thrashing, kicking, and trying too hard, I remembered the wisdom of Mengzi and my Friend:

Don't help it grow; prune it.[5] So, against all the fear in my body, I took a deep breath, submitted, and went limp. To my astonishment, I floated—face down, my arms and legs spread like a starfish. *Progress*, I thought.

Seeing that I could float—that I would, in fact, not sink and be dragged to the depths by some lurking octopus—shifted my mindset. If I could float, something I had once believed impossible, then I *would* swim. Research suggests that overcoming fear through visualization and belief rewires the brain's neurocircuitry, reinforcing confidence and ability.[6] So, like a man addicted to the ocean, I drove ten minutes to the shore every day, parked on a side street to avoid paying for beach parking like a fool, and walked an additional fifteen minutes with a book and towel in hand, thinking: *Today's the day I do it.*

Every day, I got better. Every day, I challenged myself and took more risks. Eventually, I could float on my stomach, doggie paddle, and perform a submerged breaststroke. But I was stagnant. I was afraid to tread water, afraid to float on my back. And as a result, I stopped practicing. Life took over, and before long, I got a tattoo, which kept me out of the water for some time. But I never gave up on my desire to swim.

Months later, I became an English teacher in the Jesuit tradition at Fairfield Prep, my alma mater. With my goal still alive, I bought a membership to the campus recreational complex and resumed my practice in their pool.

On my first day, I took the second lane—since an old man was effortlessly lapping back and forth in the first—and reviewed everything I had learned. After about thirty minutes of repetition, a thought struck me with the stern authority of a coach: *How important do you think floating on your back is for swimming?* Without hesitation, I answered myself: *I suppose as important as letters are to books.* With that, all fear fled. If floating on my back was fundamental, then why was I wasting time avoiding it?

I took the deepest breath, threw my head back, spread my limbs like a starfish, and went limp. The sensation was terrifying. I felt waterboarded, felt hot blood rushing to my head. But I refused to move. *This time, I need to. I won't leave until I'm swimming.*

I stayed. And I *floated*. The same grace that keeps ducks and swans peacefully adrift had finally come to me, like a mother cradling her newborn. Studies show that individuals with a growth mindset are more likely to persist in challenges, believing their abilities can develop through effort.[7] If the pool's water level had been measured that day, it would have risen with the tears that slid down my face as I lay staring at the giant ceiling fan above. When I closed my eyes, I felt *everywhere*—suspended in a void, infinite, untethered. I took another deep breath, pushed off the water slightly, closed my hands to my thighs, and kicked. At last, I, Donnel Delva, had learned to swim.

Beaming, I caught the attention of the old man in the first lane. Finally pausing his water marathon, he told me he had some tips. I warmly accepted. In time, he taught me to tread, improved my breaststroke, and then uttered the words I had been waiting to hear: *It all stems from floating. As long as you can float, all the strokes become mere expressions. Why, one could walk on this if only he filled his whole body with that buoyancy.*

THE BITTER END

I didn't care if he saw me cry at that point—he wouldn't be able to tell anyway. As he climbed out of the water, I noticed something unbelievable. *The old man had one leg!* When I asked about it, he lightheartedly said that the other had been amputated, as simple as that, without elaborating. I didn't pry. I thanked him profusely, and he smiled. The last thing he said before exiting the deck was: *If an old amputee like me can swim, then I wish I could be there for when a tall, strong boy like yourself starts lapping. Even if I can't go for a walk, I can always go for a swim—that's something no one can take away from you.*

As he gathered his crutches and left, I couldn't help but think how much he resembled a merman with his one leg in the water. He was a mythical creature, no doubt.

And so, I learned to swim—not by force, but by surrender. Research on cognitive biases explains that we often overcomplicate learning by resisting natural adaptation, which delays progress.[8] Once again, the paradoxical nature of this dimension revealed itself to me. Surrender had been my key to mastery. Studies on self-efficacy emphasize that belief in one's ability directly influences performance and success.[9] By using the nature of this reality to my benefit, I had transformed. And so can you, my beloved reader.

In the following sections, I will draw direct inspiration from *The Kybalion* to explore the Seven Hermetic Principles laid out by Hermes Trismegistus, the ancient scribe of the gods. His insights further prove the paradoxical nature of this dimension, and by understanding them, you can wield reality itself for your transformative growth.[10] Additionally, research on perception and belief suggests that our expectations shape our experiences, reinforcing the power of imagination.[11]

Mentalism

The first of the Seven Hermetic Principles is the Principle of Mentalism. It states, "THE ALL IS MIND; The Universe is Mental."

> "This Principle embodies the truth that 'All is Mind.' It explains that THE ALL (which is the Substantial Reality underlying all the outward manifestations and appearances which we know under the terms of 'The Material Universe'; the 'Phenomena of Life'; 'Matter'; 'Energy'; and, in short, all that is apparent to our material senses) is SPIRIT which in itself is UNKNOWABLE and UNDEFINABLE, but which may be considered and thought of as A UNIVERSAL, INFINITE, LIVING MIND."[12]
>
> Three Initiates

I'd like to draw your godly attention to the paradoxical implications of this first principle. Recall in *How It All Works* when I said, "Your imagination exists in some other dimension and must make its way to this dimension." (I have to admit—it feels pretty neat quoting myself.) With the First Hermetic Principle in mind (pun intended), my explanation of how your imagined desired states manifest on this third-dimensional plane reveals the paradoxical nature of reality.

All joking aside, think of "THE ALL" as your imagination itself. You can never fully know or define your own imagination—just as you can't imagine imagination itself. However, it's something you evidently do automatically. Why? Because, as I said before, your imagination is God; it is THE ALL. The paradox lies in the fact that while you cannot truly *know* your imagination (God, THE ALL), you can still inquire about it, contemplate it, and, as described in *You Are What You Believe God Is—And Vice Versa*, ascribe to it an identity that empowers you to become the person you'd like to be in your desired state.

Philosophers and mystics alike have explored this paradox for centuries. Carl Jung's work on the collective unconscious suggests that the mind is not an isolated entity but rather interconnected with all human experience, shaping and being shaped by archetypes and symbols beyond conscious understanding.[13] Similarly, quantum physicists have found that observation plays a role in determining reality, implying a deep connection between consciousness and material existence.[14]

By ascribing a new identity to THE ALL, you essentially become familiar with—or, in other words, "know"—an unknowable, undefinable entity. This aligns with Neville Goddard's teachings on imagination as the creative force behind reality[15] and Joe Dispenza's research on neuroplasticity, which shows how mental focus can reshape neural pathways to align with desired outcomes.[16]

By engaging with THE ALL through this reductionist approach (the only approach our human brains can ever hope to process), you can now utilize this new understanding to uplift, motivate, and ultimately take the necessary actions to *indubitably* obtain your desired state. This process mirrors ancient Hermetic teachings on mental transmutation—the idea that by shifting one's perception of reality, one can transform their external experience.[17]

Correspondence

The second of the Seven Hermetic Principles is the Principle of Correspondence. It states, "As above, so below; as below, so above."

> "This Principle embodies the truth that there is always a Correspondence between the laws and phenomena of the various planes of Being and Life ... And the grasping of this Principle gives one the means of solving many a dark paradox and hidden secret of Nature. There are planes beyond our knowing, but when we apply the Principle of Correspondence to them, we are able to understand much that would otherwise be unknowable to us. This Principle is of universal application and manifestation on the various planes of the material, mental, and spiritual universe—it is a Universal Law."[18]
>
> Three Initiates

This second principle connects the paradoxical nature of this dimension with the other dimensions where our desired states are nurtured. Recall in *Understand The True Cost Of Your Desired State* when I said, "Identify the value you've been operating by and that will reveal to you the type of person you currently are." Like this principle states, there is a direct connection between how you think mentally, feel spiritually, and act materially.

Modern psychology supports this principle through the concept of embodied cognition—the idea that our thoughts, emotions, and bodily states are deeply intertwined and influence each other.[19] Neurological studies also suggest that the way we think affects our emotional regulation and physical actions, reinforcing the interdependent relationship between mind, body, and soul.[20]

Our minds, bodies, and souls are interconnected and interdependent. Each one shapes and guides the other. This interrelation is seen in research on neuroplasticity, where changing one's thoughts can lead to measurable changes in brain function, ultimately influencing emotions and behavior.[21]

Through the understanding of this principle, you can use its paradoxical nature to improve your life—moving from an undesired state to a desired state. This is done by immersing yourself in the mindset of the person you wish to become. By focusing on who you would be upon obtaining your desired state, aligning your emotions to feel as if you have already attained it, and acting in ways that reflect this highest version of yourself, you align your internal and external realities. Studies on the placebo effect show that belief alone can produce physiological changes, further emphasizing the power of aligning thoughts and emotions with desired out comes.[22]

Ancient philosophical traditions and modern psychological frameworks alike emphasize the significance of aligning thoughts, emotions, and actions. This principle is reflected in cognitive-behavioral therapy, which operates on the premise that changing thought patterns leads to changes in emotional and behavioral responses.[23] By understanding and applying this principle, you gain the ability to reshape your life and bring forth your ideal reality.

Vibration

The third of the Seven Hermetic Principles is the Principle of Vibration. It states that, "Nothing rests; everything moves; everything vibrates."

> "This Principle explains that the differences between different manifestations of Matter, Energy, Mind, and even Spirit, result largely from varying rates of Vibration. From THE ALL, which is Pure Spirit, down to the grossest form of Matter, all is in vibration—the higher the vibration, the higher the position in the scale."[24]
>
> Three Initiates

While this third principle may seem straightforward at first, it is essential to understanding and utilizing the paradoxical nature of this dimension for our benefit. Science

by perception, and our ability to shift from one state to another lies in our consciousness of that transition.[33]

Like I said in *Your Imagination Is God—The Creator*, "nothing in this material, third-dimensional world exists objectively." Studies in quantum mechanics have supported this claim, suggesting that reality exists in a state of potentiality until observed, at which point it collapses into a definitive state.[34] As a result, "cold" and "hot" exist as identicals but differ in degree after your subjective observation.

The same idea applies to your undesired and desired states. Both are states of being; however, once you judge which one you'd rather be in, you can adjust the degrees of that state to match your values, mindsets, and character dispositions. Psychologists studying cognitive reframing emphasize that shifting one's perception of circumstances—rather than the circumstances themselves—can lead to radical personal transformation.[35] By recognizing that opposite states are part of the same continuum, you reclaim control over your reality. You recognize that you aren't just treading down a new path—you're already on the path—it's just that you're a bit far from where you want to be positioned.

Rhythm

The fifth principle, the Principle of Rhythm, is by far my favorite of the seven. It states that:

"Everything flows, out and in; everything has its tides; all things rise and fall; the pendulum-swing manifests in everything; the measure of the swing to the right is the measure of the swing to the left; rhythm compensates."[36]

Three Initiates

I love this principle because it provides the necessary escape from one end of the pendulum to the next, allowing us to remain in our desired states. Since everything has its natural ebbs and flows, it is universal that we unconsciously swing between undesired and desired states. However, just because the pendulum swings does not mean you must go with it.

Consider this: I'm certain you have experienced the thrill of a happy moment, only to be followed by the sorrow of a sad one, and vice versa. What often happens during these sad moments is that people allow them to erase the effects of their previous happiness, effectively resetting their progress. This tendency is comparable to the myth of Sisyphus, condemned to push a boulder up a hill, only to watch it roll back down.[37] But unlike Sisyphus, we are not doomed to this cycle.

It is possible to maintain the effects of happy moments even through periods of sadness. Imagine symbolically placing a stopper beneath the boulder—something that prevents it from rolling all the way back down when difficulties arise. This mental "stopper" allows you to fully experience sadness in a healthy way without undoing the joy that preceded it. Research on emotional resilience suggests that individuals who acknowledge and process negative emotions without suppressing them are better equipped to sustain overall well-being and happiness.[38]

Then, as the pendulum swings back toward positive moments and the metaphorical moon begins to wax, you can resume pushing your boulder forward, building upon rather than erasing your progress. This principle aligns with psychological studies on emotional set points, which indicate that people can develop strategies to maintain their baseline happiness despite fluctuations in external circumstances.[39] Learning to work with the Principle of Rhythm, rather than against it, is essential for sustaining long-term success in any pursuit, whether personal, professional, or spiritual.

Cause And Effect

The sixth principle is the Principle of Cause and Effect. It states that:

> "Every Cause has its Effect; every Effect has its Cause; everything happens according to Law; Chance is but a name for Law not recognized; there are many planes of causation, but nothing escapes the Law."[40]

> Three Initiates

Like the third principle, this sixth principle also seems straightforward at first. However, upon deeper reflection, it provides the understanding needed to utilize the paradoxical nature of this dimension for our benefit. It should be clear that every cause has an effect and every effect has

a cause, as everything that occurs results in some consequence, and every one of those consequences stems from
some prior occurrence. This fundamental law aligns with
the philosophical and scientific understanding of causality,
which has been extensively explored in metaphysics and
physics.[41]

When it comes to obtaining our desired state, however,
the causes and effects may not always be so clear. Recall how
one must prune plants to help them grow and, conversely, how pulling sprouts prematurely can wither them. Both
actions yield effects that may initially seem counterintuitive.
This paradoxical relationship mirrors the psychological principle of delayed gratification—where short-term sacrifices
lead to long-term gains, a concept supported by studies in
behavioral science.[42]

As a result, to achieve our desired effect, we must first
understand the paradoxical nature of this dimension and
subsequently perform the correct cause. Oftentimes, the
correct cause may not be what we originally assume. Psychological research suggests that human cognition is prone
to biases, often leading us to misjudge the relationship between cause and effect.[43] This phenomenon was explored
by philosophers such as David Hume, who questioned the
nature of causation and whether it is something we perceive
or simply infer from repeated observations.[44] Similarly, Immanuel Kant argued that causality is an essential framework
through which humans understand the world.[45] Therefore,
it is crucial to practice discernment before acting.

Gender

THE BITTER END

Last but not least, the seventh principle is the Principle of Gender. It states:

> "Gender is in everything; everything has its Masculine and Feminine Principles; Gender manifests on all planes."[46]
>
> Three Initiates

I find this principle to be the most creative. Annihilate the idea that gender pertains only to social constructs! That sort of thinking is base and restrictive—not to mention instituted for mass manipulation and indoctrination.[47] This principle provides liberation from imposed constructs and constraints, allowing those who understand its significance to shape both themselves and their external reality.

A misunderstanding of this principle has given rise to toxic masculinity and toxic femininity, which stem from a rejection of the balancing and stimulating aspects of their gender equivalent.[48] I find that this deeper concept of gender often perplexes those who rigidly identify with only one polarity. They foolishly believe that integrating aspects of the opposite gender—be it femininity within masculinity or masculinity within femininity—somehow diminishes their identity. This belief could not be further from the truth.

In reality, embracing both principles leads to balance and creativity. Just as nature thrives through the interplay of opposing forces—light and dark, hot and cold, expansion and contraction—so too does the human spirit flourish when it harmonizes both masculine and feminine energies.[49] The idea that balance fosters growth is not new; ancient spiritual traditions, from Taoism's Yin and Yang to Hermetic teachings, have long emphasized the necessity of dual forces working in tandem.[50]

This paradoxical concept may seem counterintuitive, but it reflects the very fabric of existence. Just as procreation requires the union of masculine and feminine forces in the physical world, so too does the creative process in every realm—mental, emotional, and spiritual.[51] By acknowledging and integrating both principles within, one gains access to a fuller range of expression, insight, and power. It is through this balance that true creation occurs.

It Doesn't Need To Be Logical To Be True

I'll close this chapter with a belief of mine that has allowed me to flourish within my desired state after overcoming my undesired state: it doesn't have to be logical for it to be true.

If I haven't made it clear by now, our dimension is composed of paradoxes. It is also composed of people. As a result, people themselves are paradoxical in nature.

Among the people I've met, interacted with, and observed, there exists a pattern so consistent that I believe it to be universal: most, if not all, act on emotion but conceal their emotional motivations within a Russian nesting doll of logic. I do not believe humans are rational by nature, as we are woven into the very fabric of this paradoxical dimension. Our surface-level logical reasoning often follows "if-then" statements, the foundation of laws and governance. However, infinite hypothetical instances casually break these supposedly strict guidelines—so much so that these so-called outliers become conventional and even expected (consider how people drive in the U.S. or how U.S. courts acquit criminals who, by all logical accounts, should be convicted).[52] These inconsistencies arise due to our emotional nature and the paradoxical universality of human behavior. By accepting our emotional nature and the paradoxical reality we inhabit, we can better harness our inherent strengths to obtain our desired states.

I have found that people fail to accept their emotional nature for two primary reasons. First, logic has been heralded as an objective, infallible approach to solving life's problems and making decisions, with proponents boasting that logical reasoning removes emotional "barriers." Second, emotions have been socially constructed as a sign of weakness.[53] Both of these assumptions could not be further from the truth.

Just think, my beloved reader, about all the times you followed the logical or mandated course of action, only to feel terrible afterward. Conversely, recall moments when you defied logic or convention and felt deeply satisfied by doing so. Now, reflect on what was true in those moments. Many assume that logic is synonymous with truth, while illogic equates to falsehood. However, as I've walked us through in this chapter, this dimension consists of infinite seemingly illogical phenomena that serve as unwaveringly true laws and principles.

The essence of the seemingly illogical and paradoxical principles governing this dimension is truth—and that is what matters most. There is nothing weak about our emotions. In fact, embracing our emotional nature is one of the most liberating and empowering things we can do for personal growth and overall well-being.[54] Those who sacrifice their emotions in pursuit of pure logic dangerously deceive themselves. Not only does perfect logical reasoning not exist, but its pursuit can create a toxic detachment that fosters emotional insensitivity, neglect, and, most dangerously, self-deception.[55]

Ultimately, there is nothing inherently true about logic if it does not align with our emotional and paradoxical nature as beings within a paradoxical dimension. Our intuition and imagination tell us why we can know something simply by feeling its essence. These faculties—often mistaken for weaknesses—are in fact our greatest tools for achieving our desired states.[56]

Immediate Action Steps

1. Reflect on the Paradoxes in Your Life: Take five minutes today to reflect on the paradoxes in your life. Identify situations where apparent contradictions coexist. For example, think about areas where striving hard has led to burnout or disappointment, and where surrender or letting go might bring freedom. Write these down and consider how they might be reframed.

2. Practice Non-Action: In moments of stress or overwhelming thoughts, choose one task to consciously "not help grow." Let it be something small, like stepping back from a relationship issue or taking a break from an urgent work deadline. Observe how this "pruning" impacts your inner state—does it bring clarity or relief?

3. Commit to a Daily Mindfulness Practice: Implement mindfulness to cultivate awareness of the paradoxes you experience daily. Each time you encounter a situation that feels "unfair" or "imbalanced," pause for a moment. Reframe the situation: *"If this is true for all, how is it fair?"* See what insights arise when you recognize the paradox within it.

4. Engage with the Power of Surrender: Choose one area of your life where you feel stuck. Think of a paradox you've noticed in this situation—perhaps

the more you push, the more resistance you feel. Take one action today that embodies the opposite of your usual approach: let go, surrender, or shift your perspective. Track the results, and notice how it affects your progress.

5. Practice Visualization and Rewiring Your Brain: Reflect on a fear or challenge you've been avoiding. Visualize yourself overcoming this fear. Imagine the steps, the victory, and the emotions you'll feel when you overcome it. Write down the visualization steps, and repeat this exercise daily to reinforce confidence.

6. Integrate Mind, Body, and Soul: Choose one practice each day that engages your mind, body, and soul. For example, meditate (mind), do a light workout (body), and connect with nature or journal (soul). Notice how each influences the others.

7. Embrace Imperfection: Identify one area where you've been avoiding something due to fear or past failure. Set a small, achievable goal for yourself, and remind yourself that it's okay to stumble. Celebrate every small victory along the way.

4

EXPAND YOUR REALM OF CONSCIOUSNESS

"But seek first the kingdom
of God and His righteous-
ness, and all these things
shall be added to you."
—Matthew 6:33

***

Have you ever wondered why some people seem to thrive no matter their circumstances while others remain stuck, despite endless efforts? What separates those who transform their lives from those who stay in cycles of dissatisfaction? The answer lies not in external conditions but in the expansion of one's internal consciousness.

Internal Vs External

For the duration of my life, my mother has had a severe case of schizophrenia. I have watched her cycle on and off psychiatric medication that caused painful side effects, check in and out of hospitals for months at a time, and, most gravely, lose complete touch with reality, forming new, distorted perceptions of the world. As a child, around three in the morning, she would sit my younger brother and me on the couch while she shouted back at the voices in her head, ensuring we'd be there in case the threats in her mind attempted to kill her. I'd sit there, dazed and confused, across from her, with my younger brother slumped over asleep on my shoulder until the sun came up. I'd listen for hours to this woman, so lost in her own reality, and try desperately to make sense of her experience, to connect any sort of dots. When I thought I had found a pattern of understanding, I would offer my consultation—always met with extreme paranoia and a prompt order to sit silent and listen, lest I become one of her phantoms.

Days became weeks; weeks, months; and before I knew it, I had sat with my yelling mother and sleeping brother for the entirety of my childhood. It became routine. Only as I grew older did I befriend the power of *internal versus external*—and only now, looking back with more developed insight, can I say that I truly understand my dear, troubled mother.

What I learned from living with my mother is this: the realm of the internal is *your* jurisdiction, your sovereign domain, whereas the realm of the external is beyond your control.[1] It's a cliché (and acknowledging that it's a cliché is also a cliché) that life isn't about what happens to you but about how you react to it. Though often repeated, it remains true. You do not control the events of this dimension, but you *do* control your reactions, outlooks, and attitudes.[2] More importantly, by changing your reactions, outlooks, and attitudes—*i.e., expanding your realm of consciousness*—you can transform not only your circumstances but also the world around you.[3]

So, how do you expand your realm of consciousness? I've distilled the answer into a simple principle: *if you can see it with your eyes or touch it with your hands, it won't make you happy.* (I got this insight from a friend who heard it from a minister online, but it remains valuable nonetheless.) Recall from *Don't Do Instant Gratification—Chip Away* how I said, *"What you need to truly understand is this: not doing instant gratification stems from the wholehearted espousal of your new mindset, virtues, character dispositions, and attitudes."* The same holds true for expanding your realm of consciousness. The way you expand your consciousness determines, over time, what brings you fulfillment. Most people stuck in undesired states gravitate toward instant gratification, whereas those striving toward their desired states practice cultivating their inner world, knowing that external pleasures only provide fleeting relief from misery.[4]

So, why does this approach work? Because, my beloved reader, if you have no enemies within, the enemies outside cannot harm you. (Like my previous insight, I borrowed this one too—this time, from an African proverb. Ironic how many of my insights originate externally, isn't it?) By overcoming limiting beliefs, you unlock dormant energy already within you. All you had to do was get those energy pools on your side instead of letting them oppose you. Your realm of consciousness expands when you recognize the limiting beliefs that keep you trapped in your undesired state and actively work to dismantle them.[5] Only when your mind, body, and soul operate in harmony can you truly expand your consciousness.

So, what do you gain from being aware of your internal energy and expanding your inner citadel? Quite simply: everything you've ever wanted. Where your attention goes, your energy flows. Once you focus entirely on your internal domain, opportunities and solutions—through people, places, and experiences—will naturally present themselves. Of course, they were always there, but now you have expanded what you're conscious of, what you *perceive*. At this stage, as long as you remain willing and imaginative enough to manifest your desired state, you can prevail.[6]

In closing, count yourself among the luckiest to know that all you need to focus your attention, energy, and efforts on is your *internal world*. Can you even imagine the debilitating overwhelm that would come from trying to decide where to drop the rain or when to send the wind? I'm sure you've completely freaked out before over which ice cream flavor to choose, where to park at the supermarket, or whether to send that risky *"You up?"* text at 2 a.m. Each of these dilemmas belongs to the *external*, the uncontrollable. There is nothing you nor I can do to change the external except by first changing the internal—our sole sovereign domain. So, throw your hands up and shout, *"THANK YOU, GOD!"* for the simple grace of having to manage only the realm of the internal. When you master the internal, your external world transforms accordingly. The doors that were always present—but previously beyond your awareness—will begin to open effortlessly, as if by magic.[7]

Interpret Parables As Your Autobiography

I originally stumbled upon this concept while reading Neville Goddard's mystical book, *Infinite Potential*.[8] In this transformational work, he explained that every parable in the Bible is, in essence, your own self-autobiography. Neville hit the nail on the head, but I'd like to push the envelope even further.

All parables, whether religious or secular, serve as your autobiography. Neville explains that by interpreting parables this way, you become all of the characters. In other words, every figure in a parable represents an aspect of yourself acting in relation to another aspect of yourself. The tribulations, victories, and lessons experienced by these characters become opportunities to learn about yourself.[9] Additionally, Neville highlights how, through a self-autobiographical interpretation of parables, we can learn to perceive parables and stories mystically. As a result, we become mystics—people who believe in the spiritual apprehension of truths that transcend logic (recall my insights from *It Doesn't Need To Be Logical To Be True*). After realizing that all parables were reflections of my own life, every text I read became a key to unlocking the doors barring me from my desired state.[10]

Nearly every parable I encountered after internalizing Neville's insights transformed my thinking and propelled me toward my greatest version of myself. Two parables, in particular, have served me tremendously: the Parable of the Wheat and the Tares from the Bible and the Parable of the Ox and the Sheep from Mengzi.

In *Matthew 13:24-30*, my Friend put forth this parable:

> "The kingdom of heaven is like a man who sowed good seed in his field; but while men slept, his enemy came and sowed tares among the wheat and went his way. But when the grain had sprouted and produced a crop, then the tares also appeared. So the servants of the owner came and said to him, 'Sir, did you not sow good seed in your field? How then does it have tares?' He said to them, 'An enemy has done this.' The servants said to him, 'Do you want us then to go and gather them up?' But he said, 'No, lest while you gather up the tares you also uproot the wheat with them. Let both grow together until the harvest, and at the time of harvest I will say to the reapers, 'First gather together the tares and bind them in bundles to burn them, but gather the wheat into my barn.'"

At face value, this parable describes how, despite the tares growing among the wheat, the owner allows both to grow to avoid harming the wheat. However, he plans to eventually gather the tares for burning and the wheat for his barn. When read mystically, this parable transforms into an autobiographical lesson, illuminating our personal journey toward our desired states.

First, in this framework, you are all the characters, each representing different aspects of yourself. The parable, then, translates to this: You have planted a good seed—an idea or goal—in your mind. As you toil toward this goal, you notice negative habits or self-doubt creeping in. You consider eliminating these bad habits but hesitate, fearing that doing so might disrupt your progress. Consequently, you persist toward your goal, carrying both good and bad habits. Finally, once you achieve your desired state, you separate and remove the negative habits, while reinforcing the positive traits that helped you succeed.[11] (I shed tears at the simplicity of this story—I pray that those who previously couldn't hear, hear now.)

In *The Essential Mengzi*, the philosopher presents the following parable:

> "While the king was sitting up in his hall, an ox was led past below. The king saw it and said, 'Where is the ox going?' Hu He replied, 'We are about to ritually anoint a bell with its blood.' The king said, 'Spare it. I cannot bear its frightened appearance, like an innocent going to the execution ground.' Hu He replied, 'So should we dispense with the anointing of the bell?' The king said, 'How can that be dispensed with? Exchange it for a sheep.'"[12]
>
> Mengzi

On the surface, this parable describes a king who orders a sacrificial ox to be replaced with a sheep because he cannot bear to witness the ox's terror. But when read mystically, this too becomes a reflection of the self.

Again, you are all the characters, representing different aspects of your internal world. The parable then translates as follows: You recognize a harmful habit that you are about to eliminate because it no longer serves your desired state. However, you also acknowledge the pleasure or comfort this bad habit provides and find yourself reluctant to give it up. As a result, instead of eliminating the core habit, you opt to remove a smaller, less significant bad habit in its place.[13] (Again, the sheer simplicity of these Teachers is remarkable—I pray that those who previously couldn't see, see now.)

All parables—whether religiously affiliated or not—function in the same manner as the ones we have just examined. Most people fail to recognize this because they have yet to expand their realm of consciousness. However, broadening your awareness multiplies your world a hundredfold! Take these parables as mere examples. Perhaps moments ago, they seemed esoteric. Yet, with just a slight expansion of our consciousness, an extension of our awareness, and an increase in our attention, we have uncovered profound insights beneath their lines.

Now, imagine the treasure troves that lie all around you—hidden within texts, experiences, and encounters—waiting to be unearthed by those who know they exist.[14]

THE BITTER END

Ascribe Proper Intent

When my mother experienced her bewildering schizo-phrenic delusions, she always made it a point to say that certain experiences were happening *to* her. The voices she heard emanated not from the chemical and neurological imbalances in her brain but from the vents, the off televisions, and the neighboring rooms. Moreover, she believed so deeply in her perceived reality that she rationalized reasons why the voices chose to bother her. *They're doing this to me because of my husband! They won't leave me alone because I'm an immigrant and it's easy to pick on me. They make me suffer for decades because I can't explain to the doctors what's going on!* Needless to say, my dear mother ascribed the wrong intent when confronting her demons. Studies on schizophrenia and auditory hallucinations confirm that individuals experiencing these delusions often externalize their symptoms, attributing them to outside forces rather than neurobiological origins.[15]

People often say that we shouldn't ascribe intent at all, but let's face it—we always do. Ascribing intent refers to taking something someone says or does and applying meaning to it based on *your* perception rather than their actual intentions. In other words, you assume (and you know what happens when you and I assume, donkey). As a result, most people attempt to avoid ascribing intent altogether, believing that it is better not to assume anything. Practicing this kind of thinking typically sounds like this: someone bumps into you while looking down at their phone and doesn't apologize; you think, "...." That's right, you have no thoughts about it one way or another. Zero. None. ... As if! Your magical brain

77

simply won't allow it—heck, neither will your base instincts. Cognitive psychology suggests that our brains are wired to attribute cause and intent, an evolutionary trait designed to assess threats and social dynamics.[16] You didn't negate all assumptions when you opened this book; you assumed it would open and not burst into flames or tears from your cruel grip. The same principle applies to everything else. So instead of trying to suppress all active or intrusive thoughts, manage them. Regulate them so that *you* become the master of your holy perception—and ultimately, your desired state.

Rather than ascribing improper intent and assuming the worst, or numbing our minds to ascribe no intent at all and hopelessly guessing at life, we should instead *ascribe proper intent*. This means coming to a conclusion that is as close to the truth as possible. To paraphrase Ray Dalio, the person who can discern what is closest to reality will profit the most.[17] I'd hate to oversimplify this because, don't get me wrong, it's very difficult. It's almost impossible to discern exactly why someone said or did something. However, there are ways to get closer to the truth.

First, you can always *ask*. This is obviously more difficult with strangers, but for friends and acquaintances, I highly suggest it. Asking removes all guesswork and assumptions. If they're honest, asking creates a clear dialogue. In the example of someone bumping into you without apologizing, you might ask, *Hey, did you notice you bumped into me?*—giving them a chance to clarify their intent rather than leaving it up to your imagination.

Next, if asking is not an option, then here's how you can ascribe proper intent: scan *yourself* for reasons why you reacted the way *you* did. Turn the lens inward. Remember, we cannot control externals; we can only govern our internal realm. If someone bumps into you without apologizing, don't ask yourself, *What made them do that?* Rather, ask yourself, *Why was I so offended?* Psychological studies on emotional regulation emphasize that our reactions are deeply influenced by our internal states and unresolved emotions, often more than external stimuli themselves.[18] *What dormant seeds were just watered and sprouted as a bad reaction? How can I improve so that someone's aimless bump on the shoulder doesn't send me into a rage?* Taking responsibility for all that happens in your life balances your perception of what is happening *to* you versus what is happening *as* you. This shift in perception is not only empowering but has been linked to improved mental well-being and resilience.[19]

Slow Down

To close this chapter, allow me to emphasize the importance of slowing down. You already know that this world operates paradoxically. As an unsurprising result, the more you slow down, the more you speed up. Moreover, slowing down serves as a catalyst for expanding your realm of consciousness and ultimately obtaining your desired state, as you will perceive the world more completely, neither overlooking nor rushing through anything. Research in cognitive psychology suggests that mindfulness and deliberate slowing of mental processes enhance decision-making and awareness.[20]

When you slow down the pace at which you perceive and operate, hurry becomes the Devil. The Devil does not obtain

79

victory through temptation and affliction alone. Rather, the Devil's strategy is distraction. With you distracted, you won't notice the laziness that crept in when you stopped going to the gym, nor will you hear the lies you tell yourself about working on your dreams, nor will you feel responsibility for the power you've neglected to use to your advantage. The Devil wants you in a constant state of hurry because hurry begets oversight and desperation. Neuroscientific studies on stress confirm that chronic urgency diminishes cognitive function, reducing both awareness and long-term goal attainment.[21]

Oversight and desperation limit your realm of consciousness because they prevent a holistic view of the world. In a hurried state, all you can perceive are problems, not progress; obstacles, not opportunity. I liken living in a constant hurried state to playing a game of *Where's Waldo?* while shaking the page—how the fuck are you supposed to find him in a blur? How are you supposed to find your desired state in a blur? Studies on attentional focus indicate that mental clutter obstructs creative problem-solving, reinforcing the importance of slowing down to gain clarity.[22]

Finally, remember this: *Kairos* is greater than *Chronos*. *Chronos* refers to quantitative, measurable time—an exact sequence of minutes and hours. For example, you have five minutes to catch the train that will take you to spend eight hours of your life in an environment that siphons your energy. *Kairos*, on the other hand, is qualitative time—moments rather than minutes. For example, eating a snack under the stars with her felt like an eternity. A life ruled by the Devil's hurry is enslaved by *Chronos*—a relentless ticking of the clock.

THE BITTER END

But a life ruled by *Kairos*—now that's the stuff of dreams and abundant success! Psychological research suggests that people who frame their lives around *Kairos*—valuing meaning over rigid schedules—experience greater fulfillment and success.[23]

Live life through *Kairos,* and you will only know *right now*—the ever-present, opportune moment, the birthplace of the greatest version of yourself.

Immediate Action Steps

1. Cultivate Mindfulness and Awareness: Start your day with 5-10 minutes of quiet reflection, focusing on your internal state. Pay attention to your thoughts, emotions, and physical sensations. Set a reminder to pause and check in with yourself every few hours. How are you feeling? What is your mind focused on? Recenter yourself when you notice it drifting.

2. Practice Reframing External Events: When you face a challenging situation, consciously reframe it. Instead of viewing it as something happening "to you," ask: *"How can I control my reaction to this situation?"* In your next stressful moment, take a deep breath and ask yourself, *"What do I control here? How can I shift my response to this situation?"*

3. Expand Your Consciousness by Letting Go of External Validation: Challenge yourself to let go of external sources of validation. For one week, limit your consumption of external validation (like social media or seeking approval from others). Replace this time with practices that nurture your internal world, like journaling or creative self-expression.

4. Dismantle Limiting Beliefs: Write down a limiting belief and the evidence that supports it. Then, list evidence that disproves it. Commit to affirming the new empowering belief daily.

5. Interpret Parables as Personal Insights: Choose a parable today and rewrite it as if you were the main character. What part of yourself does this character represent, and what lesson does the story offer you right now?

6. Slow Down and Observe: Pick one activity today (e.g., eating, walking, or working) and consciously slow down. Pay attention to every detail—taste, texture, sounds, and sensations—without rushing. Notice how this affects your mental state and perception.

7. Revisit Your Past to See the Bigger Picture: Reflect on a difficult period in your life. What limiting beliefs or external pressures were you caught up in? How did you react at the time? What could you have controlled differently? What did you learn that serves you now? Reframe this experience by recognizing the internal growth or lessons you gained from it.

8. Apply the "No Enemies Within" Principle: Identify one area of internal conflict (e.g., a fear or insecurity) and take one action this week to address it—whether through self-compassion, confronting the source of fear, or seeking support.

5

WORDS ARE CHARMED

"Not what goes into the
mouth defiles a man; but
what comes out of the
mouth, this defiles a man."
—Matthew 15:11

If your unspoken thoughts shape your actions, how much
of your life is influenced by what you refuse to say out loud?
What impact do the words you constantly repeat to yourself
have on your reality? Are you the person you claim to be, or
the person shaped by the words you never dare to speak?

7

DONNEL DELVA

Everything You Say Is A Spell

It's commonly accepted that actions speak louder than words. However, all actions originate from a series of *internal* words or *narratives* believed within the self.[1] I'll go into detail later on how our words affect us and how you can use your words to attract your desired state (for that is the purpose of this book, of course). But for now, consider the "words" and "narratives" that even seemingly inanimate objects embody.

If a rock weren't continuously affirming its identity—*rock, rock, rock*—it wouldn't express itself as a rock in the external world. Likewise, if water were to stop reinforcing its essence—*water, water, water*—and instead adopted a new self-talk, one that says internally, *fire, fire, fire*, then our planet and everything on it would instantly burst into flames. This analogy, while metaphorical, aligns with scientific principles regarding vibrational frequencies and the structure of matter.[2]

Words possess the power to change the universe because they are the fundamental medium through which God imagined all of creation. While we cannot fully comprehend God's internal self-expression, we do know that whatever God declares, becomes reality. The very fabric of existence resonates with God's creative ability. As Nikola Tesla famously said, "If you want to find the secrets of the universe, think in terms of energy, frequency, and vibration."[3] This suggests that all of creation, originating from the Word, perpetually vibrates with the universe's creative potential. Thus, for any-

86

thing to manifest, it simply requires the correct words to be spoken—the spell to be cast.

Consider spells as gravitational fields acting upon the universe's creative energy, attracting kindred realities to themselves. A word or phrase emanates a particular frequency that resonates sympathetically with corresponding frequencies in the universe.[4] So, what a rock or water or any inanimate object "says" is, in essence, its vibrational frequency. The interconnectedness of the universe is a layered tapestry of frequencies, each piece fitting together to create the world as we experience it. When you witness a mountainous riverbank with cascading waterfalls, shimmering rainbows, birds chirping, and bees buzzing, you are observing an intricate symphony of vibrations in harmony. That same scene would not appear in the Sahara or the Arctic because those environments resonate with entirely different frequencies, which manifest in the form of distinct landscapes, wildlife, and natural phenomena.

Now that we've established how spells emerge from the vibrations embedded in all things, let's examine how we can consciously use our words to cast spells that empower us. First and foremost, you are always under a spell—always. The question isn't whether you are under a spell but rather, *which* spell are you under? Since you are constantly vibrating, you continuously emit a frequency that attracts similar frequencies to you. Research in quantum physics and consciousness studies suggests that focused intention and belief can influence physical reality, reinforcing the idea that our internal narratives shape our external world.[5]

The only difference between what you attract lies in the specific frequency you decide to emit. If you begin to shift your identity toward your desired state, then your inner self-talk must shift first. You must replace the repeated inner narrative of undesired failure—*loser, loser, loser*—with the narrative of your chosen success—*winner, winner, winner*. The more consistently you sustain this frequency within, the more you will attract and maintain your desired state. Neurological research supports this, demonstrating that repeated affirmations and cognitive restructuring can rewire neural pathways to align thoughts with desired outcomes.[6]

When practiced with consistency and intent, this shift in frequency can even influence the behavior of those around you. Human consciousness operates in resonance with collective energy fields, meaning your vibrations can subtly alter how others perceive and react to you.[7] Finally, when you consistently influence the external world through your internal mastery, you will have truly mastered the art of casting spells—an art form deeply reverent to the ultimate Creator.

Choose Your Words With Agency

I'll start this section with a radical perspective shift: It is a privilege to speak, not a right. (I know what the U .S. Constitution says!). Challenge yourself and adopt this agency-focused mindset when choosing the words you express. The words you choose must pass through you first before entering the world. As a result, the energy within your words builds up inside you, affecting *you* before it permeates the world. Studies in psycholinguistics have shown that the words we use shape not only how we communicate but also how we perceive reality.[8] The fact that your words must channel through you means that all positive and negative energies impact you before they influence anything else. So, choose your words like a bouncer at a club or the warden to a prison—i.e., with agency.

You ultimately dictate what comes out of your mouth. The words you're capable of saying don't have the *right* to exist in this world; rather, they have the distinct *privilege* to be spoken into existence. In other words, you gift your words with life as you pronounce them. This concept has enlightened my world. Now, I only tolerate uplifting, life-giving energy to flow from my mouth into my desired state. Before I say things aloud, I tell my words, *If you want to go out into the world, then you have to go through me first!* This is the kind of disposition you need with your words to foster your desired state—a heroic stance that protects the true meaning of what you want from parasitic energies. Studies on self-affirmation theory confirm that the words we choose, especially in self-talk, reinforce our beliefs and behaviors.[9]

Let's face it—we must admit this about ourselves—humans practically burst at the seams with parasitic energy that desperately seeks to weaken the world. These parasitic forces live within us all and spring up at the first chance to spread negativity. Neuroscientific research suggests that negative speech patterns activate the brain's stress response, reinforcing cycles of fear and pessimism.[10] These parasitic seeds lie dormant within us and awaken when stirred. Our task is to safeguard the gate between these parasites and our desired states. Ask yourself: *Am I really going to let everyone into my lavish party?* Is just any old parasite worthy of your divine attention?

It is your duty to be discerning with your words, ensuring they contribute to the reality you wish to create. As scripture reminds us, "Let no corrupt word proceed out of your mouth, but what is good for necessary edification, that it may impart grace to the hearers. Let all bitterness, wrath, anger, clamor, and evil speaking be put away from you, with all malice" (Ephesians 4:29, 31). The wisdom of both scripture and modern psychology aligns: the words we allow to manifest shape not only our external world but also our internal state.[11]

Don't Share A Plan You're Uncomfortable Revealing

In your pursuit of your desired state, you will undoubtedly develop many plans. If you've been following this far, you'll notice that planning has been a primary factor in becoming the type of person who consistently obtains their desired states. Plans are essential because, without a structured approach to guide your future decisions, achieving your desired state will be left to chance.[12] While planning is necessary—even when things go awry—*sharing* those plans with others is not. In fact, revealing your plans prematurely can often work against you.

When I began my life as a student life coach, I nearly fell into the trap of telling everyone my plans. Since my passion was already teaching English to high school students (and coaching football), I decided to expand my reach by connecting with online student audiences—those I couldn't reach in my classroom or on the field. As a result, I began posting TikToks aimed at empowering students to flourish. While in the infancy of my coaching journey, I stumbled upon a piece of wisdom from an online source that said something along the lines of, *your first hundred videos won't get any views—just focus on improving one thing in each video, and by the hundred-first video, you'll have something.*

Hearing that insight, all stress and overwhelm immediately left me. Why? Because I didn't feel the burden of telling others about my coaching plans until I had already become more prolific. By keeping my plans to myself, I was able to focus on the process, refine my craft, and ultimately yield higher results when others needed me most. Research in psychology suggests that prematurely sharing goals can create a false sense of accomplishment, reducing motivation to follow through on actual execution.[13] Approaching success in this way allows for organic growth without the external pressures of expectation.

Do not tell anyone a plan you're not comfortable sharing because every thesis (your desired state) summons its respective antithesis (your undesired state).[14] When you share your plans with others, you first permit certain energies to pass through you into the world through words. Upon the arrival of these words, their energies are immediately counterbalanced to create equilibrium—the natural state of the universe. Psychological studies on goal intention suggest that verbalizing aspirations can lead to unintentional self-sabotage, as external validation replaces the internal drive to accomplish those goals.[15]

What counterbalances the energy you release into the world is the skepticism and doubt that inevitably arise in the minds of those you confide in. When you share with someone, *I will achieve success*, they can't help but—despite their congratulations and goodwill—imagine a world in which you do *not* succeed. It's an automatic cognitive response, much like when someone says, *Don't think of a pink elephant*—you immediately visualize one.

Create Mantras

One of the most important aspects of creating a mantra is understanding that all things constantly repeat mantras; as a result, mantras shape the reality they manifest. As I mentioned before, every seemingly inanimate object is repeating to itself its inherent spell—the energy that defines its existence. Mantras function in almost the same way. They take the frequency or vibration of a state of being and convert that energy into words best suited for the individual.[16]

Because of this specificity, certain mantras will be highly effective for some people while having little to no effect on others. For example, one mantra that has been especially transformative for me in my pursuit of my desired state is one I first discovered while reading Emile Coué's *Self Mastery Through Conscious Autosuggestion*: "Every day, in every way, I get better and better."[17] Just reading that mantra fills me with an energy I find difficult to put into words. However, when I advised my buddy from college to adopt this same mantra to break his habit of sloth, he found that repeating it was completely ineffective. This is because different mantras resonate differently with different people.

Finding the right mantra is a deeply personal process. Some may respond to long, affirming phrases, while others may find power in a single word—or even a single letter. When I'm doing planks at the end of my workout, sometimes simply repeating my name keeps me locked in a level of focus and clarity that allows me to endure. Neuroscientific research supports this—repeating personalized mantras can activate brain regions associated with self-regulation and resilience, reinforcing endurance and mental fortitude.[18]

Regardless of how your mantra is tailored to you, make sure it is *lifegiving*. Too often, people trapped in their undesired states focus on the negative aspects of their situation rather than envisioning a life where they have achieved their desired state. This fixation on the negative only reinforces their current condition, further entrenching them in their suffering. Cognitive behavioral research has shown that negative self-talk perpetuates undesired mental states, making it more difficult to shift into new, constructive patterns of thinking.[19] For instance, a weak mantra may sound something like, *Someday, in some way, I may get better*. A mantra like this does not put your desired state front and center—it keeps it at a distance, reinforcing doubt rather than transformation.

Instead of repeating words that focus on moving *away* from pain, focus on words that emphasize moving *toward* pleasure. This shift in language is crucial. Studies in positive psychology highlight the impact of affirmative, forward-focused statements on achieving personal growth and succ ess.[20] This is why I tailored Coué's mantra to fit me more snugly: *Day by day, in every way, I get better and better—and I better!* This version not only reinforces my steady progression but also commands me to expect nothing less than continuous improvement.

My Bronze Rule

You've more than likely heard the old adage, "If you don't have anything nice to say, don't say anything at all." Of the life rules that exist (often attributed to metals), I call this aforementioned adage the Bronze Rule because, while it provides crucial advice for, let's say, children and/or U.S. Presidents, it often proves ineffective when it comes to expressing your honest beliefs—a necessary characteristic for obtaining your desired state.[21] Nonetheless, this rule still supports the essence of what it means to choose your words with authority, like a bouncer at a nightclub, standing at the door of your reality, deciding what gets in and what stays out.

My variation of the Bronze Rule follows the same vein, and I remind myself of this every day: If what you say isn't inspiring, loving, helpful, or even generally important, then keep your mouth shut! Studies on the power of words and their psychological impact show that language not only influences others but also shapes the speaker's thoughts and emotional state.[22] To reiterate, the words you allow to enter this world do not have the *right* to exist; rather, they have the *privilege* of being here. Now, vet the words that beg to enter this world. Ask them: *Who and what do you inspire? Will you love or be loved? How helpful are you? To whom? Are you even important?* If the energy your words carry doesn't pass your vetting with flying colors, then you get to keep your mouth shut. Neuroscientific studies indicate that verbalized thoughts and expressions create neural pathways that reinforce either positive or negative emotional states.[23] I can't tell you how much pain I've avoided simply through silence. Bless yourself and all those around you with that same gift of "addition by subtraction."

Now, take your vetting and gatekeeping a step further: don't just use the Bronze Rule for others—use it for yourself. The energy carried in your words always affects *you* first before they have a subsequent effect on the world.[24] So ask those aforementioned questions inside your heart-mind because you're the one who has to deal with them first. Psychological research on self-talk and cognitive behavioral therapy (CBT) confirms that the words we say to ourselves directly shape our behavior, emotional resilience, and self-concept.[25] So don't just vet your words and bounce them—create an environment where they don't even *want* to come. What would a bad vibe want with a good vibe party? By carefully curating your speech and thoughts, you ensure that negativity has no space to thrive in your reality.

Self-Talk Is All-Talk—And Vice Versa

To close this chapter, I'd like to offer an outlook on life that I adopted when I truly understood that my words are charmed. That is: self-talk and all-talk are the same. What you say to yourself is what you say to others, and inversely, what you say to others reflects what you say to yourself.

95

This concept aligns with research on self-perception theory, which suggests that our behaviors and words reinforce our self-concept over time.[26]

I have a friend named Jen who once told me that I was fond of "spraying and praying." I was immediately offended, for two reasons. First, I am never desperate. Second, she mistakenly attributed my fondness for giving compliments—something I do as a form of positive self-talk—to a desperate attempt to pick up girls. Her misinterpretation reminded me how easily people misunderstand the power of words and intention. As a result, I explained to her the following, which embodies the essence of what it means not only to understand that words are charmed but also to wield that responsibility with the utmost authority:

Do you think I give people compliments, calling them beautiful and lovely, only to turn back to the mirror and say, *Donnel, you son of a bitch, you worthless piece of shit*? Absolutely not! I compliment people because I am constantly complimenting myself, and as a result, I can't help but extend that energy to others. Research on positive affirmations shows that self-directed positive speech has the power to rewire the brain, reinforcing confidence and emotional well-being.[27] I have created an environment where positive talk flourishes. Like a bouncer at a nightclub or a college admissions counselor, I only allow words and energies that promote love, helpfulness, and happiness to enter my world.

So, I concluded my conversation with Jen in this way: *When I choose only to say things that uplift and help, then maybe, in a way, I do "spray and pray." But what am I spraying, and what am I praying for? I am projecting myself outward—I pray for my desired state.* Studies on the law of attraction and the psychology of spoken affirmations suggest that verbalized intentions shape the subconscious mind, reinforcing belief patterns that lead to real-world manifestations.[28] When I think of something kind to say to someone and *don't* say it, I do myself and the world around me a huge disservice.

People so often let their words slip and fail to watch their tongues when it comes to negativity and belittling energies. They do not hesitate to bash someone—or, more often, themselves. But strangely, they hesitate to praise both themselves and others. Why is it so much easier to be negative than positive, fearful rather than faithful, hateful instead of loving? Studies in cognitive psychology indicate that the human brain has a negativity bias, meaning it is wired to focus on negative experiences more than positive ones.[29] People who find it easier to hate themselves than to love themselves have accumulated a rotten heap of energies in their environment—in other words, within themselves. And that rotten heap has primarily manifested through words.

By cleaning up the words you say, you directly influence the energy you put out into this world and the energy that inevitably shapes your desired state. Neuroscientific research on language and cognition suggests that the words we repeatedly use shape our neural pathways, reinforcing emotional and behavioral patterns over time.[30] Thus, mastering self-talk is not just about personal affirmation—it is about crafting reality itself.

Immediate Action Steps

1. Observe Your Internal Dialogue: Spend a day paying close attention to your inner conversations. What narratives do you notice? Are they empowering, or do they hold you back? Write down a few examples and reflect on how they might shape your reality.

2. Create Your Own Personal Mantra: Based on what resonates with you, craft a mantra that embodies your desired state. It could be a word, phrase, or affirmation that empowers and motivates you. For example, *"Every day, in every way, I get better and better"* or something more personal. Repeat this mantra daily.

3. Speak Words with Authority: Practice speaking with intention. Before you speak, ask yourself: *"What energy am I about to project into the world?"* Take a moment to check if your words align with the energy you want to create. If not, rephrase them to reflect positivity, intention, and agency.

4. Limit Negative Self-Talk: Today, commit to reframing or eliminating negative words you say to yourself. If you catch yourself thinking something self-limiting or harsh, pause and replace it with something positive or constructive.

5. Guard Your Words in Conversations: Notice how you speak to others. Practice giving compliments, offer-

ing positive feedback, and speaking with intention. What energy are you sharing with the world through your interactions? Make a commitment to only allow words that support and uplift to leave your lips.

6. Don't Share Untested Plans: Reflect on your current goals and plans. Ask yourself: *Am I ready to share this with others, or do I need to keep refining it?* If you're not comfortable sharing yet, take a step back, focus on the process, and work on improving your craft before revealing your ambitions to others.

7. Affirm Your Progress: Every night, write down one or two things you've accomplished that day toward your desired state, no matter how small. Acknowledge your progress and celebrate it.

8. Be Mindful of the Energy You Allow In: Like a bouncer at a nightclub, monitor what words, people, and energies you allow into your space. If something feels off, kindly remove it from your environment. This could mean saying no to negative conversations or limiting time with energy-draining people.

PART II: TRANSFORMATION

6

Solitude Builds Strength That Becomes Power

"But you, when you pray, go
into your room, and when
you have shut your door,
pray to your Father who
is in the secret place; and
your Father who sees in secret will reward you openly."
—Matthew 6:6

***

Who are you when you're alone with yourself? Can you sit in silence without discomfort? Without anyone to validate you, would you feel invisible—or more present than ever?

DONNEL DELVA

Strong And Powerless

I'm willing to argue that most people often fail to act on their own. From my observations, this failure stems from two primary reasons: either they dislike themselves and seek constant companionship with others who likely feel the same way about themselves, or they fear confronting their own inadequacy. Research in social psychology suggests that people often rely on social validation to regulate self-esteem and avoid the discomfort of self-reflection.[1]

After noticing these trends in the people I've been fortunate to meet, I began to believe that solitude might be the single most useful asset when it comes to inner strength. Human beings evolved in communities, just like everything else that calls Earth its home. As a result, solitude tends to feel inherently unnatural. Neuroscientific studies show that our brains are wired for social connection, making prolonged solitude challenging for many.[2] However, those who embrace solitude demonstrate an exceptional strength—one that is necessary to obtain their desired state.

I started acting on my belief that solitude is strength when I began going to watch movies in theaters alone. The first time the concept was brought to my attention was when I kept pleading with my younger brother Carl to watch a movie with me. After repeatedly asking him, I finally questioned why I even needed someone to go with me. At that moment, an epiphany struck me: *I don't.* Since then, I've seen at least ten movies alone. Whether it's watching a movie by myself or walking through a desolate forest, I've found that embracing my solitude has been one of the most empowering practices for obtaining my desired state.

Being, and really just *being*—existing—with myself has allowed me to synthesize all the principles in this book into a seamless medley of growth and success. I no longer need validation to act, nor do I compare myself with others. I couldn't tell you the last time I felt the fear of missing out. I don't chase anything or anyone; I allow the universe to bring blessings to me like a magnet. Psychological research on self-determination theory suggests that people who develop intrinsic motivation—acting based on personal values rather than external validation—experience greater long-term fulfillment.[3]

I am never surrounded by insincere people with negative energy; if I'm not alone, then I'm with my loved ones. Solitude, for me, has become my greatest addition by subtraction. This aligns with spiritual and philosophical teachings that emphasize solitude as a path to enlightenment and self-mastery.[4]

However, while one can cultivate strength through solitude, that strength means little if it is not converted into power. When my Friend was baptized, He withdrew into the desert to be tempted by the Devil for forty days and forty nights. But, as He often does, He returned. *Returning* to others is what transforms strength into power.

If, for some reason, you find yourself strong in your solitude yet unable to stand others and their energies at large, then you are strong—but powerless. You have tempered your spirit to not only tolerate solitude but to relish in it. However, by focusing solely on that—on the love you feel with yourself alone—you risk isolating yourself entirely. This, in turn, results in powerlessness. Studies on emotional intelligence suggest that true personal power lies in the ability to balance self-awareness with social adaptability.[5]

Weak And Powerful

On the flip side, you can be both weak and powerful. This paradoxical combination means that while you struggle with solitude, you possess an uncanny ability to influence others. I pity these types of people the most because, on the surface, they appear to thrive in groups and crowds, yet they struggle to face themselves in the mirror.

If you are weak and powerful, then you are, quite honestly, an anomaly to me. How is it that you feel more alive in the presence of others than in your own company? The answer is simple: you thrive by expending all your energy outward. While you would never be caught watching a movie alone in a theater, you are more than capable of persuading a group to watch a movie they had no prior interest in. This phenomenon is an anomaly because, typically, it is inner strength and self-love that enable people to influence others. However, in your case, it is inner weakness that compels you to overcompensate and exert influence.

Existing in this state makes it nearly impossible to attain alignment or your desired reality. Without inner strength and imagination, you lack the creative power necessary to manifest your ideal state in this dimension. Psychological research suggests that those who rely heavily on external validation often struggle with self-actualization, as their sense of identity is shaped by external forces rather than internal convictions.[6] You become subject to the whims of external validation, people-pleasing, and the ever-changing expectations of those around you. When the collective desires conflict, you are pulled in multiple directions, leaving you fragmented and unfulfilled. This aligns with findings in social psychology, where individuals with high social dependency tend to experience lower self-esteem and increased emotional exhaustion.[7]

Despite this, you still retain the power to direct the herd. The difference is that your power originates from a place of lack rather than abundance. Rather than leading from inner conviction, you manipulate external forces to maintain your relevance. Studies in leadership psychology indicate that those who lead from a need for validation often struggle with consistency in their influence, as their authority is dependent on fluctuating social dynamics rather than a stable internal compass.[8]

While this state allows you to wield influence, it ultimately renders you powerless over yourself. True power is not derived from controlling others, but from mastering one's own thoughts and desires. Without that mastery, you remain at the mercy of the world around you, constantly adapting, yet never truly becoming.

Strong And Powerful

Most, if not all, people who have obtained their desired states are both strong and powerful. Being in this state is synonymous with being in the zone or experiencing a flow state.[9] Psychological research suggests that flow states occur when an individual is fully immersed in an activity, balancing skill and challenge seamlessly, which leads to peak performance and fulfillment.[10] If you're strong and powerful, then you can both love your solitude while also influencing others.

People in this state almost never overcompensate because they do not rely on external validation, yet they naturally attract others to follow them. This phenomenon aligns with research on self-determination theory, which posits that intrinsic motivation and personal authenticity lead to greater life satisfaction and influence.[11] Ironically, what fuels their ability to attract others is their knack for remaining independent. Since they do not fold under the pressure of contradicting beliefs and values, they exude sincerity, which in turn invites new opportunities. Most people who even seek a "desired state" in the first place tend to display leadership characteristics, so it's no surprise that strong and powerful individuals often find themselves in positions of influence.

If you're strong and powerful, then you have a responsibility to help others reach their best selves as well. Not everyone actively seeks to become the greatest version of themselves, and that's a sobering reality. Psychological studies on self-actualization, particularly in Maslow's hierarchy of needs, suggest that only a small percentage of individuals reach their fullest potential due to limiting beliefs and environmental factors.[12] However, those who are both strong enough to embrace solitude and powerful enough to influence others must serve as a lighthouse for those still searching. A significant aspect of strength and power is an unwavering commitment to justice.

The best indication that you are thriving in your desired state is your ability to lead others toward their own. It's one thing to be strong, but the "powerful" aspect emerges when you illuminate the light within yourself to guide others. As leadership research suggests, true power is not dominance but the ability to inspire and uplift.[13] The world needs more strong and powerful people—individuals who have mastered themselves and, in doing so, positively impact the lives of others.

Weak And Powerless

I'll keep this section brief: these types of people are in serious trouble. Since they lack the inner strength to be alone, they rarely take the time to reflect on what they truly desire. Without introspection, they remain disconnected from their own goals and aspirations, drifting aimlessly through life. Research in psychology suggests that individuals who struggle with solitude often experience heightened anxiety and difficulty in forming independent identities.[14]

Similarly, their lack of influence over others keeps them from ever stepping into the spotlight. They avoid actions that would draw attention because they fear judgment and lack the confidence to assert themselves. Studies on social anxiety and self-efficacy confirm that those with low personal agency tend to avoid situations that require leadership or decisiveness.[15]

I feel completely justified in criticizing such parasitic people because I know they will never read this book. People who lack personal power often avoid challenging material, as it forces them to confront uncomfortable truths about themselves.[16] Their aversion to growth keeps them stuck in cycles of mediocrity.

Avoid these types of people at all costs. They do not contribute to your growth; they are only good for consuming and tainting your energy. Research in behavioral psychology indicates that surrounding yourself with unmotivated individuals can have a detrimental impact on your own ambitions and mindset.[17]

Discover What You Value—Then Protect It

When you continue to love your solitude, you will be graced with the discovery of what you truly value. Not only will you gain the clarity that accompanies seclusion, but you will also develop an unwavering faith in those values.[18]

During my pursuit of my desired state, I've learned that the twofold appreciation of my values—discovery and faith—are paramount. Before I could ever fully believe in what I hold dear, I first had to know what those values were. At this point in my life, as a bewilderingly handsome twenty-four-year-old English teacher, author, brother, and friend, I hold this belief: that Freedom and Truth are identical—they are the same word, possess the same essence, and both fill me with the same passion and love for myself, God, and others in the world.[19]

THE BITTER END

This realization did not happen by chance; I discovered it through severe addition by subtraction—solitude. When I first began to embrace my solitude, taking myself on solo dates to the movies and sitting alone for table-for-one dinners, my mind was like white water rapids, constantly racing, fearful of missing out on experiences and memories with others. Now, as I type these words in the shared nook office in the back of a high school cafeteria, my mind is as clear and still as the waters at Walden Pond—that polished mirror that Thoreau described in 1854, proclaiming that "Heaven is under our feet as well as over our heads."[20]

So, what do you suppose is the natural response to discovering something of immense value? Protection, defense, conservation. I liken the safeguarding of one's values to a safe. Picture this: before you stand two identical safes—both adorned with finely embroidered treasure chests, their edges lined with gold and diamonds. They are mysteriously alluring, yet somehow already fulfilling. However, inside one safe lies your undesired state, while inside the other rests your desired state. The former leads to ruin, or worse—complacency. The latter leads to the promised land of your unwavering imagination. Yet, in this scenario, you do not know which is which. The only clue you are given is this: one safe remains unguarded, while the other is encircled by Seal Team Six—or better yet, the Straw Hat Pirates—armed, alert, and unwavering in their defense.[21]

Treat your values like the second safe in this scenario—with your utmost care. Think about it: it's no wonder that you wouldn't protect your values while in your undesired state. That would be like guarding a safe with nothing valuable inside. However, when you discover what you value most, your faith in those values will naturally lead you to protect them, just as someone would defend a safe filled with untold riches. Human beings are wired to play defense rather than offense—we are often more inclined to protect ourselves from pain than to pursue pleasure.[22] So why not use that instinct to your advantage? Since you are already protecting something—whether it be your self-interests or your limiting beliefs—you might as well discover what it is that you have been defending all this time. Then, in the blissful silence of solitude, do the inner work necessary to clarify your values, strengthen your faith in them, and establish how you will guard them against anything that attempts to diminish them.[23]

How You Treat Yourself Sets The Standard For How Others Treat You

As you continue to strengthen yourself through your relationship with solitude and impact others with the power that comes from discovering what you value, you will naturally begin to treat yourself with tenderness and the utmost respect. When you start saying "no" to lifestyles that don't serve you and "yes" to personal growth, people will take notice and adjust their behavior accordingly. Like I said at the beginning of this book, when you use your imagination to visualize and magnify your desired state, those involved in your life will naturally align with the roles they are meant to play.[24]

However, getting people to play their role in your life starts with how you treat yourself. I wish I could say that just by going to movies alone and enjoying dinner-for-ones, people magically took notice and stepped into the roles of lover or friend in my life. Newsflash: that did not happen—at all. But what did happen was beyond and better than anything I had imagined (as it often is).

Since people see how I cherish my time and don't wait for their approval to enjoy personal experiences, they have learned to cherish my time as well. They see how unwaveringly I take care of my body and cultivate my relationship with God, and in turn, they respect those aspects of my life.[25] Because I have established firm boundaries and consistently say "no" to events and places that do not serve me, people have adjusted without me needing to explicitly tell them. They no longer invite me to activities that don't align with my values, not out of resentment, but because they recognize that I have set a clear standard for how I spend my time.

Moreover, those who once invited me to such events, upon sensing the consistency of my choices, have removed themselves from my life altogether. Since they perceive my absence as rejection, they no longer seek me out as a companion. This natural selection process refines my relationships, leaving only those who align with my values and energy.[26]

You stop tolerating subpar treatment from others the moment you stop tolerating it from yourself. Let's face it: who in your life has let you down the most? Cheated you the most? Given up on you the most? Lied to you and fallen short on promises the most?

You, yourself.

The moment you decide that enough is enough, your identity shifts—from passive to intentional, from lukewarm to on fire—and the entire universe takes notice.[27] Remember what I said about self-talk and how it's all-talk: do you think I'm out here lifting people up just to turn around and tear myself down in the mirror? Of course not. I build others up and love them because I build myself up and love myself first.

This type of self-respecting relationship creates a cycle of perpetual growth and blessing. Because I love people as an extension of my own self-love, people love me. Now, why they love me—I don't always know. I like to think it's because they, too, love themselves. But perhaps they simply love being loved by me. Either way, this cycle benefits us all.

Since people—these autonomous manifestations of the universe—love me, they also forgive me when I need time for myself instead of overextending my energy for things that do not enliven me. They support me when they see I'm struggling. Ultimately, they step into the roles I need them to play in my life, effortlessly and in divine timing.

Throughout my life, I have needed a lover, a friend, a mentor, a healer, a listener. Although I had no idea who these people would be, I have always found someone to fill each role precisely when I needed them. And this is not a coincidence. It is a direct result of raising my own standard for how I want to be treated.[28]

Strength Is In What You Let Go—Not What You Carry

THE BITTER END

I first heard this concept while watching a phenomenally impactful YouTuber who truly helped propel me toward my greatest version: Infinite Waters, formally known as Ralph Smart.

I was in college at the time and believed that strength came from what I could carry and accomplish. In a single day, I'd exercise at the gym, go to class, do homework, meet with my residents as an RA (resident assistant), hang out with friends, play video games I felt obligated to, and occasionally take a trip off-campus. Of course, I would never get every single thing done, and I struggled with that reality. At night, when I got down on my knees to pray, I'd ask my Friend for the strength to carry the responsibilities I needed to fulfill—not to remove them, but to help me bear their weight. Then, one day, when my heart felt particularly heavy, I watched one of Ralph Smart's videos where he seemingly spoke directly to me: *"Strength isn't what you can carry, but what you can let go—let go!"*[29]

That simple request brought me to tears. I felt guilty for not accomplishing the hundreds of things I wanted to do daily. And now, here was a very successful mentor of mine telling me that I should, in fact, do *less*. A part of me was freed at that moment. As a result, I boiled down my list to only the essentials: gym, class/homework, and RA responsibilities. My friends and professors became noticeably aware of my shift, as I deepened my focus on these few, simple tasks. Research in cognitive load theory suggests that reducing mental clutter enhances productivity and well-being, as the brain performs best when it isn't overwhelmed by excessive tasks.[30]

DONNEL DELVA

As a twenty-four-year-old English teacher and author, my approach has remained the same despite the essentials shifting: reading a book, writing my book, and expanding my knowledge. Exercising at the gym has long since become a part of me—so much so that I no longer need to list it as an intentional priority. This philosophy aligns with studies in habit formation, which indicate that deeply ingrained behaviors require little active decision-making and instead become automatic, freeing cognitive resources for other pursuits.[31]

I also realized that this same concept—strength coming from letting go rather than carrying more—applies to solitude. When obtaining your desired state, your strength comes not from who you can carry into your new lifestyle, but from who you can *let go*. Studies on personal growth and transformation emphasize that significant lifestyle changes often involve shifts in social circles, as relationships must align with new values and priorities to be sustainable.[32]

Paradoxically, there is a heavy burden that comes with isolating yourself for self-improvement. You may feel guilty and begin to doubt whether you are even *allowed* to experience such tremendous growth and freedom. Let me tell you right now, my beloved, beloved reader: YOU ARE WORTHY! YOU ARE ENOUGH! Psychological research on imposter syndrome and self-worth affirms that many individuals struggle with feeling deserving of success, especially when it requires distancing themselves from past influences.[33]

You don't need to be around people who fail to bring out the best in you. Not only *can* you seek out isolation in the name of your desired state, but you *ought* to. Your desired state—and the best version of yourself—exists on the clearer side of what you've let go. Psychological theories on self-actualization, particularly Maslow's hierarchy of needs, highlight the necessity of removing distractions and limiting beliefs in order to reach higher levels of fulfillment.[34]

There Are Twice As Many Vices Than Virtues

All virtues exist as a perfect median between two extremes. I first encountered this idea during my time studying philosophy in college, and that simple yet profound insight transformed my understanding of solitude. With this newfound knowledge, I began to practice solitude with greater intentionality, recognizing its value in a world overshadowed by vice.

I still clearly remember the day this realization truly resonated with my spirit. I had just received some disheartening news about an altercation between two friends of mine, both of whom I deeply admired. Allegedly, one friend had sexually harassed the other, shattering the image I once held of the aggressor and irreparably damaging my relationship with them. As I reported this information to my college's Resident Life and Housing Department, the epiphany struck with the tap of each letter on my laptop:

There are twice as many vices as virtues.

For example, take the virtue of courage. On either extreme of courage lie the vices of cowardice and rashness. This concept, rooted in Aristotelian ethics, asserts that virtue is a mean between two moral failings—one of deficiency and one of excess.[35] If virtues are infinite, then the number of vices must be twice as infinite—one virtue, two vices. So what the fuck makes you think that surrounding yourself with people, in a world doubly covered with vices, will lead you toward virtue? Statistically, more people will gravitate toward vice, as virtue is like a compass needle that must be finely calibrated—too far in either direction, and it loses its true north.[36]

This epiphany reinforced my appreciation for solitude. If virtues rained down like clouds while vices scorched the earth, then two-thirds of the planet would be a desert. Research in social psychology suggests that environments heavily influence moral behavior, and individuals surrounded by moral corruption are statistically more likely to conform to it.[37] I don't ever want to be in that desert. So, I ensure that I stay to myself—an area so teeming with life that others gather near, like an oasis.

Enter The Cave—But Return From It

To close this chapter, I'd like to leave on a more uplifting note. As you obtain your desired state, you will inevitably enter a period of sustained solitude—one that you will not only come to love but may even become addicted to. However, let this serve as a warm warning: while you must go into the cave, you must also return. Your desired state depends on it.

Throughout history, many great figures have sought solitude for deep reflection and discernment. Jesus Christ retreated into the wilderness for forty days. Buddha meditated beneath the Bodhi tree until he attained enlightenm ent.[38] St. Ignatius withdrew into a cave in Manresa for nearly a year, shaping his *Spiritual Exercises*.[39] Even the nameless protagonist of Ralph Ellison's *Invisible Man* isolates himself to gain a deeper understanding of his identity and society's illusions.[40] Plato's *Allegory of the Cave* serves as another illustration of this concept, wherein the journey to enlightenment requires one to first withdraw from the illusions of the world before returning with new-found wisdom.[41] Despite their deep introspection, what unites these figures is not just their time in solitude, but their eventual return to the world—bringing back knowledge, truth, and transformation. Solitude is essential, but action is what solidifies the change.

I do not lock myself away and hoard my good energy in gluttonous isolation. That would never lead to my desired state. True transformation requires engagement with the world. I take action toward my goals. I work. I interact with the world around me and, in doing so, change it. As I become the person who has already obtained his desired state—by embodying all the necessary characteristics, attitudes, and competencies—the world itself shifts in response to me.[42]

Yet, returning from solitude is not easy. This world has a way of draining one's spirit, exhausting even the most resolute souls. But do not be disheartened. For as my Friend says, "Enter by the narrow gate; for wide is the gate and broad is the way that leads to destruction, and there are many who go in by it. Because narrow is the gate and difficult is the way which leads to life, and there are few who find it" (Matthew 7:13-14).

DONNEL DELVA

Since you, my beloved reader, desire more for your life, you are among the few who choose the narrow gate—the path of life—over the broad road of death. Every living thing struggles to survive, but not all take the necessary actions to thrive. So do what most people refuse to do. Take the difficult path. Cultivate discipline. Embrace the solitude that allows for deep transformation, but do not remain there. Return, embody your truth, and walk freely into the world—flowing with abundance, happiness, and unshakable freedom.[43]

Immediate Action Steps

1. Spend One Hour Alone Each Week: Commit to spending at least one hour per week in complete solitude. No distractions, no social media, just time with yourself. This could be a quiet walk, sitting in nature, or simply being with your thoughts in a quiet space. The goal is to cultivate comfort in your own presence.

2. Reflect on What You Value: After each solo session, write down what truly matters to you. What are your core values? This will help you define what you want to protect and prioritize in your life.

3. Practice Letting Go: Identify one thing—whether it's a relationship, a habit, or a belief—that no longer serves you. Make a deliberate choice to let it go.

4. Take One Solo Action a Week: Do something alone that you've always relied on others for. Whether it's going to the movies, dining alone, or taking a solo trip to the park—take action without needing validation.

5. Set Boundaries That Reflect Your Values: Look at your social interactions and commitments. Are you honoring your values by saying yes to the right things and no to the wrong ones? Practice saying no to events or people that drain you, and yes to your

personal growth and solitude.

6. Start Journaling for Self-Reflection: Take five minutes every day to reflect in a journal. Ask yourself: *What did I learn today? What did solitude reveal to me? How can I move closer to my desired state?*

7. Visualize Your Desired State: Spend time in silence, imagining what your ideal life looks like. Envision yourself in your most empowered state, strong and independent, and ask yourself: *What does this version of me do differently? How can I start to embody that now?*

8. Strengthen Your Inner Circle: Evaluate the relationships you currently have. Do they align with your values? Do they support your growth? Let go of toxic connections and nurture the relationships that add value to your life.

7

THINK FOR YOURSELF

"For what will it profit a man
if he gains the whole world,
and loses his own soul?"
—Mark 8:36

***

How much of your desires are even yours? If you were gaslighted since birth into believing certain perspectives, would you notice? Or would those figments of your imagination go with you into the grave, altered and estranged?

DONNEL DELVA

You Can't Spell Culture Without Cult

Around 1620, millions of humans from Africa were forcibly taken, packed into ships, and sold into slavery in America. Another group of humans then purchased those slaves and cruelly put them to work on plantations. When slave owners realized they could expedite their yield by producing new slaves through the wombs of enslaved women rather than outsourcing from overseas, those women were systematically raped and forced to reproduce. Their children grew up malnourished, terrorized, and bound to a life of atrocity. This industry prospered for roughly 250 years.[1]

What do you suspect endorsed such a system? Was it productivity? The carefree life that comes with a booming economy? Certainly—those benefits bolstered morale. But what did that morale, in turn, strengthen? The culture. The culture of the American people. The culture of the human race.

As Terence McKenna famously said, "Culture is not your friend."[2] He hit the mushroom right on its top, which leads me to my central point: while culture can be a beautifully freeing aspect of your life and identity, it can also be the single most restrictive force holding you back from achieving your desired state.

Imagine you're me, a bewilderingly handsome Haitian man. One day, you decide that you enjoy the flattery that comes with wearing a sombrero, a broad-brimmed straw hat typically worn by Mexicans. Or perhaps you become captivated by the elegance of a hijab, a head covering worn by

Muslim women, and wish to experience such grace yourself. Would you wear them? Should you?

These were not trivial musings—I genuinely pondered them. Much to her mortification, I consulted the girl I was dating at the time. She majored in anthropology, the study of human societies and cultures, so I believed she'd have the best perspective. In a slew of carefully chosen words, she explained that wearing a sombrero or hijab for fashion's sake would deeply offend Mexicans and Muslim women, respectively. She argued that unless I understood the cultural significance of both garments, I should never wear them. After our discussion, I ultimately agreed—to keep the peace—and have never worn either.

While my past lover's perspective may have spared people discomfort, it also reinforced the rigid boundaries of a cultish social construct. If someone were offended by me wearing clothing they believed I shouldn't, simply because I am not of their culture, who was truly wronged? How would they even know I wasn't Mexican or a Muslim woman? By the color of my skin? By my perceived background? If only Mexicans can wear sombreros and only Muslim women can wear hijabs, where do we draw the line?

Remember, there was a period in American culture when only white people were allowed service at restaurants.[3] There was a time when schools and education were exclusively reserved for white men.[4] The boundaries of culture are fluid, yet history has shown us how they can be weaponized to justify exclusion, oppression, and even atrocity.

To obtain my desired state, I had to learn to unshackle myself from cultural and mental restraints. If I had conformed to the cult-like groupthink that dictates much of the world, I would never have pursued higher education, pierced my ears four times, or even written this book. I might have chosen viciousness over self-awareness and further plagued the world with ill intent. By reclaiming my power of imagination and choice—by thinking for myself instead of allowing culture to think for me—I freed myself.

Don't Be A Sheep—Avoid Groupthink

The irony has not been lost on me as I beseech you to *think for yourself.* In any case, I hope this section of the book reinforces that you can decide whether or not to take my advice. Critical thinking is your most powerful tool in constructing your reality, and without it, you may find yourself unknowingly swept into the beliefs and behaviors of the masses.

Imagine you're in a room with nine strangers observing a canvas that has a green triangle drawn in the center of it. As you appreciate the artwork, you overhear more and more from the nine strangers how red the triangle appears. Their appraisal becomes the overwhelmingly singular reality among them, to the point where you clearly know they all believe the triangle is red, while you know that they know that you still believe the triangle is green. Now, one of them blatantly asks you: *what color is the triangle?*

According to Polish-American Gestalt psychologist Solomon Asch's conformity experiment, which examined the extent to which social pressure from a majority could affect a person's willingness to conform to groupthink, seventy-four percent of people would conform in the aforementioned scenario and respond with red.[5] The people who conformed knew their beliefs were being invalidated but chose to conform to better fit in and avoid ridicule.[6] This phenomenon, known as normative social influence, reveals just how deeply ingrained our need for social belonging is—even at the cost of truth.

The results of this experiment shouldn't surprise you. Again, in a world doubly covered in vices than virtues, it is easier to act viciously (i.e., lie to fit in) than to act virtuously (i.e., uphold integrity despite social pressures). Consider the percentage of Americans who conformed for over two hundred years to the notion that Africans weren't human when they knew, upon looking into the eyes of a slave, that they too were in fact a person. Groupthink, when left unchecked, has led to some of the greatest moral failings in human history.[7]

Recall what I shared in chapter one about your un-wavering imagination and how your desired state moves through dimensions to become your reality. Based on memetics—the study of how ideas and cultural informa-tion spread—our ideas are perceived as:

"a kind of virus, sometimes propagating in spite of truth and logic. Its maxim is: Beliefs that sur-vive aren't necessarily true, rules that survive aren't necessarily fair, and rituals that survive aren't necessarily necessary. Things that survive do so because they are good at surviving."[8]

James Gleich

In other words, the longevity of a belief or practice does not inherently validate its truthfulness or necessity; it only confirms its ability to persist.[9]

As a result of an idea's need for our divine attention to survive, it will do whatever is necessary to remain relevant, moving light years through space and time to cling to you. Some ideas serve you, while others serve only themselves.

So, avoid groupthink like you avoid the flu. Cover your mind with energies that reinforce your desired state, not an undesired state that desperately seeks your attention to exist. In doing so, you become the shepherd of your mind, body, and soul—not the sheep that mindlessly follows wherever it's nudged or beckoned, only to be lost to ravenous wolves. Or worse still, lost to its own idleness and ineptitude, needing desperately to cling to a life source.

Delete Social Media

In December 2020, I deleted all social media apps from my phone. For me, that included Snapchat, Twitter (now X), Facebook, TikTok, and Instagram. This decision was not made impulsively or in a manic fashion; rather, it was the result of deep reflection and an understanding of how these platforms influenced my mental and emotional well-being.

A couple of months before I deleted social media, I went through a breakup with the girl I had been dating for a year and a half during college. That breakup hit me hard, and by Thanksgiving, I found myself at my cousin's house, enduring a depressing dinner where everyone made sure to point out how much weight I had lost. That night, I decided that I would not carry that negativity into Christmas break. I wanted a reset, a way to refocus my energy inward. As a result, I deleted all social media apps to avoid seeing her, her life without me, or the possibility of her moving on. Instead, I wanted to focus on my own resurrection—a personal transformation untainted by digital distractions.

Although my initial motivation was the fear of seeing her happy without me, the benefits I gained from that decision extended far beyond my breakup. In fact, I hadn't even realized how much I was lacking until I started flourishing without social media.

The first major benefit was an increase in my freedom to do what I wanted with my time. Without mindless scrolling consuming my attention, I became more intentional with how I engaged in the essential matters of my life. Studies have shown that excessive social media use is linked to reduced attention spans and difficulties in goal-directed behavior, as constant dopamine stimulation from online platforms diminishes the brain's ability to focus on long-term rewards.[10] Additionally, I found that I engaged in daily tasks with more patience and peace since I no longer relied on my phone for instant gratification. Research suggests that prolonged social media use can rewire the brain's reward system, making users more prone to seeking short-term stimulation at the expense of sustained attention and delayed gratification.[11]

Next, I experienced an ironic increase in autonomy by *not* being in the loop. One day, during the following summer, I decided to take learning to swim more seriously and made some friends at the beach. Eventually, they asked me to make a TikTok with them using a trendy sound and dance. I had no idea what they were talking about. They laughed, explained it to me, and encouraged me to join. I politely declined, amused by how disconnected I had become from digital trends. In that moment, I realized that my lack of exposure to social media allowed me to show up to social spaces with nothing but my own energy. I wasn't weighed down by comparison, expectation, or an awareness of the latest trends dictating how I should act. Psychological studies indicate that excessive social media use fosters conformity and erodes individual autonomy, as people tend to mirror online behaviors to gain social approval.[12] To my surprise, my new friends respected me more for it—they saw me as someone with a strong sense of self rather than just another person following the herd. Their reaction validated my decision, reinforcing my confidence in rejecting digital conformity.

So, if you're not going to delete social media for the benefits, at least consider doing it to avoid the detriments—because there are plenty. The first and most glaring issue is how social media fries your brain. The constant exposure to high-intensity, fast-paced content rewires cognitive functions, reducing attention span and increasing impulsivity[13]. You end up consuming vast amounts of toxic content without realizing how much time has permanently slipped away. Research has linked prolonged social media use to an increased risk of anxiety and depression, particularly due to the comparison trap and the addictive nature of these platforms.[14]

Beyond that, excessive social media use leads to a disturbing level of conformity. You begin to absorb and internalize the opinions, behaviors, and manufactured lifestyles of others at an alarming rate. Most of the content online is simply someone trying to convince themselves—and everyone else—that their life is amazing. The reality, however, is that most people's lives are mundane. Rarely do we see a post that reads, *Had an average day today.* Instead, we're bombarded with highlight reels, curated perfection, and exaggerated portrayals of success. This cycle reinforces unrealistic expectations, breeding dissatisfaction and envy.[15]

So why consume something that is both fake and parasitic? Social media, like processed fast food, is engineered for addiction, providing a quick dopamine rush but leaving you nutritionally (or intellectually) starved.[16] By removing it from my life, I reclaimed my time, autonomy, and mental clarity—benefits that continue to shape me to this day.

Don't Watch The News

Similar to my experience with deleting social media, I realized that after I stopped watching the news, I began to discern for myself what was truly important. The constant stream of information had shaped my perception of reality, and stepping away allowed me to reclaim control over my own thoughts and priorities. Research in cognitive psychology suggests that excessive media consumption can influence cognitive biases, leading individuals to perceive the world as more dangerous or negative than it actually is.[17]

News channels promote negativity and polarization—not because they are inherently evil, but because that's what the majority of people are conditioned to engage with. Sensationalism drives ratings, and higher ratings drive even more sensationalism. Studies in media psychology confirm that negative news elicits stronger emotional reactions, increasing viewer engagement and leading to a cycle of heightened negativity in reporting.[18] The more tragic a headline, the better the ratings. And as ratings climb, so does the intensity of the negativity, as networks compete for attention in an oversaturated information market. This vicious cycle persists because many people have allowed their consciousness to be completely compromised by external narratives. As a result, their emotions and internal state are dictated not by their own discernment but by the latest crisis broadcasted on their screens.

As I coupled my social media purge with my news detox, I regained control of my mind, body, and spirit, which allowed me to effortlessly manifest my desired state. Studies on mental health and digital detoxes show that reducing exposure to negative media correlates with lower stress levels and improved emotional well-being.[19] By stepping away from constant external stimuli, I was able to cultivate inner peace and clarity. Again, I'm still waiting for someone to approach me and say, *I just watched the news, and I feel so much better.*

Now, I honor what's truly important to me by first thinking for myself. I no longer allow external influences to dictate my worldview. Instead, I take the critical step toward my desired state by turning inward. Neuroscientific research on mindfulness and self-reflection suggests that individuals who practice introspection develop stronger cognitive autonomy, reducing susceptibility to external manipulation.[20] I choose to be the creator of my reality, rather than a passive consumer of the world's chaos.

Go Within

If you're one of those people who believe that they need to stay connected with social media or the news to know what's going on in the world and to stay aware of what's around them, trust me when I say that everything you need to know is within yourself. You don't need to reach outside of yourself to understand the universe. All you need to do is master and know yourself to discover your destiny. Research on introspection and self-awareness supports this idea, showing that deep self-reflection enhances problem-solving abilities and decision-making.[21]

All the answers to your questions reside within you because you are made up of the same laws and forces that govern this entire universe. Recall the principles discussed in *We Live In The Paradox Dimension*. Those principles are as present in you as they are in nature. Neuroscience has demonstrated that the brain is wired to recognize patterns in nature, suggesting that by understanding oneself, one can gain insights into larger universal principles.[22] As a result, by deeply studying yourself, you can uncover the forces that shape the world around you.

By going within, you reduce the amount of toxic energy you consume while simultaneously increasing the size of your internal oasis. This shift reinforces that *you*—not the news, not social media, not the distractions of the world—are the source of your desired state. Psychological studies show that individuals who disengage from constant external stimuli and cultivate inner awareness experience reduced stress and increased emotional stability.[23] You determine your internal conditions, which then, in turn, reflect in your external environment. Likewise, by isolating your positive energy from the negative, you strengthen your resolve to obtain your desired state. The people of this world start to act in your favor, playing the role you'd like them to play in your life.

I especially noticed how going within transformed my state when I began meditating. At first, the slightest discomfort would throw me off, and I'd lose my concentration. However, as I meditated more and more, my visualizations became so vivid that I was able to alter my reality in real time. Neuroscientific studies on meditation confirm that consistent practice enhances cognitive function, improves emotional regulation, and even alters neural pathways associated with perception.[24] It was like I was literally able to view my body from the inside and perform surgery all from my seated position on my couch.

Going within is the critical first step in deciding for yourself what your desired state even *is*, and, more importantly, why you need to become the person whose life has all they could ask for. Without self-reflection, you risk pursuing desires that are not truly your own but are instead shaped by external influences. Philosophical and psychological research on self-actualization suggests that individuals who engage in deep introspection are more likely to achieve fulfillment and long-term success.[25]

The Only Change That Matters Is Self

Last summer, I had the privilege of watching *The Seven Deadly Sins*, an anime following the dynamic love story of Meliodas and Elizabeth. During Meliodas' quest to reassemble his chivalry, he shares with a comrade, "What matters isn't what others think of you, but what you think of others." His wisdom hit my ears like a boom underwater.

If you believe others—family, friends, peers, the universe, God—act benevolently whenever possible and strive to aid, then you will encounter a loving world where others help you wherever they can. Studies in cognitive psychology suggest that individuals who hold a generally positive outlook on human nature experience more fulfilling social interactions and greater overall well-being.[26] On the other hand, if you believe others are malevolent and constantly out to get you, well then, you'll continually see yourself getting fucked ... over and over. This aligns with research on confirmation bias, which shows that people tend to seek and interpret experiences in ways that reinforce their preexisting beliefs.[27]

If you want to change the world, then start by changing yourself. You will never control how others think, feel, or act. However, you always have control over your thoughts, emotions, and actions. Studies in neuroplasticity confirm that individuals can rewire their brain patterns through intentional thought processes and repeated behavior.[28] Depending on what you decide to think, how you choose to feel, and what you decide to do, you will determine whether you exist in your desired or undesired state. So, I should rephrase my topic sentence: If you want to change the world, then you *only* have to change yourself.

Let's face it—we all know that one unattractive person who somehow attracts lover after lover, or the depressed millionaire who seemingly has it all but remains unfulfilled. What makes or breaks one's life is one's sense of self. Psychological research on self-concept and self-efficacy suggests that people who hold a strong, positive sense of self are more likely to succeed in relationships, careers, and overall happiness.[29] The instant that you accept all negative aspects of yourself will be both the beginning and the end of your struggles. You will no longer misuse your energy fighting battles that do not serve you but rather enter a state of flow, governed solely by your own thoughts, emotions, and actions. This concept aligns with the philosophy of self-actualization, which suggests that personal fulfillment arises from self-acceptance and alignment with one's true nature.[30]

Taboo Is The Only True Taboo

In order to think for yourself, you must remove the clog in your mental drainpipe: taboos. A taboo is a social or religious custom that prohibits or forbids discussion of a particular practice or association with a particular person, place, or thing. In other words, taboos are social clogs or roadblocks that restrict independent thought and personal growth.[31]

During seventeenth-century America, it was widely considered taboo to regard Africans as people. The prevailing social custom dictated that Africans were property, no different from cattle. Similarly, there were deeply ingrained customs that forbade all women from voting or attending college in this country. Even expressing opposition to these norms was often met with severe social consequences, sometimes even exile from one's community.[32] History has shown us time and again that what is deemed "taboo" is often merely a tool of control, designed to maintain the status quo and suppress progress.

When you choose to live into your desired state, you will inevitably oppose others and potentially offend them. These discomforts are both necessary and, in fact, bonuses. Since you cannot simultaneously exist in both your undesired state and your desired state, you must neglect the life that no longer serves you and commit to the one that uplifts and supports your growth. Doing so may provoke backlash from individuals or even entire communities, as they perceive your transformation as a threat to the established order. This kind of resistance is a sign that your internal condition has become firmly rooted in reality—so much so that it has begun to disturb the opposing energy.[33]

Psychological studies suggest that societal norms, including taboos, play a significant role in shaping human behavior, often leading individuals to conform even at the expense of their personal aspirations. Those who break free from these constraints frequently experience initial resistance but ultimately pave the way for broader cultural evolution.[34] The persecution you may face for breaking taboos is, in some sense, proof that you are making an impact. The greater the resistance, the more deeply you know you are carving a new path.

Lastly, thinking for yourself and pursuing your desired state is an act of true freedom. You cannot honor the voice in your mind while simultaneously gaslighting yourself into believing what the majority believes. You must develop unwavering resolve in your efforts to obtain your desired state—especially when that state challenges your previous habits and lifestyle. Embracing taboos, rather than fearing them, is the key to breaking free from self-imposed limitations.

For example, openly discussing financial success, such as becoming a millionaire, is often viewed as taboo in certain social circles. However, research in behavioral economics indicates that those who actively visualize and speak about their financial goals are significantly more likely to achieve them.[35] By giving life to the idea of honoring your worth and prioritizing your well-being, you shift the paradigm for yourself. When you establish a new standard of thinking, others will either adjust to align with it or remove themselves from your space. If they refuse to adapt, more power to them—because in your oasis of abundance, they are merely playing the role of the desert.

Beware Of Claims About Human Nature

As you continue to think for yourself and take consistent actions that guide you closer to your desired state, you will inevitably encounter sweeping claims about bad habits and unproductive lifestyles, all attributed to human nature. For example, phrases such as *"It is what it is"* and *"C'est la vie"* tend to serve as excuses, giving people a pass when it comes to failing to reach their goals. These statements are often accepted without question, subtly reinforcing a mindset that limits growth and progress.[36]

My biggest problem with these phrases is how they generalize life and, in doing so, diminish the potential accomplishments that people can achieve. You rarely hear these expressions in response to success stories. Instead, they are used as a blanket narrative to justify why people remain in their undesired states. Research on learned helplessness demonstrates that when individuals believe outcomes are beyond their control, they are less likely to take meaningful action to change their circumstances.[37]

The reality is that such phrases tend to cast a negative outlook on people and attribute that pessimism to human nature itself. I am always cautious when I hear claims—especially discouraging ones—about what is supposedly *natural* in human psychology and behavior. Psychological studies indicate that people tend to adopt limiting beliefs based on cultural conditioning and personal experiences rather than objective truths about human nature.[38] Therefore, unless someone making such a claim has conducted extensive, global research—surveying at least a third to half of the world's population—I refuse to accept an unreasonably small sample size as definitive proof. In most cases, what is being presented as a universal truth about human nature is actually a reflection of an individual's personal disposition toward a given subject. Studies in cognitive bias suggest that people frequently project their own experiences onto broader populations, falsely assuming their perspective represents a universal reality.[39]

Not All Characters In Your Favorite Show Are The Same

I love anime. I've seen roughly thirty different anime and have enjoyed them all to some extent. One major aspect that makes the best anime stand out is having a strong protagonist supported by a compelling cast of characters. All the anime that I absolutely love—*Naruto*, *My Hero Academia*, *Fullmetal Alchemist*, *Demon Slayer*, *One Piece* (to name my top five)—effectively utilize the fact that not all characters are the protagonist.

I am extremely fond of anime characters and use their lives as living examples of how to achieve great success and obtain my desired state. I genuinely consider these created characters to be real life people whose decisions and philosophies dictate mine. For example, Minato's sacrifice taught me the best can come out of the worst; Almight's legacy taught me that we can be chosen, even if not destined, for greatness; Edward taught me that Truth doesn't outweigh our love; Rengoku taught me to set my heart ablaze; *One Piece* at large taught me the power of friendship. However, at no point during my love of any particular anime did I wish that *all* of the characters were my favorite characters. Imagine that—one thousand chivalrous Sanjis! None of them are the least bit happy (since they're all dudes and not ladies). This highlights a crucial lesson: diversity in character roles makes a story compelling, just as diversity in personal success makes life meaningful.[40]

As you obtain your desired state, you will notice how your success will be different from others' success. What you desire will be different from what others desire. If you obtain your first million, you'll feel a lot different than Warren Buffett down to his last million. The journey you take to reach success can and will be different from others' journeys. Psychological studies on goal-setting and personal fulfillment suggest that individuals derive meaning from different pursuits, reinforcing the idea that success is not universal but personal.[41]

We are literally parts of infinity, yet we often act as if we must follow the same path. People will advise you based on what has worked for them, but as an educator, let me tell you why that is a flawed approach. Achieving your desired state is not a one-size-fits-all system. Just because something worked for someone else does not necessarily mean it will work for you. However, what *will* work for you is *you*. Research in cognitive behavioral therapy (CBT) has shown that self-awareness and personal agency are critical in achieving long-term success, rather than blindly following external advice.[42]

If you won't hear it from me, listen to what Paul writes in the Bible:

"There are diversities of gifts, but the same Spirit. There are differences of ministries, but the same Lord. And there are diversities of activities, but it is the same God who works all in all. But the manifestation of the Spirit is given to each one for the profit of all: for to one is given the word of wisdom through the Spirit, to another the word of knowledge through the same Spirit, to another faith by the same Spirit, to another gifts of healings by the same Spirit, to another the working of miracles, to another prophecy, to another discerning of spirits, to another different kinds of tongues, to another the interpretation of tongues. But one and the same Spirit works all these things, distributing to each one individually as He wills. For as the body is one and has many members, but all the members of that one body, being many, are one body, so also is Christ. For by one Spirit we were all baptized into one body—whether Jews or Greeks, whether slaves or free—and have all been made to drink into one Spirit. For in fact the body is not one member but many. If the foot should say, 'Because I am not a hand, I am not of the body,' is it therefore not of the body? And if the ear should say, 'Because I am not an eye, I am not of the body,' is it therefore not of the body? If the whole body were an eye, where would be the hearing? If the whole were hearing, where would be the smelling? But now God has set the members, each one of them, in the body just as

He pleased. And if they were all one member, where would the body be?"

(I Corinthians 12:4-19)

Not only will your desired state look different from others', but each unique expression of an individual's desired state needs to manifest in its own way to complete the bigger picture. Just like an anime needs a diverse set of characters to tell a compelling story, life needs diverse expressions of success to be meaningful. Studies on self-determination theory support this, suggesting that intrinsic motivation—one's personal and unique drive—is key to lasting fulfillment.[43]

Embrace that! Cherish the fact that no one will achieve success *your* way. Celebrate the success of others, and gladly play the role they need you to play. Because without our individual successes, no one can ever truly win.

Max Out *Your* Archetype

This section complements the previous one by reemphasizing the need to obtain your unique desired state. While this may sound redundant, it is better to over-explain than to risk confusion.

I first recognized this concept while playing *NBA 2K23*. I spent time and attention creating my own player to compete online against random opponents. As I designed my player, I realized that sacrifices were necessary due to the game's new "MyPlayer" system, which imposed stricter caps on player attributes. After hours of research, discussions with my four equally sweaty friends who also had "MyPlayers," and plenty of testing, I settled on playing with a 6'8" small forward.

What influenced my decision the most? Was it my teammates' input? The opinions of YouTubers? No. What I considered most was: *What am I naturally good at in this game?* On my team, I excel at defense and cutting to open spots to score effectively. As a result, I tailored my player to reflect my playstyle, maximizing what *I* was already skilled at. The result was a dominant player who thrived when I allowed the game to flow naturally—waiting for the primary ball handler and other scorers to pass up their shots and set me up for easy buckets. This approach led me to shoot around seventy percent from everywhere on the floor.

Not once did I envy or covet being the point guard or center. I focused on maximizing my own archetype. At the end of the day, no player could create a "MyPlayer" with a ninety-nine rating in every category—it's impossible.

I liken the covetousness of archetypes to a note on a piano desiring to be another note. Just because a C note isn't a D note doesn't mean the C note should rename itself D-flat-flat. It remains a C note and must be a C note to contribute to beautiful music as part of a larger instrument and ensemble. If a C note rejects its frequency and attempts to alter itself, it falls out of tune, creating dissonance that affects the entire composition. The world suffers every time someone strays from the truest version of themselves, as authenticity fosters harmony both individually and collectively.[44]

The same principle applies to genres. Genres in any art form serve as archetypes—structures that, when fully realized, can be "maxed out" in a sense. Imagine if your favorite country song was suddenly in Japanese and played at twice the speed. Or if your go-to workout rap playlist consisted solely of Barney remixes. Would you feel robbed, cheated? Most likely. Just as music depends on each note playing its proper role, audiences rely on genres to maintain their integrity.[45] A genre's authenticity forms part of its identity, and when it strays from its essence, it risks alienating those who depend on it for a specific experience.

To The Ocean, The Desert Is Evil—To The Desert, The Ocean Is Evil

As you become the person who most closely embodies your ideals, you will inevitably interact with those who oppose you. This opposition is not just incidental—it is a necessary component of your growth and self-realization.[46] I think of Tom Brady, the greatest football player of all time, when I imagine a person who simply excels yet is met with constant hate. All that GOAT did was win football games, and people hate his guts for it. Genuinely, even if I weren't a Patriots fan, I could find no logical reason to bash him.

Then it finally dawned on me: even if one stands for their highest ideals, there will always be those who stand for the antithesis of those ideals.[47] For example, to an ocean, a desert is evil. An ocean teems with life, while a desert is desolate. Oceans are wet, while deserts are dry. An ocean is essentially a desert filled with water; a desert is an ocean without it. If I had to mediate the quarrel between an ocean and a desert—sitting between slurs of insults and heated remarks—I'd have to concede that both are right. It is in each of their natures to be as they are. A desert cannot sustain itself in the presence of an ocean, and an ocean cannot exist within the confines of a desert.[48]

The same dynamic applies to authentic self-expression. To a go-getter entrepreneur who works out six days a week, laziness and wasted opportunities are evil. To a Mountain Dew-drinking couch potato, physical activity and sunlight are evil. No matter what you choose to honor as your desired state, its antithesis will inevitably rise to oppose you.[49]

However, the beauty and magic of thinking for yourself and using your unwavering imagination is that you do not have to compete with your opposition—you can encourage it. Recognize your opposition as a litmus test for your success, not as a competitor. Their necessary existence fuels your necessary existence. In a way, by striving toward good, you will always summon its counterpart, evil.[50]

The real peace and joy come from recognizing when and where you can do the most good with the energy you embody. The task, then, is not to eradicate darkness but to discern when and where to bring light into the world versus when to leave the darkness where it stands.

At the end of the day, you are not mediating the existence of oceans and deserts. As I mentioned before, we can never choose when and where it rains (thankfully). However, what we do mediate is the circumstance for their existence. Despite both parties calling the other evil, if I asked Mother Earth, she'd say she created both because she needs them—always.

You Know The Answer—How You Arrive Is Up To You

In the spirit of this section, I'll keep my remarks brief: at all times, you already have the answer within yourself—you just need to recognize which course to take.

I liken the idea of already possessing the answers to solving a math problem. Let's say that the number 4 represents your desired state. Four is who you want to become and the lifestyle that reflects your inner resolve. Four is the solution—you already know what you want and why. Your desired state isn't what you're discovering or solving for. The fun part now is figuring out how to get there.

Since 4 represents your desired state, the next step is identifying whether you have an excess or a deficiency in relation to 4. Are you at 10 when you want to be at 4? Ten can represent overindulgence when you need discipline, overstimulation when you need peace, or overcommitment when you need free time. In that case, subtract or remove 6. If, on the other hand, you're at 1 when you want to be at 4, then you need to add 3. Three could represent courage when you've been hesitant toward a decision or conviction when you've doubted your ability to grow beyond who you currently are. Either way, you already know the answer—the path to its attainment is infinite.

This concept is powerful because it frees you to pursue your desired state in any way that suits you. Psychological studies on decision-making and goal achievement suggest that clarity in desired outcomes significantly enhances mo-tivation and persistence.[51] When you think about it, 4 repre-sents many people's ultimate goals: happiness, abundance, freedom. But we all stand in a different relation to 4. Even if someone's path is as complex as $x^2 - 8x + 16 = 0$ (solve for x), with enough imagination, they too will reach 4. Research in cognitive flexibility supports this notion, showing that there are multiple pathways to problem-solving and personal gr owth.[52]

Avoid Parking Lot Science

I first stumbled upon this concept when learning more about food and how to eat better. Michael Pollan's beautiful-ly written and jarring book *In Defense of Food: An Eater's Manifesto* opened my eyes to a key concept: parking lot science. In an interview later posted online, titled *Michael Pollan Debunks Food Myths* by Onnesha Roychoudhuri, Pollan explains that:

> "You measure what you can see, and you in-evitably decide that what you can see is what matters. Cholesterol is a classic example. It's the first factor related to heart disease that we could measure. So, the science got obsessed with cho-lesterol, and cholesterol became the cause of heart disease, and dietary cholesterol was what you had to eliminate. This is parking lot science. It's based on the parable of a man who loses his key in a parking lot at night. He spends all his time looking for it under the lights even though

he knows that's not where he lost it because that's where he can see best."[53]

In essence, parking lot science is the opposite of thinking for yourself. It limits your perspective, causing you to evaluate your circumstances only through the lens you've grown most accustomed to. This cognitive bias—where people focus only on the most easily accessible information rather than seeking a broader understanding—is well documented in psychological research.[54] Worse still, you then use those limited perspectives and undesired mindsets to declare that your desired state is impossible or beyond your reach simply because that's all you know—all you can see. This phenomenon aligns with what psychologists call *confirmation bias*, where individuals selectively focus on information that reinforces their existing beliefs, ignoring evidence that contradicts them.[55]

The trick is to resist the urge to assume that just because you've spent significant time in an undesired state, you cannot improve. Studies on neuroplasticity show that the human brain is capable of remarkable adaptation, meaning change is always possible, no matter how ingrained past behaviors or thought patterns may seem.[56]

Rather than measuring reality solely based on what you can currently see, recognize that your perspective is only a fragment of the truth. Many breakthroughs in psychology, neuroscience, and even quantum physics suggest that perception is malleable and deeply tied to what we choose to focus on.[57] The truth is that you can transform your life and obtain your desired state in a single moment. Research in cognitive-behavioral therapy (CBT) supports this, demonstrating that even a single shift in thought patterns can significantly alter emotional states and behavioral outcomes.[58]

You Can't Gauge The Weather Through A Window

When you think for yourself, you act and discover what's possible for you by participating. While I attended College of the Holy Cross in Massachusetts, I naively tried to gauge the weather by observing how students dressed outside. The problem, of course, was that students wore all sorts of clothing regardless of the actual weather—there was zero correlation between their outfits and the temperature. It would be freezing, and I'd see two people walking side by side, one bundled in a parka and the other casually wearing a white t-shirt (not an exaggeration). Time and time again, I found myself confused, often running back inside to grab a jacket.

This experience taught me a fundamental lesson: when striving to reach my desired state, I must take direct action rather than relying on external cues. Psychological studies support this idea, showing that individuals who take initiative and engage with the world directly develop stronger problem-solving skills and self-efficacy.[59] After graduation, my commitment to action took the form of volunteering at my high school to co-teach and coach.

After graduating college with the intent of becoming an English teacher and professor, I realized that, despite my deep understanding of the subject, I had no real experience teaching basic English curricula. Instead of passively enrolling in a master's program where I'd sit in a classroom learning, in theory, how to teach, I chose to volunteer at my high school's post-undergrad program to gain firsthand experience. Research on experiential learning suggests that hands-on practice significantly enhances skill development and retention compared to theoretical study alone.[60]

Taking this leap of faith—and I mean *mega* leap, considering how little money I made—propelled me toward my desired state at an accelerated pace. Immersing myself in real-world teaching provided insights no theoretical class could have. Neuroscience research on embodied cognition supports this, showing that learning through direct experience enhances cognitive processing and decision-making.[61] I now know when it's below zero outside and when it's sweltering hot by actually stepping into the world, rather than merely viewing it from a distance.

Before Reaching For A Key—Grab The Doorknob

This motto has been instrumental in transforming my life, particularly in terms of thinking for myself. Much like the previous section, reaching for the doorknob before a key means getting into your desired state on your own—not by reading about it or vicariously living through other fulfilled people.[62]

I learned this lesson the hard way when I once sat outside an open door for an hour, waiting for a friend. You should have seen the embarrassment on my face when they unhesitatingly popped the door open with a casual *"C'mon, bro, I wouldn't have left you waiting! That's why I left the door open!"*

Since then, I've sworn to always reach for the doorknob, even if only to confirm that the door is, in fact, locked. When you're journeying toward your desired state, you may mistakenly believe that open doors are closed. Unless you jiggle the knob yourself, you may end up keeping yourself outside of your desired state for no reason other than your own mental limitations and beliefs.[63]

I liken this image to a fly trapped inside a house, bumping against a window. Every time I've had the opportunity, I've opened those windows, hoping for the fly's freedom. I once did this with my car window when a fly was trapped inside. Guess what? The fly didn't immediately rush to its promised land. Each one I've observed has always kept crashing into the window before realizing it's open. They unnecessarily prolonged their suffering (which I'm sure is quite substantial in fly-time).[64] Whenever I witness such needless suffering, I always, always ask myself: *How many people are like this fly right now, crashing needlessly into their own window?*

So, before you decide that there's nothing you can do to attract your desired state, and that it's time to throw in the towel and sit outside by an open door for no reason, please check to see if that belief is true. Don't let your own mental barriers keep you from stepping into the life you want.[65]

Wear Your Own Glasses

To close this chapter, I'd like to share a timely bit of insight that kept me pushing forward toward my desired state. One day, I logged onto a live YouTube event hosted by Dean Graziosi, where he invited Trent Shelton to speak to the audience's soul (he sure spoke to mine). Trent shared that when you have a mission and try to convey it to others, people will call you insane. They don't judge you because your idea is unobtainable, but because they are viewing it through their own prescription lens.[66]

He continues to explain that everyone has their own unique prescription, and just like when switching real glasses, trying to see through someone else's lens will lead to headaches and confusion. As a result, it's best to wear your own glasses. Think for yourself. *Your* mission, *your* desired state, is crystal clear for *you*. Others may try to look through your lens and see nothing. They will think that you cannot be healthy, joyous, wealthy, abundant, nor free by following the desired state that you see so clearly. But you know what? That's *your* desired state—the one tailored specifically for *you!* Not only is it clear and obtainable, but you genuinely, wholeheartedly cannot imagine any sort of life without it.

So, go forth knowing that every day you're a step closer to the reality that has drifted and found immense refuge in your unwavering imagination and your divine attention. That state cannot exist without you, and your life isn't truly your life without your desired state.

Immediate Action Steps

1. Identify the Cultural Beliefs You've Absorbed: Reflect on the societal norms or beliefs you've inherited from your culture, family, or peers. Write down any that you believe are limiting or no longer serve you. Challenge these beliefs by asking: *Are these true for me? Or were they imposed on me?*

2. Question Groupthink: When you find yourself in a group setting and feel pressure to conform, pause and evaluate the situation. Ask yourself: *What do I genuinely think about this, separate from the influence of others?* Make it a habit to express your honest opinion, even when it differs from the majority.

3. Delete One Social Media App: Take a break from the constant stream of social media. Start by deleting one app that you feel is draining your mental energy. Spend the time you would have spent scrolling on a hobby, physical activity, or engaging in deep self-reflection.

4. Practice Mental Detox from the News: Try going without the news for a week and notice how your mood and perception of the world change. Reflect on what you were previously conditioned to believe and whether it was beneficial to your growth.

5. Engage in Daily Self-Reflection: Dedicate 10-15 min-

utes every day to reflect on your thoughts, actions, and emotions. Journaling or meditative practices can help you align with your inner desires, and you'll be better equipped to make decisions that align with your desired state.

6. Revisit Taboos You've Internalized: Write down any taboos or social restrictions that you feel limit your thinking. Consider where these taboos come from and whether they are truly beneficial or simply out-dated social constructs designed to maintain control. Challenge one of them this week.

7. Examine Your Beliefs About Human Nature: Notice when you unconsciously accept limiting beliefs about human nature, such as *"people are selfish"* or *"life is unfair."* When you catch these thoughts, pause and replace them with more empowering beliefs, like *"people are capable of growth"* or *"life presents opportunities for learning."*

8. Refuse to Conform to External Success Models: Instead of trying to mirror someone else's success, create your own unique path. Spend some time defining what success looks like for you—what will it feel like? What will you be doing? Write down your personal definition of success, independent of what others expect from you.

9. Max Out Your Archetype: Dive deep into who you are. What are your strengths, quirks, and values? Embrace them fully, and commit to amplifying your

authentic self in every area of your life.

10. Challenge Your Reality with a New Perspective: Choose one day each week to look at a familiar issue or problem from a radically different perspective. This could be from the lens of a completely different culture, an opposing viewpoint, or an entirely fictional scenario. Let the new perspective shift your thinking.

8

OVERCOME NEGATIVE EMOTIONS

"The lamp of the body is the
eye. If therefore your eye is
good, your whole body will
be full of light. But if your
eye is bad, your whole body
will be full of darkness. If
therefore the light that is in
you is darkness, how great
is that darkness!" —Matthew
6:22-23

***

What are you running from? What harsh truths do you stubbornly refuse to embrace? What irreconcilable conflicts torment your soul? Why do you persist in shunning the darkness within you? How heavy is the burden that your heart carries in silence?

Feel—Understand—And Accept Negative Emotions

Many people in their undesired states are constantly running from the one person they can never escape: themselves. The very act of rejecting the wretched parts of themselves only brings them face to face with what they don't want. They believe that by suppressing their ugliness, they can be made beautiful. However, the truth is this: the only way they can free themselves from this pitiful state of suffering is by embracing the fact that they are ugly and wretched.[1] (I know—*what?*)

Now, before you get offended, let me ask you: if you were perfect, if your poop didn't stink, why did you decide to read this book on obtaining your desired state?

The fact of the matter is this: all of us are imperfect; we are walking contradictions to our highest ideals. Sometimes it's hard to believe there's any semblance of the divine within us. But here's what the Redeemer says about that: "I have not come to call the righteous, but sinners, to repentance" (Luke 5:32). Thank God for coming to redeem *us sinners!* If my Friend came only for the Saved among us, He'd be preaching to a duet, let alone a choir.

It's the greatest gift in the world to be given the opportunity to obtain our desired state through our imagination. The very fact that we can envision a life beyond our current circumstances is nothing short of divine grace.[2]

So, what should we do with that chance? Step one: feel your negative emotions to their fullest depth.

Right now, in this moment, confront that beast of your mind and be still with it. It's been there all along, siphoning off and misusing your energy. But now, give it the attention it needs. Acknowledge it! *Feel, feel, feel!* Cry and lament because this awful creature is your baby, your creation, you. Behold it in all its immense pain and fear. Let it know you're there *with* it now, never again to neglect it. Be its parent at last (you bum!). Nurse it. Then, once you've felt what it's like to be decrepit and alone, move to step two: understand what it is and why it's come to be that way.

Now that you're sympathetically resonating with the beast of your mind, inquire into its very nature. What external events sparked the internal reaction you had to create such an awful outlook? It's this reality of co-creation that you need to embrace in order to understand that you decide what the events of your life mean. You decide! All the downs and negative emotions you've ever felt have been your decision—and no one else's to engage in. So, what was it? What happened? Do not, do not leave your pitiful beast without discovering this. Take as long as you need to answer this question. When exactly did you give birth to such vileness? When's its birthday?

Once you've understood the nature of the beast's existence, move to the final step: accept the negativity for what it is!

At last, in this empowered moment, with your closed eyes streaming with tears, say to it as I did: *"You are not that ugly!"* The negativity, the pain, and the fear—the beast of your mind—is not that ugly! Free it! Watch it demolish and dissipate back to its native nothingness. You've given it an awful life through your constant neglect. Now that you're back in its life, it's finally given the opportunity to flourish. To thrive. And like all the children whose parents gave them heaven on earth, watch it go away. The energy that was once misused now returns to you one hundredfold! Your mind, body, and spirit are now full of light. Every cell in your body is filled with the light Christ teaches us never to cover! It's yours again![3]

Bend The Twig

Oftentimes, people stuck in their undesired states will describe their situation with deflecting phrases like, *"I suck!"*, *"I'm the worst!"* or *"It is what it is,"* and *"This is just who I am!"* However, these beliefs are fundamentally wrong. Research suggests that people do not exist in an undesired state because they are inherently "the worst" or because they "suck." Instead, they are simply exercising certain parts of their character disposition more than others.[4]

For example, if you find yourself addicted to smoking cigarettes, vaping nicotine pens, or engaging in similar behaviors, you may be telling yourself the same old story: *"I'm just an addict."* Again, that's not true. Studies show that addiction is often a symptom of underlying behaviors and dispositions, not an inherent part of who you are.[5]

Similar to the last section, to discover the root of this demeaning story, you must first feel the essence of what you're doing. What are you *really* doing when you consume the substance of your addiction? Are you relaxing from a stressful moment? Are you stimulating your boredom? Are you celebrating? Or, perhaps, are you attempting to cope with deeper emotional pain? By understanding the root of your actions, you can begin to address the true cause of your behavior.[6]

Once you have the essence of your action settled, inquire about the character disposition you exercise to complete that action. Let's say you smoke (or consume any particular negative substance) every time you feel stressed or, conversely, when you rejoice. Which character disposition do you perform that action with? What mode of self or state are you operating from? Do you lack or are you deficient in a certain trait, or do you possess too much of a certain character? For instance, are you an impatient person, always in a rush? If so, then your rushed personality—stemming from your impatient character disposition—may perpetually lead you to seek quick escapes from stress or enter celebratory moments too often. In this case, your addiction may stem from impatience (a lack of patience) and has become a mode of self-expression to exercise that state.

So, now it's time to bend the twig.

Now that you've come to terms with the reality of your addiction (from *"I suck!"* to *"I'm impatient!"*), you must bend the twig. The beauty of shifting your internal narrative from a limiting one to one that more accurately reflects reality is that you can take new action toward your desired state. This step is where you implement new actions that radically align with your desired state. Research indicates that taking massive, radical action is essential to disrupting old patterns and fostering new ones.[7] You want to begin with radical, massive action to counterbalance your bad actions with good ones. Thus, you bend the twig from one crooked angle to the left to a new crooked angle to the right so that the muscle memory of the twig eventually brings it back to a new, leveled baseline. Both extremes—impatience and ambivalence—fail to serve you, whereas only virtuous patience can guide you toward a balanced life. Where you once lacked patience, you now substitute it with an excess of patience—but just for the time being. With enough practice, you will naturally "average out" and find the middle path.[8]

As a result, by understanding that your addiction has been an impatient version of yourself practicing a hurried lifestyle, you can begin to practice a patient lifestyle. So, the next time you go for a puff (or a sip, or a light, or a prick, or a stroke, or a flick), pause for a moment. Be more patient. Restrain yourself in that moment by using your newfound knowledge of yourself. Say to yourself, *"I'm not an addict; I'm just impatient and want this sadness to go away now—or I want to celebrate now. But, if I'm just a bit more patient right now, I'll be a step closer to living the life I desire most. I can live my best!"*

Just Because Something Bad Happened Once Doesn't Mean It Will Again

Something, I'll say conveniently, happens to your brain after experiencing something bad: traumatization. I call this reaction to negative events "convenient" because that trauma can be both a protective barrier and a limiting prison. Research suggests that the brain's tendency to shield us from perceived harm is a survival mechanism.[9]

THE BITTER END

When you burn your hand and learn that excessive heat causes pain, your brain remembers that bad experience and keeps you from repeating your mistake. However, just the same, if you hand your heart over to a lover who cheats on you with your best friend, the pain experienced during that traumatic event may prevent you from romantically loving again. Studies show that trauma in romantic relationships can significantly affect one's ability to trust and love again.[10]

The brain doesn't differentiate between experiences. It simply stores information for better or for worse, but your brain always assumes it's for better. This science of the brain retaining information is called neuroplasticity.[11] Neuroplasticity is the ability of the brain to form and reorganize synaptic connections, especially in response to learning or experience or following injury.[12] Neuroplasticity in the brain is like a path created in a grassy plain: only after repeated journeying does the trampled grass finally give way. Neuroplasticity is also like weather for your brain. So, to use the previous examples, when you feel burned by the heat and your lover, the weather in your brain becomes cold, icy. The cells in your body remember how much those experiences hurt, so they keep a jacket on to endure that kind of weather.[13]

The objective, then, is to remove those layers and bask in the sun of warmer mental weather by remembering that a bad experience doesn't automatically beget other bad experiences. Studies show that re-exposure to positive, affirming experiences can gradually rewire the brain, allowing us to replace old patterns with healthier, more adaptive ones.[14]

When journeying toward your desired state, you will inevitably have bad experiences. Your brain and every cell in

163

your body will shy away from feeling that again. But does that mean you should give up? Never. Your desired state will test you every opportunity it gets until you finally align yourself to it. You've seen your desired state in your imagination; you know the true cost and foster the attitudes and character dispositions to obtain it. As a result, until you finally reach that breakthrough where you completely embody what it means to be the person in your desired state, you will need to be tested and tempered over and over. So don't quit—especially not right before the miracle happens.

Shake off the cold weather of your mind and warm up! If you lose, must you necessarily feel defeated *too*? If your heart's broken, does that mean you also *have* to feel disheartened? Do those feelings come in tandem, like some cheap two-for-one fast food deal? Your downcast feeling toward an event is not required after the event unfolds. You are allowed to burn your brightest after you've been burned. You can decide for yourself what that event means for you. It's not just a power you have—it's the *only* power you have.

Radical Truth And Radical Transparency

I first came across this insight while reading Ray Dalio's book, *Principles*.[15] In it, he shares that his success in managing the world's largest hedge fund has come from his radical commitment to truth and transparency. Radical truth and radical transparency are not only great ways to discover what you don't know; they are also linchpins in your path toward overcoming negative emotions. Psychological research supports this idea, showing that self-honesty is essential for emotional regulation and personal growth.[16]

When you are radically honest with yourself, your negative emotions transform from points of dissonance to paths toward harmony. When you feel like a pile of dog poop stepped in by a careless passerby, you own that feeling. When you feel like sunlight, you radiate. The worst thing you can do is bury your emotions—whether it's the negative ones or the positive ones. Studies indicate that suppressing emotions leads to increased stress and psychological distress.[17] Allow all feelings to surface sooner rather than later.

Additionally, radical honesty fuels your self-esteem and confidence. You are never afraid to tell the truth and acknowledge how you really feel because all feelings simply become a matter of fact. You just are. And so you will be—freer and more alive than ever. In bringing to the surface that which troubles you most, you free yourself from all the side effects caused by emotional suppression, which research has linked to anxiety, depression, and even physical illness.[18]

When you are radically transparent, you not only acknowledge your truth but also allow others to see how you really feel. Similar to the freedom that follows an honest lifestyle, when you're transparent with who you are, you become invulnerable through sheer vulnerability. This may seem paradoxical, but research on emotional authenticity confirms that people who are open about their emotions experience greater psychological well-being and stronger interpersonal relationships.[19]

The moment you become fearless in letting others in, you can never be hurt by them again. I liken this sort of nonresistant approach to a butterfly. With its incomprehensibly fragile body, it flows with the wind, making little effort to control its ultimate destination. However, despite its seeming helplessness, its ability to maneuver effortlessly with the wind causes it to be untouchable. Similarly, your negative emotions will never consume you once you learn to let them in. Psychological resilience studies show that individuals who accept and process emotions rather than resist them are more adaptable to stress and hardship.[20]

Additionally, most people are drawn to this kind of transparency because it exudes confidence and cultivates trust. Research in social psychology suggests that authenticity and vulnerability foster deep connections and improve interpersonal relationships.[21] When you let others in, you create a virtuous cycle of genuine interactions.

All of this happens because you finally stop hiding from yourself. Nothing will hurt when you declare: *Here I am!*

Reflex—Reaction—Response

A very simple indicator of all your suppressed negative emotions comes in the form of three words that, while similar, carry distinct meanings: reflexes, reactions, and responses.

Your reflexes to events serve as your principal guiding force. These are the split-second actions that occur after an external stimulus, revealing the truest state of your internal condition—pure, thoughtless motivation. Reflexes expose your true colors, much like seeds sprouting in a garden. Your mind is fertile soil for these seeds. If you plant good seeds, your reflexes will be good; if you plant bad seeds, your reflexes will be bad. In these instances, external stimuli act as the water that cultivates what was already inside of you.[22]

For example, if someone steps on my shoes and my first reflex is to throw a Floyd Mayweather-style haymaker at them, then that external stimulus (my big toe getting crushed) simply exposes that I am truly an irritable person, always ready to lash out. On the other hand, if someone slaps my beloved ice cream out of my hands and my reflex is to forgive them and buy another one, then that same external stimulus (someone treating my ice cream like a tee-ball) has instead revealed that I am truly a peaceful and abundant person. Psychological studies on emotional regulation support this idea—our immediate emotional responses are a product of ingrained habits and past conditioning.[23]

Similar to reflexes, reactions also indicate how our emotions manifest, but they involve more cognitive processing. Where reflexes are thoughtless, reactions require a bit of thought. If I continue the garden analogy, then reactions are like budding plants rather than mere sprouts. They are closer to maturity but not quite there yet. Reactions also have the ability to override reflexes.

So, even if my initial reflex was to throw a punch at the person who crushed my big toe, I still have the opportunity to pause and choose a more composed reaction. In this way, reactions serve as the "weeding" process of the garden—where reflexes may expose bad seeds, reactions give us the chance to uproot them. Neuroscientific research suggests that reactions emerge from the brain's limbic system but can be moderated by higher-order executive functions in the prefrontal cortex.[24]

Lastly, the highest form of action after an external stimulus comes in the form of responses. Responses are like fully grown oak trees—rooted, unwavering, and patient. Unlike reflexes and reactions, responses reflect a state of complete maturity. They occur only after careful thought and consideration of the circumstances.

People develop measured responses by consistently tending to their internal garden, fertilizing only good seeds while refusing to cultivate bad ones. When your internal soil is properly maintained, you won't even entertain a negative response. If someone decides to Aaron Gordon under-the-legs windmill dunk your scoop of ice cream, instead of anger, you will cheer them on. Your response remains grounded because you are internally grounded.

Now, you might be thinking, *That's impossible! No one can always respond correctly.* But before you rush to dismiss this as unrealistic, let me ask you this: Would you find it reasonable, fair, or even possible for an apple tree to produce oranges? Or for a rattlesnake's venom to bring someone back to life? Nature follows the patterns of what is cultivated, and so do we. Behavioral psychology reinforces this—habitual responses become ingrained through neuroplasticity, shaping our automatic behaviors over time.[25] The way you respond to life is merely a reflection of what you have nurtured within yourself.

Get Back Up

THE BITTER END

To close this chapter, I'd like to end with a deep conviction of mine:

We never get to the place where we never fall again; we only get to the place where we always get back up.

Everyone falls. People fall every day. Everyone struggles with their negative emotions. They hate to feel bad, so they suppress their emotions like landmines. But the more they suppress, the more pressure builds beneath the surface. Eventually, with enough explosions, they reach a breaking point. And in that moment, they decide to stay down. They give up and remain negative for life, because for them, at least this way, they'll never have to fall again.[26]

But! My beloved reader, there is a turning point in life that comes after you accept that you are a falling creature: the point where you always get back up! Once you understand that falling is inevitable, you can shift your focus. Sure, you'll always fall down, but if you make it a habit to rise every time, then each fall occurs at a higher place than the last. This is a concept often seen in trading, referred to as *higher lows*.[27] In an upward trend, the market may decline at times, but the low points become progressively higher. The same applies to life: if you keep getting back up, you will always land on a higher level than before.

This is how real progress happens. If you feel like every two steps forward result in one step back, think about where you'll be after fifty steps. The answer: sixteen steps ahead! It may not be the fifty you hoped for, but had you stopped after your first setback, you'd be just one step ahead. Persistence compounds over time, building resilience and creating lasting change.[28]

DONNEL DELVA

No one ever gets to the place where they never fall again. That would be the dream—perfect, uninterrupted progress. But reality is different. Life is filled with mistakes, setbacks, and moments of doubt. Yet, despite all of that, we can reach the place where we always, *always* get back up. And that, my dear reader, is all that truly matters.

We get there because that's the only place our desired state resides. Our dreams, our highest aspirations, and the life we long for—they all exist at the end of a road paved with persistence. When a city of gold atop a hill on Mount Olympus in Valhalla beckons us, how could we possibly stay down? Even in our lowest moments, we are drawn forward by the undeniable force of our own imagination and belief.[29]

Immediate Action Steps

1. Feel Your Emotions Fully: Sit with your negative emotions in silence. Close your eyes and feel every sensation—fear, anger, sadness—without judgment. Let the intensity wash over you, knowing that by feeling deeply, you are beginning to break free from suppression. Allow yourself to cry, breathe deeply, or even scream if needed.

2. Understand the Origin: Take a step back and reflect on the situation that triggered your emotions. Ask yourself: *What external event sparked this reaction in me?* Think deeply about the meaning you've attached to this event. Write down the experience that caused this negative emotional state. When did it begin, and why did you react in the way you did?

3. Examine Your Behavioral Patterns: If your emotions have been influencing specific behaviors—whether addiction, avoidance, or self-destructive actions—take a close look at what these behaviors are. What are you doing when you feel the urge to engage in this behavior? Are you trying to avoid pain, seeking relief from stress, or perhaps numbness from past wounds? Write down the behaviors, and connect them to your emotional triggers.

4. Recognize Your Internal Dialogue: When negative emotions arise, what story do you tell yourself? Do

you label yourself as *"the worst,"* *"broken,"* or *"unworthy"*? Consciously challenge these thoughts. Write down the story you've been telling yourself and rewrite it with compassion and self-empowerment.

5. Radically Embrace Your Truth: Acknowledge the full extent of how you feel—whether positive or negative. Admit your anger, frustration, fear, or sadness without shame. Write it down in a journal or say it out loud to yourself.

6. Practice Reframing the Narrative: Reframe the way you view past pain. When you think of past pain, ask yourself: *What lesson can I extract from this? How did this experience serve me in my growth?* Write down the new, empowering perspective on those events.

7. Respond, Don't React: The next time you feel triggered by an external event, practice response over reaction. Pause and take a deep breath before you act. Give yourself the space to choose a response that aligns with your highest self. Reflect on the situation and ask: *What is the wisest response in this moment?* Write down how you can better handle similar situations in the future, creating a more mindful and intentional response.

9

THE UNIVERSE IS AN AIDING FORCE

"Therefore do not be like
them. For your Father knows
the things you have need
of before you ask Him."
—Matthew 6:8

***

What keeps you up at night worrying? What stresses you out well beyond repair? What necessities did you yearn for, only to be denied? Has the universe *ever* given you anything you did not need?

You Are Not A Victim Of The Universe

Not a single part of this book would be possible to put into practice if you believed that you were a victim of this universe. How could you begin to imagine a reality that you can co-create if you are caught in the illusion that the universe has already designed a living hell for you? Would you ever think for yourself if you believed the universe had its mind set on tormenting you? Absolutely not! Studies on learned helplessness suggest that those who feel powerless in their circumstances often fail to take action, reinforcing their own suffering.[1]

Only those who believe that they are not merely co-creators of this universe, but the very means of its existence, will rise to live the life they desire. Without you, again, the universe implodes on itself, returning to its native nothingness. With you, however, the glory of this universe is realized and made manifest. This concept echoes ancient philosophical and spiritual teachings that describe consciousness as the fundamental force shaping reality.[2] Even modern quantum physics suggests that the observer plays a crucial role in determining the outcome of events, further supporting the idea that we are active participants in shaping our world.[3]

The Universe Wants To Help You

This chapter at large isn't knowledge you don't already experience every single day. I love to liken this experience to something we have all witnessed in our bodies: it heals itself.

What happens when your body is cut? Does the wound stay open forever, becoming increasingly infected and eventually fatal? Nope. It heals itself. Better said: the universe, of which we are an integral part, heals the cut for us. The body's natural regenerative abilities have been widely studied in medical and biological sciences, demonstrating how cells instinctively repair damage to maintain life.[4]

Since we *are* the universe, what it does for itself, it does for all of us. The universe sends hurricanes and wildfires, and you may step back and wonder: *why all the destruction?* What seems to be devastation, in this paradoxical land, turns out to be the very force that promotes life. Research in ecological science confirms that natural disasters often play a crucial role in renewal—wildfires enrich soil, and hurricanes regulate climate patterns.[5] Out of the cinders come new sprouts, nurtured by the now-fertile soil. The winds of the hurricane test many trees so that they may grow stronger over time. This resilience is reflected in natural selection and evolutionary biology, where environmental pressures shape stronger, more adaptive organisms.[6]

As a result, when your body—when any creature's body—is cut, the oxygen in the air meets the oxygen inside you to create new cells. Without any effort on your part, those cells know how to repair the living organism. They *know*. That understanding is due to the universal intelligence constantly aiding life! Cellular regeneration and the role of oxygen in healing have been key areas of study in biomedicine, showing how physiological responses work to repair and enhance survival.[7] It is a beautiful thing!

And do your cells return your body to its previous state? Not quite. Your cells *know*—the universe *knows*—to repair living organisms to a *higher* level, making similar injuries less fatal next time. The hurricane, the wildfire, the cut—they ultimately make you and this planet stronger and more resilient. Research on post-traumatic growth suggests that human beings also adapt psychologically in response to hardship, emerging more capable and wiser than before.[8]

Nothing has the power to keep that cut open forever, nor the power to keep the winds bellowing or the fires burning eternally. Others would have you believe that life is one long hardship with rare moments of bliss. That couldn't be further from the truth. But again, for many, the struggles in life feel like the dominant reality.

Well, I guess the bad is always there ... but so is the good. So, in actuality, life is endless bliss and a stream of miracles accompanied by rare moments of hardship. It's not a constant shitshow with commercial breaks of peace. It's *constant peace* with occasional advertisements of shit you don't need.

So, the next time your plan goes awry or you feel behind, imagine that you are right on track because the universe is always helping you. Ask yourself: *How is this helping me? How is this all part of the divine design?* The answer to those questions will set you on the abundant path to your desired state.

The Universe Is Always Moving Towards Equilibrium

THE BITTER END

When you observe the universe around you and notice how it unceasingly aids itself and supports life, you may assume this process happens without thought. However, recall the principle that ALL IS MIND—everything that exists is a product of consciousness. Therefore, this aiding process is an ongoing thought the universe perpetually has.[9]

You may not consciously think about your nostrils drawing in oxygen or your arteries carrying blood to your organs, but the universe does. In this way, you are participating in this process, even if unconsciously. The universe ensures that every living organism is sustained and that life is supported. This is the will of the universe—an intrinsic, intelligent force that operates toward balance and fulfillment.[10]

The universe does not judge; it simply reflects. It provides people with exactly what they continuously focus on and ask for, whether consciously or subconsciously. If negativity dominates your internal world, the universe responds by supplying a never-ending stream of negativity. Studies in cognitive psychology confirm that our focus shapes our reality—what we repeatedly concentrate on becomes reinforced in our neural pathways, affecting perception and behavior.[11] Conversely, if gratitude and service to others define the best parts of you, then the universe supports the life of the one who supports life. This concept aligns with research on positive psychology, which shows that gratitude fosters greater well-being, resilience, and success.[12] When your will aligns with the benevolent will of the universe, you will accomplish everything you desire.

You may also fall into the belief that chaos and suffering are permanent fixtures of existence. If so, remember that since the universe is always moving *toward* equilibrium, disorder is *temporary*. All negativity, all chaos, is in a constant state of dissolution. Research in systems theory and thermodynamics suggests that all complex systems—whether social, biological, or cosmic—naturally progress toward states of balance and stability.[13] In due time, false realities will inevitably return to their native nothingness, for the universe wills it so.

Abundance Is The Natural State Of The World

Everyone—every living organism in this world—is meant to experience abundance. No one is meant to merely scrape by; rather, everyone is supposed to have more than enough. The truth is, there is more than enough for everyone.[14]

You see this plentiful reality everywhere. Look at the orange tree. Look to the orchard. When that tree, in all its fury, grows and expands, does it toil endlessly to produce just *one* solitary fruit? Of course not. A tree that springs from a single seed produces hundreds of fruits. This is nature's blueprint—expansion, multiplication, and overflow. Ecological studies confirm this phenomenon, showing that natural ecosystems tend toward growth and self-sustaining abundance when undisturbed by artificial constraints.[15]

We see the same principle of abundance in finances. This is why we never need to compete to obtain our desired state—because there is more than enough money in the world to support the life of our highest ideals. Are we still passing around the same currency that the first American presidents originally printed their faces on? No. New bills are printed constantly, as needed, to meet economic demand. The global money supply expands as productivity and financial systems grow, demonstrating the ever-renewing nature of wealth.[16]

Likewise, there is also more than enough of *you* to go around. Many people get trapped in the illusion that their time is scarce and wish there were two of them to manage all their responsibilities. However, that scarcity mindset is just that—an illusion. Since abundance is the natural state of the universe, there will always be more of *you* to go around when you tap into the infinite energy that permeates the world. Quantum physics and metaphysical studies explore this concept, suggesting that consciousness itself is not bound by physical limitations and that energy—once directed—creates expansion.[17]

Beyond your individual efforts, unseen forces are always at work, aiding you along your journey. The world itself operates with an intelligence beyond human comprehension, orchestrating events, connections, and opportunities. Psychological studies on synchronicity and the law of attraction support this idea, indicating that when individuals align their beliefs with abundance, they become more attuned to opportunities that reinforce that mindset.[18]

$$E = mc^2$$

In 1905, Albert Einstein introduced the world to his theory of relativity, encapsulated in the now-famous equation: $E = mc^2$. Straight from the genius himself, Einstein explained in an interview that this equation states mass and energy are simply different manifestations of the same thing.[19] More specifically, $E = mc^2$, in which energy is equal to mass multiplied by the square of the velocity of light, demonstrates that a very small amount of mass may be converted into an enormous amount of energy, and vice versa.[20]

While I am certainly no scientist, the implications of this equation extend far beyond physics. When it comes to obtaining our desired state, this principle suggests that the energy we release and absorb directly correlates with the physical manifestations that follow. In other words, our thoughts, emotions, and intentions create an energetic output that influences the reality we experience.[21] This concept is ever-present, observable in the way we attract people and events into our lives based on the energy we radiate.[22]

We are always engaged in a symbiotic dance with energy. The energy we exude and attract materializes in this dimension when we metaphorically "square" our speed of light by itself. But what does that mean? In layman's terms: when you use your imagination (represented here as the speed of light, a constant) to visualize and emotionally experience a desired state, you amplify its effect by reinforcing it through repetition and belief.[23] Neuroscientific research supports this, demonstrating that mental imagery and repeated visualization strengthen neural pathways, making imagined experiences feel real to the brain.[24]

Picturing your imagination functioning this way may sound advanced—or like complete hocus pocus—but at its core, the force that brings your desired state into your imagination is itself. Since the universe operates on mental principles, your unwavering, godly imagination must be the thinking force acting upon its own thoughts.[25] When this happens, you become the vessel—the physical matter—that energy needs in order to manifest in this dimension. And remember, this manifestation is not optional; it is law. Since it must happen, you might as well use it to your benefit.[26]

Synergy

When you observe the universe aiding life, you may be tempted to believe that processes occur in a closed system. Paradoxically, it sort of is: a closed system that possesses the ability to create more of itself within the closed system. However, there exists a magical element that allows for more and more life to be supported: synergy.

Synergy is the interaction or cooperation of two or more organizations, substances, or other agents to produce a combined effect greater than the sum of their separate eff ects.[27] In other words, 1 + 1 = 3. One of the most well-known examples of synergy is the relationship between bees and flowers. While bees need the pollen from the flowers, the flowers need the bees to spread their pollen, ensuring the proliferation of plant life. Without their cooperation, ecosystems would collapse.[28] However, if the process simply stopped there, their relationship would be a simple mutual exchange—but it's not! The synergy from this relationship extends far beyond just the bees and flowers; it leads to the flourishing of entire ecosystems, creating a ripple effect that sustains countless other species.

This principle applies to various aspects of life. Consider music, which consists of two fundamental components: sound and silence. On their own, they are simple elements, but when combined with intention, they create melodies that move the soul.[29] The same holds true for exercise—muscle expansion and contraction appear as basic opposing movements, yet their interaction results in strength, endurance, and vitality.[30] Even sex is an example of synergy, blending both the rhythmic and the physical—almost like musical exercise (beautifully so, but I digress).

The same synergy applies to manifesting your desired state. You may interact with your imagination and bring that energy into physical matter, but that exchange does not end there. What results from that transaction is a reality greater than the sum of your initial efforts—your desired state not only manifests for you but also ripples outward, shaping the world and influencing others. This very book is an example of synergy. Long after I have finished typing these words, something far greater than the sum of my fingers and this MacBook will remain: your experience reading it (and, with tremendous faith, the benefits you will reap from it).[31]

In most, if not all, synergistic relationships, we have the easy part. To be or not to be—that's it. We either perform the action necessary for the magic to unfold, or we don't. There are only two options, nothing more. Yet, the results of those two choices extend far beyond the choices themselves.

THANK GOD! That means all I have to do is be or not be. And guess what? I am *already* always being or not being. Who I am either aligns with the actions necessary for my goals to materialize or painfully contradicts them. If the conditions for creating your desired state were any more difficult—if you actually had to supply the third "1" to generate

"3"—then this universe would still be without form and void. Because when God spoke light into existence (God's "1"), if the universe had responded, *Sorry, but you have to turn the lights on yourself—figure it out, bud*, then nothing would have happened. Instead, the universe allowed itself to be acted upon, and the synergistic result is the beauty and glory that now permeate this life of yours without end.[32]

Law Of Dissonance

There's a well-established cognitive theory known as *cognitive dissonance*, which posits that people experience psychological discomfort when they hold contradictory beliefs, attitudes, or behaviors. To alleviate this discomfort, they often adjust their beliefs or behaviors to create consistency between them.[33] If you're reading this book to inevitably obtain your desired state (or if you're merely part of the "ninety-eight percent"), then you're probably experiencing some form of dissonance within yourself.

In this experience, once again, the universe aids you. The very fact that you feel discomfort from a lack of congruence should serve as a signal: the universe naturally pushes you toward equilibrium. The goal is peace—not discord. So when you're "on a diet" and find yourself creeping into the kitchen late at night, you—whether consciously aware or not—will experience a hellhole of dissonance ... and this is by design. Your remarkable body instills this discomfort as a form of protection. Nothing is more dangerous than a machine that contradicts itself. Research in neuroscience supports this, as studies have shown that unresolved cognitive dissonance activates stress responses in the brain, pushing individuals toward resolution through behavior or belief changes.[34]

Think about it: what would you do if your pair of scissors cut a piece of paper, only for you to open them back up and find that the very same scissors have somehow *repaired* your slice, leaving the paper in its original, overweight and plain condition? This paradox would disturb you because it contradicts the fundamental laws of cause and effect. Similarly, when your actions and beliefs contradict each other, your mind and body revolt against the inconsistency, urging you to bring your reality back into alignment.

So, always regard all signs of dissonance as a starter's gun for improving your life. Instead of thinking, *I'm so weak; I can never stick to a diet; let's just finish this pack of doughnuts with the bats,* decide, *Hey, this feels weird—hogging down these doughnuts at three in the morning. That discomfort is telling me something. I'm throwing all these sweets away and going to sleep.* Studies in behavioral psychology suggest that recognizing cognitive dissonance in real time and taking corrective action strengthens self-discipline and long-term behavior change.[35]

Law Of Experience

During my first year out of undergrad, when I began teaching English to high schoolers, I faced a critical decision: should I further my education in grad school, or should I step directly into the classroom? Being the diehard student that I was, I applied to Harvard's Graduate School of Education. Lo and behold, I was promptly and utterly rejected. This was the first time in my life that a major educational plan I had set my sights on did not come to pass. Up until that moment, I had moved seamlessly through my academic journey—I applied to and attended just one high school, Fairfield Prep, and then one college, College of the Holy Cross, without a hitch. I was riding high on a perfect two-for-two track record, and most underratedly, a stress-free one.

So, in perfect Donnel fashion, I took that rejection not as a failure but as a divine redirection—a lead door closing so that a golden one could open. And, as if by cosmic orchestration, I coincidentally ran into the campus minister from my alma mater, who presented me with the perfect opportunity: a chance to teach English at Prep as a volunteer. I immediately seized the opportunity, and it led me to one of the most profound realizations of my life.

I learned more from my year of service about teaching English than I ever could have at the best graduate school in America. Why? Because I experienced it. Research in educational psychology supports this notion—experiential learning often surpasses theoretical instruction in developing practical expertise and retention of knowledge.[36] A year of hands-on experience in your desired field—whether it's playing one game, performing one surgery, or leading one battle—yields exponentially more knowledge and expertise than two years of studying theory in a classroom.[37]

Again, the universe aids us in acquiring ample experience so that we may master our desired state. Did I earn an M.A. in secondary education after that year? No (though I am currently completing one at Fairfield University's School of Education & Human Development). But did I learn how to be an effective teacher, balance work and life, and flourish as an adult? Absolutely. After all, experience is the best teacher, a sentiment echoed in psychological studies emphasizing learning-by-doing as the most effective method of skill acq uisition.[38]

Law Of Fearful Confrontation

But what if I'm so scared I pee my pants until I fill the Grand Canyon? I hear you—though I wouldn't want to smell you.

Dun ta da dunn! The universe saves the day again with a simple strategy to overcome that fear: exposure therapy. The principle behind exposure therapy and the law of fearful confrontation is to gradually acclimate yourself to whatever you fear through incremental steps. Research in behavioral psychology has shown that systematic desensitization—gradual exposure to a feared stimulus—can significantly reduce fear responses over time.[39]

For example, despite being a natural-born teacher, I was still nervous about instructing students on my own, even in a very low-stakes summer orientation course for incoming freshmen. The class was literally just about helping students acclimate to the school, and my job was to make that transition easy and fun. But it was the first class I ever ran solo, and it ended up teaching me more than it taught my students.

I started off slow. At first, I only addressed them from the teacher-facing left side of the classroom. I must've looked so awkward, standing all the way in the corner, pointing at the projector in the middle of the class. But gradually, I exposed myself to more and more direct interaction with them. Now, after a year of teaching English, I practically dance around the classroom, shaking the answers loose from them. Research suggests that repeated exposure to challenging situations not only reduces fear but also strengthens confidence and performance over time.[40]

Incremental exposure to what you fear is the universe's way of cultivating strength and courage within you. "God will not have his work made manifest by cowards,"[41] so don't expect to reach your desired state while remaining in fear. If you're afraid of spiders, find out exactly how deep that fear runs. Do you feel faint just looking at one on TV? What about tiny ones? Did *Harry Potter and the Chamber of Secrets* traumatize you beyond repair, leaving you quaking like a leaf? If so, you're not alone—research indicates that phobias often stem from early traumatic experiences or media exposure.[42]

Find out where your limits are. Learn about yourself. Discover how much you can take before you start calling for mommy. Through gradual, controlled exposure, you will overcome that fear. And once you do, you'll find yourself standing on the side of town where your desired state lives.

Law Of Inertia

If you don't already know Newton's famous first law of motion, it very simply states: objects in motion stay in motion, and objects at rest stay at rest, unless acted upon by an external force.[43]

The universe abides by this law without exception. If you're in your desired state—making love, making money, making fun—then you're going to find it easier and easier to sustain that momentum. You'll keep getting lovers to orgasm, organizations to donate to, and new places to travel. Conversely, if your sex life is as real as the dinosaur outside—meaning it only exists on screens—then you're going to find it alarmingly easy to stay in that state as well. Studies on behavioral inertia in psychology confirm that habitual behaviors, once established, tend to reinforce themselves, making change increasingly difficult over time.[44]

The universe facilitates the expression of our desired states without discrimination. It doesn't judge between hot and heavy or alone with your phone—it simply enables you to keep doing what you're already doing. Neuroscientific research shows that repeated behaviors and thoughts form neural pathways, reinforcing patterns and making them more automatic.[45]

So, get started already on your desired state. See exactly what you want in your imagination and understand the internal shifts required to get there. Then, take action. Once you find your mojo—or momentum—let the gift of inertia carry you to the promised land. The principles of cognitive momentum suggest that once an individual initiates action toward a goal, it becomes significantly easier to maintain progress.[46]

Law Of Nonresistance

Per the nature of this section, I'll make the message brief and effortless. What's the easiest way for a hose to come gushing with deep water? Is it by stuffing your finger in the passageway and clogging it? How about folding it in half and squeezing the living daylight out of it? No and no. The answer: by clearing a way for blissful, orgasmic nonresista nce.[47]

You want your desired state. That's clear enough. But don't want it so badly that you stunt your own growth. Research suggests that overexertion and forceful behavior can actually hinder progress rather than accelerate it.[48] There will come a time on your journey when you realize that your forceful nature is what causes all your mishaps. Sit back. Let the universe help you. Go with the flow. If you've done all the necessary visualization, internal cultivation, and physical preparation—if you've planned the date, paid for dinner, and set a super relaxed tone at your place—then the universe will, by all means, bend time and space to give you the sexiest, most magical reality you can ever think of. Studies show that the law of attraction and nonresistance are key to manifesting what you desire.[49] It's the kind of reality that makes you scream and bite into your own pillow, for God, for more, to keep going, and to please, don't stop.

Believe me, with a universe that wants to bring everything to you, you have always been closer to that reality than you care to realize.[50]

Immediate Action Steps

1. Adopt an Internal Locus of Control: Reflect on areas of your life where you may feel like a victim. Write down specific instances where you felt external circumstances were controlling you. Now, rewrite those stories from a perspective where you, not the outside world, determine your response. Identify one area where you can take immediate action to move from feeling like a victim to feeling empowered.

2. Recognize the Healing Power of the Universe: Observe how your body automatically heals small cuts or bruises. Use this as a metaphor for the challenges you're facing. Reflect on a current problem or challenge and think of one small, positive action you can take that reflects your own natural ability to heal and improve.

3. Embrace Abundance: Take a moment today to acknowledge the abundance already present in your life. Whether it's the food on your table or the relationships you nurture, jot down three examples of abundance you experience. Visualize how expanding your mindset can attract even more of this into your life.

4. Tap into the Energy of Your Thoughts: Use the $E = mc^2$ principle to assess your thoughts and energy. Write down a current goal or desire, then consider the

energy you are sending out into the world regarding this goal. Are your thoughts and actions in alignment with this vision? If not, write down one specific action you can take today to align your energy with your desired outcome.

5. Create Synergy: Identify a relationship in your life—whether personal or professional—that could benefit from more collaboration. How can you create synergy within that relationship? Reach out to that person and suggest a way to work together to create something greater than the sum of your efforts.

6. Balance Dissonance and Harmony: If you've been experiencing internal dissonance (cognitive discomfort), acknowledge it. Write about what the discomfort is trying to teach you. Then, take one action to either align your beliefs or behaviors, moving toward a greater sense of inner harmony.

7. Fearful Confrontation: Think of a fear that has been holding you back. Break it down into small, manageable steps. Take the first step toward confronting this fear, no matter how small. Document your experience and how you felt before, during, and after taking that step.

8. Use Inertia to Your Advantage: Reflect on a positive habit you've established. How can you use the law of inertia to keep that momentum going? Set a small, achievable goal today that will reinforce that positive momentum. Alternatively, identify a negative habit

you want to break and take one deliberate step to create a shift in momentum.

9. Practice Nonresistance: Identify an area of resistance in your life—something you've been forcing or struggling with. What would it look like to approach this with ease instead of force? Take one action today to allow things to flow more naturally in this area.

10

DON'T BELIEVE IN EXCUSES

"And another also said,
'Lord, I will follow You, but
let me first go and bid
them farewell who are at
my house.' But Jesus said to
him, 'No one, having put his
hand to the plow, and looking back, is fit for the kingdom of God.'" —Luke 9:61-62

What fake excuses are you using to feel comfortable in your undesired state? How scary does it sound to become lovely, successful, healthy? Do your excuses provide a blanket you can tuck snugly under when the going gets rough? How do your excuses help you achieve your goal of comfortable mediocrity?

Never Give Up

At some point during your journey, you will want to desperately quit. You'll rue the day your heart erupted and you were swept into action. The whole journey will feel like a waste of time, and you'll cry—ugly, ugly cry. Please, allow me to be a single voice among many urging you: keep on going!

Remember when I said in *Don't Do Instant Gratification–Chip Away*, that I don't care if you quit one percent into a task versus ninety-nine percent—if you quit, you get zero results? Yes, I meant that, and I need you to summon whatever gusto you had up to continue reading to this point.

You want something unconventional, extraordinary. Do you think you can become that person by doing conventional, ordinary things? If you answered no, then you're wrong. Actually, obtaining your desired state does in fact require very simple and often banal things—good habits, decent character, pleasant attitudes, etc. The mystery that haunts people stuck in their undesired state is the dizzying routine hidden beneath the tip of the iceberg. Work out once, still fat. Work out every day, god-tier health, sexual attraction, you name it.

The people you admire and replicate can easily be mimicked. After a minimal amount of digging, you'll find that they've laid out the treasure map to their riches. They accomplished the peace of their desired state with aspects of human existence that everyone has access to: imagination, inner understanding, right conduct. However, where they blow people out of the water lies in their irrational ability to persist, to chip away, to never give up on their ultimate goal.

Their uncanny will to grit when others have long given up is truly irrational.[1] Our brains are designed to comfort us. The goal for our brains is to feed us information that protects us. Studies show that the brain's primary function is survival, so it naturally steers us toward safety and away from discomfort.[2] Remember, *It Doesn't Need To Be Rational To Be True*? It still doesn't. If I'm blowing thousands of dollars on my startup, spending countless days on my book, and see nothing to show for it in a year or two, logic and basic self-preservation instincts will alert my whole body to chill out and quit.

But here's the thing: you only need to be correct once. One company that took thousands of dollars and hours to begin, one book that took years to complete, can produce an abundance of wealth, health, happiness, and love that spans generations. What you have endured represents a stint of the good to be experienced by humanity. If you give up, you'll not only rob humanity of something we need, but strip yourself of the calling that the dimension of dreams has laid out for you. That world of imagination, of endless possibilities, needs you to exist—so please, keep going! You're closer than you think. You couldn't be any closer, since the desire has literally planted itself inside of you. Only you can be its hero and set it free. It knows that and chose you; now, you know it chose you—so create it.

Don't Avoid Problems—Find Solutions

You've already identified the true cost of what you want. I have no doubt that your desired state attracts its set of problems—all desired states do. However, there are problems that you happily accept as well as problems you begrudgingly tolerate. For example, a smoker may happily accept the increased chances of death but not be too happy about having to shell out a bunch of money—none of which ever slows their next puff. Studies in behavioral psychology indicate that people often engage in cognitive dissonance, accepting risks when the perceived reward outweighs the consequences.[3]

The goal of obtaining your desired state isn't to reach a place where problems don't exist (that place never comes), but to reach the place where you have solutions for the problems you face. Psychological research suggests that those who focus on problem-solving rather than avoidance experience greater resilience and well-being.[4] Looking at the dragon you need to slay without any sort of protection or weapon will always be daunting. Approaching Goliath with a sling will always make you hesitate. The difference between your newfound troubles and those of the past is that now you're armed with much more than external forces.

You attracted your desired state; it manifested for you because you wield the internal prowess necessary. That dragon may burn your skin and pierce your flesh. Goliath may crush your bones and grind you between its teeth. But what cannot be touched is your innermost self. Research in neuroscience highlights that individuals with strong self-efficacy beliefs—trust in their own abilities—are more likely to persist in the face of challenges and shape their reality.[5]

THE BITTER END

The universe now answers your every call and satisfies your every need—um, hello!—nothing outside of your unwavering, magical self can ever shake you. Studies on the law of attraction suggest that focusing mental energy on solutions rather than obstacles increases the likelihood of achieving one's goals.[6] Your imagination will attract what's needed to bring you back to equilibrium, your natural state. Cognitive science supports this, showing that visualization techniques can enhance problem-solving abilities and promote emotional balance.[7]

Failure Doesn't Mean Defeat

Consider all failures as stepping stones toward accomplishing your ultimate goal: obtaining your desired state. When the realization of your desired state remains your true objective, minor failures pale in comparison to the reality that you are continually moving closer to living as the person you seek to become.

Since your desired state is a way of life rather than a tangible, limited thing, whether or not material possessions manifest before you will not sway you from your journey. You are not after a mere object—you are becoming someone. This transformation means that your identity, not external validation, defines your desired state. A person who has truly become this version of themselves is incapable of defeat. Research on identity-based habits suggests that when we align our sense of self with our goals, we are more likely to sustain motivation and resilience in the face of setbacks.[8]

Often, if not always, when we embody the person we aim to be but have yet to attract certain material possessions, it signifies that we have grown beyond our original conception of success. For example, during my journey, I once desired a Tesla Model S. I saw it as a symbol of convenience, luxury, and the forward-thinking appeal of electric cars. However, as I continued my path, I became something far greater—an authentic, vibrant person full of life. Yet, the Tesla has not arrived. Do I feel like I have failed? Admittedly, a bit. But do I feel defeated? I scoff at even considering an answer. Studies in positive psychology highlight that true fulfillment comes not from material acquisition but from internal growth and purpose.[9]

The things we once desired were never the ultimate goal. What we truly seek is to become someone who cherishes everything—every moment with a loved one, every good anime, every sunrise. If a mansion is necessary for you to enjoy fresh air or if a Rolls-Royce is the only way you can appreciate a smooth ride, then you are still trapped in an undesired state. Materialism alone does not equate to happiness; many who seem to "have it all" struggle with emptiness. Research on hedonic adaptation suggests that external acquisitions provide only temporary satisfaction before individuals return to a baseline level of happiness.[10] Consider celebrities who have amassed fame and wealth yet succumb to despair—despite achieving everything externally, they remain unfulfilled internally. From the beginning, they were destined for defeat, no matter how much they seemingly accomplished.

When you remain true to your transformation, you will find that what you attract is precisely what you need—be it people, opportunities, or circumstances—at the exact moment they are meant to arrive. In that uncanny way, the reality that unfolds before you will far surpass every lofty ideal you once envisioned. This phenomenon occurs because, while you are too close to the painting, engulfed by the trees, the universe is always observing the full, expanding picture. Research in systems theory suggests that complex networks operate beyond our immediate perception, orchestrating connections and outcomes we may not anticipate.[11]

What you see is not what the universe sees. In its ceaseless effort to foster and support life, it will always bring you what you need when you need it most. In that effortless way, you will, in all cases, reign victorious.

Just Because It Didn't Work Once Doesn't Mean It Never Will

What you're doing—improving yourself, bringing out and nurturing the best version of yourself—is hard work. You will find that many attempts to change will land you flat on your face, sometimes even worse off than where you started. After all, when you were a piece of shit, at least you were a piece of shit simply existing in its smelly presence. But now? Now you're broken up, scattered, unpleasant to be around, and all over the place. It's easy to get discouraged and think, *I tried to become a temperate person, but I cannot stop smoking; I give up!* But here's the thing: try again this time.

It didn't work the first time because failure isn't the end of the process—it's part of it. There are lessons in each misstep that will serve you later down the path. Think of it like climbing a ladder: the bottom steps don't physically touch the top steps, but they are still necessary to get there.[12] When you throw in the towel, you're walking away from an opponent on the verge of defeat, one that is begging for your conviction to waver. You're closing the book five chapters in when the full story has ten chapters that keep getting better and better. The lessons learned in the fifth chapter will get you through the next one—not just the last one.[13]

Your ultimate success comes not from what you've most recently learned, but from the accumulation of everything you've learned along the way. If you think that just because you've learned to walk, you can immediately compete in long-distance Olympic games, then you're funny. It will never work right now. Growth doesn't happen instantly; it requires consistent effort, adaptation, and time. Psychological research on habit formation suggests that true behavioral change is achieved through repeated efforts, setbacks, and adjustments.[14]

In other words, you can't just snap your fingers and turn half the universe's population to dust. (Though, let's be honest, that would be pretty cool.) But eventually—through perseverance, refinement, and gathering the necessary tools—it *will* work. Like collecting the Infinity Stones, your journey requires accumulating the character dispositions, attitudes, and disciplines necessary to fully become who you say you are. Each piece of the puzzle builds upon the last until, finally, you can rest knowing you've made it. (This is the part where you say, *Fine, I'll do it myself.*)

Easier Done Than Said

Ninety-nine percent of the time, creating without competing allows you free range to attract the life you desire without the pressure of having to "put your money where your mouth is." That freedom exists because, if you're being truthful with yourself, obtaining your desired state is easier to do than it is to talk about. Research in cognitive psychology suggests that action-based goal pursuit is often more effective than verbal affirmations alone, as it bypasses cognitive resistance and reinforces belief through experience.[15]

For starters, much of what you want is shaped by external influences—ideals plagued by the perceptions that others impose on success. Do you really want a mansion, or has that idea been so flaunted in your face that you were subliminally led to believe it is what you *should* want? Studies on consumer psychology show that societal norms and media heavily influence personal aspirations, often leading individuals to chase material success that doesn't align with their intrinsic values.[16] Much of what you want will be difficult to articulate or define precisely. Despite that challenge, many self-help experts adamantly proclaim, "gEt ExTreMeLy SpEcIfIc WiTh WhAt YoU wAnT!!" Oh brother—not this again.

I can't tell you—or better yet—please let me tell you how much I've manifested by simply doing rather than saying. With this mantra on my every breath—*easier done than said, easier done than said*—I've transformed my anxiety-ridden life from one of comparison to one of great peace, fulfillment, joy, and romance. Neuroscientific research on habit formation and behavioral change suggests that repetitive action reinforces neural pathways, making success more likely when effort is focused on doing rather than over-analyzing or verbalizing goals.[17] One by one, I started seeing results form in my life. I loved the surprised expressions people gave me when they saw things that should've taken such a long time just appear. From their perspectives, my successes must have seemed to come from thin air. But I know the truth: by simply refraining from discussing my ambitions, my years of diligence effortlessly turned into sexy points of conversation and overall fun.

So, there's no need to write something down when your access to what's to come is so limited. Studies in goal-setting theory indicate that while writing goals down can be helpful for clarity, excessive verbalization can sometimes create a false sense of accomplishment, reducing motivation to take real action.[18] You don't know what you don't say. You know what you do or don't do. Every cell in your body knows if you're moving towards your desired state or not—so shush.[19]

Never Tolerate—Never Settle

Too often, you'll encounter people who have resigned themselves to mediocrity, settling for subpar standards in their lives. The life you aspire to live is desirable because of its greatness. No one dreams of a mediocre existence, yet many tolerate the lackluster behavior of those who have long since given up striving for more.[20]

When you allow mediocre standards into your life, you inadvertently send a subconscious signal to yourself: *This is what we're worth*. Over time, this repeated exposure to low expectations conditions your self-worth and, consequently, your actions.[21] The human brain adapts to the standards we reinforce, and when we normalize mediocrity, we subconsciously begin to expect and accept it.[22] Conversely, when you refuse to settle, you demand a higher standard—not just from yourself, but from others. This principle is why I advocate for top-tier restaurant service. The establishment's exclusivity is irrelevant; if I am there as a guest, then I expect to be treated accordingly. I am never unkind to servers, and I will gladly accept a mistaken order of equal value. However, I am meticulous when it comes to the small details.

The seemingly minor ways people honor or neglect your worth speak volumes about the value you assign to yourself. For instance, I once dined at an Asian restaurant where the server accidentally spilled a drop of my lover-at-the-time's miso soup. It was a negligible amount, yet I requested a fresh bowl for her. The server was visibly displeased but complied. While the difference in soup quantity was trivial, the impact on my partner was profound—she felt valued. This gesture reinforced an important truth: the way we allow ourselves and our loved ones to be treated shapes the way we see our worth.[23]

Similarly, while eating at Buffalo Wild Wings with friends, the server set our table with plastic utensils, claiming they had "run out" of silverware. However, a quick glance around the restaurant revealed that every other table had proper silverware. Unwilling to accept this silent devaluation, I firmly requested real utensils. After ten minutes of persistence, the server relented. Some might view this as an insignificant battle, but it was a matter of principle—accepting subpar treatment in small matters paves the way for accepting it in larger, more consequential areas of life.[24]

Raising your standards not only elevates your own quality of life but also uplifts those around you. When you carry yourself with dignity, others take notice and adjust their behavior accordingly. Additionally, your sense of justice sharpens. While I can overlook a server's forgetfulness, what I refuse to accept is a deliberate lowering of standards. A spilled soup or plastic utensils in a setting where others receive better treatment sends one clear message: *You are not worth the extra effort.* Excuse me? Absolutely not.

My loved ones—those closest to my heart—are worth everything to me. Therefore, no matter the discomfort or awkwardness I may face, I advocate for them just as I advocate for myself. Some may misinterpret this as arrogance, but it is quite the opposite. I stand up for them because I stand up for myself. I love them because I love myself. I never settle when it comes to their well-being because, as you might have guessed, I refuse to settle when it comes to my own.

Avoid People Who Point Out Your "Privilege"

When you decide to break away from your undesired state and enter into your desired state, you will inevitably encounter people who credit one hundred percent of your success to privilege. Privilege is a controversial topic, but in the grand scheme of obtaining one's desired state, it is irrelevant. Anyone who aggressively pushes the notion of privilege in your face is not woke—they are jealous.

As flourishing people, you are now in the business of not believing in excuses. You no longer subscribe to excuses, just as you no longer believe in the Easter Bunny—meaning, you do not allow outdated, unearthed ideas to dictate how you celebrate your life. Excuses, like all ideas, draw their life force from the attention we give them. Psychological research has demonstrated that beliefs shape reality through cognitive biases and self-fulfilling prophecies.[25] Therefore, if we choose not to acknowledge excuses, not to believe in them, and instead place our faith in our imaginations, then any and all potential excuses simply convert into one more reason why we overcame.

On the other hand, those suffering in their undesired states will resent flourishing people and attribute all overcoming to privilege. They cling to excuses as if they were gravity itself—always there to pull them down whenever they have climbed too high. Research in learned helplessness shows that repeated failures can create a psychological state where individuals feel powerless to change their circumstances, reinforcing the belief in external barriers.[26] Their jealousy is fueled by the belief that they are equal to all flourishing people but have been denied their desired state due to the color of their skin, where they were born, their socioeconomic status, or any other box they can check. But I call bullshit. Hogwash. Malarkey. Pigwater, I tell you!

Something as arbitrary as a deviation in genetic makeup will not deter you from obtaining your desired state. Studies on neuroplasticity confirm that the human brain has the ability to rewire itself and adapt, regardless of background or initial disadvantages.[27]

As a rule of thumb, you should generally seek to associate yourself with grateful people. Gratitude has been scientifically linked to higher levels of success, mental well-being, and resilience in the face of adversity.[28] Those who frequently mention privilege fail to recognize their own privilege—their ability to perceive realities beyond their immediate circumstances and ultimately shape the life they desire. There is no force greater than our uniquely human capacity to imagine a life and bring it into existence. Historical accounts of individuals overcoming immense systemic barriers—ranging from Holocaust survivors to self-made entrepreneurs born into poverty—demonstrate that external oppression does not have the power to permanently suppress someone determined to flourish.[29]

So when someone credits your flourishing to "privilege," kindly remind them that the same miracle or privilege that brought about the sun, the moon, and the stars also brought each of us into existence with the capacity to live abundantly and joyfully.

Avoid People Who Think Being "For Real" Means Being Negative

Steer clear of those seemingly "realistic" types who mask their negative sentiments as precautions. *I'm going to write a book,* you'll say. Their response: *Cool—if people still read. Plus, you'll need a publisher, which will likely reject your manuscript along with hundreds of other rejected pieces. Plus, with your schedule, I can't possibly imagine when you'd find the time. And let's say you're the one percent that does get published—it's not like you'll ever be a bestseller considering most books on shelves sell less than a thousand copies. Besides, who still reads?* Excuses, excuses, excuses. This is the moment in the conversation where you are legally allowed to walk away.

People who believe being "for real" means being negative often argue that life is not all sunshine and rainbows. But if we're *actually* being for real, life *is* also sunshine and rainbows. The problem isn't that they acknowledge life's difficulties; it's that they refuse to acknowledge its possibilities. Research in cognitive psychology suggests that individuals with a pessimistic explanatory style tend to focus on obstacles rather than opportunities, reinforcing self-fulfilling cycles of negativity.[30]

As flourishing people, we must not condemn those stuck in their undesired states. It's not entirely their fault that they perceive life through such a negative lens. Our experiences shape our worldview, and repeated exposure to adversity without resilience-building strategies can make negativity seem like the only rational perspective.[31] Honestly, if I faced their situations and chose to give up on the sunshine and rainbows, I too would become rather "realistic" real fast.

The issue is that, for those agonizing in their undesired state, the most *real* thing in their lives has become negativity. One tragedy after another has plagued their hearts beyond their capacity to perceive a better world. Studies show that chronic stress and trauma can rewire the brain's response to optimism, making it harder to imagine or pursue positive outcomes.[32] The longer they remain in this state, the more difficult it becomes to shift their focus toward hope and opportunity.

As a result, avoid them—not with judgment, but with wisdom. There are *loads* of people like this; it's the reason why Shakespeare's *tragedies* are cultural touchstones while his *fantasies* remain practically unheard of. Negativity is seductive because it validates suffering, and suffering, for many, is easier to accept than the possibility of something better.[33] Surround yourself with those who recognize both the hardships and the potential for joy—those who choose to see the sunshine and rainbows *despite* the storms.

Avoid People Who Don't Let You Respond

Since you've learned how to develop your reflexes into thoughtful responses (recall *Reflex—Reaction—Response*), I'll keep this advice brief: do not use someone's taunting as an excuse to lose your equanimity and brazenly react. Instead, exercise control over your emotions and maintain your composure—this is a hallmark of emotional intelligence.[34]

There are certain individuals who thrive on arguments—not just any kind of argument, but particularly those in which they prevent others from fully expressing themselves. This behavior is rooted in a need for dominance and control, often seen in aggressive communication styles.[35] I've witnessed these types of interactions as a third party, and they are never pleasant. Likewise, I've been the target of such verbal attacks, and the feeling that lingers is much like being stung by a gadfly—sharp, irritating, and designed to provoke a reaction.

People who provoke you in this way crave attention. Research on conflict psychology suggests that such individuals often seek to manipulate discussions to maintain a sense of superiority.[36] When someone refuses to let me speak and pressures me to respond without adequate time to think, I follow a simple yet effective approach. I calmly say: *"You're not listening to anything I'm saying, and I find that disrespectful. I'm done talking to anyone who doesn't respect what I have to say."* Then, I walk away without another word. Studies on boundary-setting indicate that disengaging from toxic conversations is one of the most effective ways to maintain personal integrity and mental well-being.[37]

I highly recommend that you adopt this approach. It's a life hack that not only protects your peace but also reinforces your self-respect.

The Accountability Conundrum

This concept may be the most important of all the advice I could give about not believing in excuses. There is no recovery after someone falls into this trap. The only remedy is preemptive. Those who commit this grievance suffer; the bystanders suffer; the victims suffer. Everyone loses something, especially a portion of their humanity.

The *Accountability Conundrum* is a phenomenon I frequently observe, occurring when people fail to take responsibility due to pettiness, fatigue, or, worse still, a distorted sense of justice.[38] Consider this example: you and your roommates have a system for rotating trash disposal once the bin is full. The agreement is simple—when it's your turn, you take the trash out, even if the dumpster is a quarter of a mile uphill. Everyone agrees.

Now, what would you do if you saw the trash overflowing from your kitchen into your bathroom ... and it's *not* your turn to take it out? If you step up and dispose of it anyway, I commend you, my hero. We're in the same clean boat. But if you're one of those petty villains who say, *I'll gladly step around the trash, plug my nostrils, and climb into bed because it's not my turn to throw it away,* then this section serves as a wake-up call.

Imagine now that every roommate begins thinking like you, waiting indefinitely for the person whose turn it is to finally take action. This situation creates the Accountability Conundrum: everyone is using an external condition as their excuse to avoid acting. Research on group behavior and social loafing suggests that when responsibility is diffused among multiple people, individuals are less likely to take action, assuming someone else will step up.[39] In most cases, those caught in this conundrum act out of pettiness. Their home could turn into a landfill, and they would still refuse to throw out the trash because *it's not their turn*. But at what cost? While the designated person should act, your refusal only worsens the situation, leading to an even less desirable state. You are choosing one form of discomfort over another when a simple solution is available. Plus, by taking action, even when it's not your responsibility, you lead by example, which often compels the slacker to act as well.[40]

You solve the Accountability Conundrum with a true sense of justice. Justice means doing what needs to be done regardless of circumstances. Should you have to take out the trash? No, it's not your turn based on the original agreement. Should the slacker be *walloped* across the face? Maybe. I don't know. Should you—or for the love of all that is clean, *someone*—just take the trash out? Absolutely. Why? Because it needs to be done. End of story.

So please, get over yourself. No more excuses. I used a harmless example (if you're not my mom, you'll find it harmless). But the Accountability Conundrum occurs in far more serious situations, with consequences too grave to be ignored. Every day, people starve to death while those with the means to help debate *who* should take responsibility.[41] We drive our cars while listening to podcasts about climate change and irreversible environmental damage, never failing to miss the irony.[42] Seriously? Every single person involved in such a conundrum suffers because we are all heroes refusing to put on our capes. So please, be the hero who finally takes some form of responsibility.

The Last Thing A Tree Bears Is Fruit

I constantly remind myself that the mission—the thing I want—is accomplished at the *end*, not in the middle, not four-fifths of the way through, but at the very end. In a profound way, your entire life is the fruit of the labor of millions of ancestors. The human race, governed by God's divine design, has progressed to this point because of the energy and toil of countless individuals we will never meet. The fact that you are reading this book, breathing, exercising, or simply lounging is the resultant fruit of all their blood, sweat, and tears.

Therefore, when the realization of your desired state seems to take longer than expected, remember this: beautiful, enriching sustenance is the byproduct of hard work—not the hard work itself. This idea is deeply rooted in spiritual wisdom. "You have the right to work," states the *Bhagavad Gita*, "but for the work's sake only. You have no right to the fruits of work."[43] That is the mystery behind obtaining your desired state—the unseen third element that miraculously emerges. After identifying what you want, embodying the characteristics of a person who lives such a life, and committing to months or even years of consistent effort, a moment arrives when you suddenly find yourself in possession of what you sought. You wake up beside your adoring lover and cry out, *THANK YOU, GOD!* for granting you the strength to relinquish all excuses.

Yet, the truth remains: the fruit borne by a tree does not belong to the tree. You have no inherent right to your desired state. You only have complete sovereignty over your internal condition, which in turn brings forth all milk and honey.[44] This process is breathtaking because trees, with their roots plunged deeply into the soil, physically grasp at the earth, helping to hold it together. The same is true for our aspirations. By becoming the kind of people who embody their highest ideals, we contribute to the fabric of humanity's better half, creating a more stable and harmonious world.[45]

Consider what would happen if trees, rather than freely offering their fruit to the earth, became entitled to it—hoarding it instead of sharing. If they uprooted themselves in an attempt to live independently, disconnected from the ecosystem, the result would be catastrophic. Quite simply, the earth would be *fucked*. Mountains would collapse, sinkholes would form, and the very fabric that holds our world together would unravel.[46]

Likewise, if you succumb to excuses and forget that what you seek will find you when you are ready, you do not only jeopardize yourself—you risk destabilizing the world around you. Your growth, like the fruit of a tree, is not just for you; it nourishes the collective whole.

It's Darkest Before The Dawn—But Sometimes The Darkest *Is* The Dawn

Things often come to fruition when circumstances become most challenging. Just before dawn opens her pinkish mouth, the night sky reaches its deepest black. Many people, in their desperation, strike the last match they have, grasping for control in an uncontrollable situation. Yet, the trick I have found most effective in navigating my own *dark nights of the soul* is to surrender to the darkness. The darkness, like all things, is fleeting—so rather than resisting, follow it out; show it the door.

Coming face to face with your struggles will always seem like the most difficult feat when you resist what troubles you. Psychological research on acceptance-based coping strategies suggests that avoiding or suppressing negative emotions only amplifies their hold over us, whereas embracing them allows us to process and move through them more effectively.[47] Expose yourself to the darkness, and it will not comprehend it. Resistance—the opposition, the Devil—will persecute you up to the very gates of heaven, and many have denied themselves divine union just when they were about to receive it.[48]

Therefore, show gratitude for the darkness. This may sound counterintuitive, but studies in positive psychology reveal that gratitude, even in adversity, rewires neural pathways to foster resilience and long-term well-being.[49] Whenever I find myself feeling *down bad*, I thank God for such a feeling, knowing that it too shall pass. By reframing suffering as a necessary stage in my evolution, I strengthen my ability to endure hardship.

What's more, I have learned that gratitude for my lowest moments cultivates my highest pleasures. This aligns with the psychological principle of contrast theory, which suggests that we derive greater joy from positive experiences after enduring hardship.[50] So, rather than using difficult situations as an excuse to retreat, take time to truly experience the darkness—immerse yourself in it, learn from it—and when the sun finally rises, it will shine so brightly that you'll wish you had some sunglasses.[51]

Are You Truly Defeated?

To close this chapter, I'll leave you with a drop of sun that has never failed to light my way through the promised land. Whenever I feel like I've failed to accomplish something, I ask myself two questions: *Have I been defeated? And can I still smile right now?*

If I can still smile—truly, genuinely smile—regardless of the answer to the first question, then I haven't been truly defeated. The way I see it, no one who has ever been truly defeated can smile. In other words, if you can still smile, then you have not been defeated—not by a long shot! Research in positive psychology suggests that the ability to maintain a genuine smile despite adversity is linked to resilience and emotional regulation, which are key factors in overcoming setbacks.[52]

True defeat happens internally. External conditions—excuses—cannot defeat you. If the buzzer sounds and your opponent's score is greater than yours, then you've lost the match. That's all. Losing in the external world is simply a data point, a moment in time—not a definition of who you are. Psychological studies on learned helplessness demonstrate that individuals who internalize external failures as personal deficiencies are more likely to experience long-term discouragement and disengagement.[53] However, those who view failure as an event rather than an identity are more likely to persist and achieve success in the long run.

But what if this was the most important match of your life? What if this championship victory was supposed to crown you as the Goddess of Everything? You know what? If this competition recurs, then train for it and compete again next time. Failure is often a stepping stone to mastery, as evidenced by research on expertise development and deliberate practice.[54]

But, but, but—no buts! At the end of the day, you can only be defeated on the scoreboard, in the data spreadsheet, or in the outside world. True defeat, however, is a choice.

Studies in cognitive behavioral therapy suggest that our interpretation of events, rather than the events themselves, determines our emotional and psychological responses.[55]

No matter what external circumstances say, like everyone else in their own magical way, you, too, will have your tailor-made moment to shine. Your moment is only as far away as your willingness to continue moving forward.

Immediate Action Steps

1. Embrace Your Resilience: Recall the moment you wanted to quit in the past. Did you give up then, or did you push through? Today, ask yourself if quitting will truly bring you closer to your desired state. If the answer is no, then *don't quit*. Instead, write down what was hardest for you in the moment when you felt like giving up, and next time it comes up, pull that list out and use it to fuel your perseverance.

2. Identify the Cost of Your Excuses: Look at your life right now—where have you been tolerating sub-par conditions or actions? Identify one area where you've allowed excuses to hold you back. Is it in your health, work habits, or relationships? Today, take one specific, small action to start solving that problem—whether it's scheduling a workout, organizing your workspace, or having a difficult conversation.

3. Turn Failure Into Feedback: List out your failures and consider what you learned from them. Write down one insight from each failure and how you will apply it to your next step forward.

4. Rewire Your Thinking: Find a moment today where you catch yourself thinking negatively or focusing on the barriers. Instead of accepting that as fact, challenge it: What's the alternative? What if you saw this as an opportunity to grow or improve? Shift your

perspective from the obstacle to the opportunity. Write down what you need to remind yourself when your mind starts focusing on excuses, and create a new mantra that empowers you to take action.

5. Reaffirm Your Standards: Take a moment to evaluate the standards you've set for yourself in different areas of your life. Are you tolerating mediocrity? Are you letting others set low standards for how you should be treated? Choose one thing in your life where you're settling for less than you deserve, and today, take a stand. Demand a higher standard for yourself and actively seek ways to elevate that aspect of your life.

PART III: PRESERVATION

11

Focus Only On The Desired State

"Therefore do not worry
about tomorrow, for tomorrow will worry about its
own things. Sufficient for
the day is its own trouble."
—Matthew 6:34

***

Do you waste the present worrying about future dreams to avoid action? Why worry about dreams if you won't act? Why stress over what might go wrong? Why use the present to fear the future? If you know what you want, then why expend so much energy ruminating over what you don't want?

DONNEL DELVA

You Are The Alpha And The Omega

First off, I'd like to congratulate you for reading this far into the book (I'm only talking to those who didn't skip to here!). So far, we've discussed how you can use your imagination to visualize what you desire. Once that picture is developed and deeply felt, we explored what it really takes to attract what you want: internal conditioning, not external circumstances. Now, it's time to understand how to stay focused while integrating everything into your lifestyle.

One of the keys to focusing only on your desired state is embodying the fact that you are the alpha and the omega, the first and the last. C. S. Lewis highlights how effortlessly you can embody such a principle. In *Mere Christianity*, he writes:

> "The Christian says, 'Creatures are not born with desires unless satisfaction for those desires exists. A baby feels hunger: well, there is such a thing as food. A duckling wants to swim: well, there is such a thing as water. Men feel sexual desire: well, there is such a thing as sex. If I find in myself a desire which no experience in this world can satisfy, the most probable explanation is that I was made for another world. If none of my earthly pleasures satisfy it, that does not prove that the universe is a fraud. Probably earthly pleasures were never meant to satisfy it, but only to arouse it, to suggest the real thing. If

that is so, I must take care, on the one hand, never to despise, or be unthankful for, these earthly blessings, and on the other, never to mistake them for the something else of which they are only a kind of copy, or echo, or mirage. I must keep alive in myself the desire for my true country, which I shall not find till after death; I must never let it get snowed under or turned aside; I must make it the main object of life to press on to that other country and to help others to do the same.'"[1]

C. S. Lewis

If there is a desire in your heart, then the object of your desire—the ideal state of your desire—exists and can be met. This principle aligns with the philosophical and psychological understanding that our desires stem from perceived gaps between our current and ideal states.[2] You only recognize a desired state as *unrealized* because you are meant to pursue and manifest it. (And I'm going to assume your desires are earthly—otherwise, yeah, you totally came to the wrong place, Brother/Sister/Father/Mother/Saint.)

You initiate the crystallization of your desire when you become aware of it. In your awareness, you collapse a point in the chaotic other dimension that eventually makes its way over to you—because it must.[3] Neuroscientific studies support this: our brains actively shape our reality based on repeated thoughts and visualizations, reinforcing neural pathways that guide our actions.[4] In that sort of roll-call relationship, you are the alpha—the beginning. Everything that eventually becomes reality starts with your divine attention.

On the tail end of the process, you are also the omega—the end—when you embody and match the frequency of your desired state. Studies on quantum cognition suggest that our beliefs and expectations influence not only our perception of reality but also our outcomes.[5] When it's all said and done, the desired state exists because you created it. Without you, it's empty and void—all potential and no actualization. You were there when it first popped into this dimension as a desire and a vision, and you are there now that it has become the way you express yourself.

Concentrate on that fact: that through the raising of your frequency and constant embodiment, you start and complete your desired state. It's easy to worry about what will happen if you miss a payment, fail to write a thousand words, or falter in some way. But for the love of all that is sexy: chill out! You're doing your thing now because you've long proved to yourself that you can be trusted with such a worthy state of being. Research in behavioral psychology shows that consistent identity-based habits reinforce long-term success more effectively than momentary motivation alone.[6] Don't trick yourself out of your desired state. Stick to what has worked, and I assure you it'll keep working—so long as you keep improving what is working.

Revisiting The Past Doesn't Guarantee Learning

As you live out your desired state, you'll encounter people who insist that revisiting the past is essential for present growth. You may even find yourself tempted to linger in the past longer than you know you should. Often, it's the memories of mistakes and missteps that replay in your mind. Other times, it's the ways you've been slighted or abused. Either way, one truth remains: dwelling on the past diverts your attention from your desired state in the present. And if we're being completely honest, more often than not, revisiting undesirable memories doesn't lead to growth—it only reinforces old wounds.[7]

This idea isn't the easiest to accept, but then again, nothing about transformation is easy. So allow me, my even more beloved reader, to be that radical voice that inspires your dramatic self-improvement. When you ruminate on past actions and realities, you unconsciously reinforce what did not work for your growth. Psychological studies on rumination confirm that excessive focus on past failures and regrets is linked to heightened stress, anxiety, and even depression.[8] Instead of seeing your path as blessed and full of possibility, you fill your mind with the clutter that once obstructed your progress.

Don't be swayed by the naysayers who argue that societies must study the past to better understand the present. Here's my counterpoint: where has that truly gotten us? It's widely accepted that history repeats itself, but why? Some suggest it's because human nature is inherently cyclical, but I offer a different perspective: we ingrain the mistakes of the past so deeply into our collective consciousness that we unknowingly perpetuate them.[9] The mind operates in patterns—when you continually reinforce certain thoughts and narratives, they become the dominant lens through which you see reality. Neurological research on memory and cognition supports this idea, revealing that the brain strengthens neural pathways associated with frequently recalled memories, making them feel more immediate and emotionally potent.[10]

So here's my groundbreaking suggestion: focus on the present—your desired state. Did you recently get laid off? Shift your focus toward the jobs and opportunities seeking you out. Did your lover betray your trust and hurt you? Direct your attention to the endless possibilities of love and connection awaiting you. Were people who look like you, act like you, or believe as you do historically subjected to systemic discrimination? Instead of fixating on past injustices, recognize how those same groups now flourish, excelling in spaces once closed to them.[11]

When you dwell on the past, you quite literally bring the past into your present. Neuroscientific research suggests that reliving painful memories can activate the same neural pathways as the original experience, reinforcing emotional distress and keeping individuals trapped in a cycle of suffering.[12] But when you focus on what life is like right now, you unlock limitless possibilities to prosper in meaningful ways, grow in every aspect of your life, and uplift the people you love most. The past does not need your attention to persist—but your future certainly does.

Bringing up the past brings the past. Focusing on the present manifests the present into reality.

Crucify Your Savior

THE BITTER END

When my Friend and Teacher, Jesus, died on the cross, he shattered the veil and forever allowed everyone to share in the abundance promised to us all. This was not an accident. He suffered a painful, humiliating death as a guiltless man for the sake of we guilty, guilty sinners. His passion and example are exactly what we are called to follow when it comes to manifesting our desired state—crucify it for the redemption of the life you are destined to live (Matthew 27:50-51).

You want your desired state to save you, but you must first make it suffer. *"But I want it quick and easy,"* you say. Well then, I think you're looking for a Double Quarter Pounder with Cheese—that sure gets to you quick and easy. But transformation is not a fast-food transaction. Your desired state must endure suffering because you are essentially transmuting your base nature into pure gold. Like any alchemical process, this transformation requires time and energetic invigoration.[13] Imagine this shift from the perspective of a base metal: it is being subjected to extreme heat, agitation, pressure, and force. That same tempering is necessary within yourself if you are ever going to possess the Midas touch.

Rooted in all your base characteristics are the seeds of great virtue. If you are lazy but aspire to become productive, then you must cast all burdens of laziness onto your productive savior and believe that this new version of yourself has the power to redeem you from your old lifestyle. In this redemptive process, your new lifestyle "dies" for you so that, in its spirit, you can flourish.[14]

The psychological process of shedding an old identity and assuming a new one is well-documented. In neuro-science, studies on neuroplasticity confirm that sustained focus on a new identity can rewire the brain and create new behavioral patterns.[15] Additionally, in religious and philo-sophical traditions, the concept of death and rebirth as a means of transformation is central to spiritual enlightenm ent.[16]

It is only when you release the energy of the best ver-sion of yourself that you can finally begin to attract and sustain the life you truly desire. This concept is supported by research in quantum cognition, which suggests that the way we observe and believe in a future state influences our reality.[17] Your task, then, is to raise up the new you, filled with love and positive energy, so that this version of yourself can release to you the power needed to live in your new, abundant life.[18]

Assume You Have What You Desire

As you live out your desired state, you may feel like assuming you already possess what you desire goes hand in hand with delusion. I'm here to tell you that it is not delusional to behave in a way that reflects already having what you want—it's the secret ingredient to the Krabby Patty formula.

You assume you have what you want because you *literally* do have what you want. You imagined and saw your desired state in your mind; therefore, the life you desire is a real reality. Research in cognitive psychology supports this—mental imagery has been shown to activate the same neural pathways as real-life experiences, reinforcing belief and behavioral alignment.[19] The objective now is to live out a life that reflects having, in this third-dimensional world, what you already have within you.

Remember, what you imagine in your heart and mind must manifest in this world, so expect it to. Expectation is a powerful force in shaping outcomes. Studies in neuroscience show that expectation and belief influence perception, decision-making, and even physical performance.[20] When a couple is pregnant with a child, what terminology do they use for the infant's arrival? "On its way," like a package delivery? "Coming soon," like a movie to a theater near you? Incorrect. The couple, doctors, family, and spoiling friends all describe the infant's arrival as *expecting*. Everyone expects the infant to be birthed, for that creation to be realized. The same mindset needs to be applied to your desired state. You need to expect it to crystallize in the same way a mother does with her newborn: by nesting.

Nest the world around you in anticipation of your desired state. Behavioral psychology research suggests that structuring one's environment to align with goals significantly increases the likelihood of success.[21] If you see yourself in shape, then nest your kitchen by removing all Twinkies and Mountain Dews. If you imagine that your life is meant to be abundantly wealthy, then nest your bank account by divvying up your money in an investment portfolio. This principle aligns with studies on the law of attraction, which indicate that actions reinforcing a belief system help turn that belief into reality.[22]

I could go on and on with different areas of your life that you can nest, so simply fill in the respective blanks for yourself. But the bottom line is this: when you desire a certain lifestyle, act in accordance with that life before it crystallizes in this world. Neuroscientific research shows that the brain responds to repeated behaviors and thoughts by strengthening neural connections, making desired outcomes more attainable.[23] When you align your life with what you want, you send signals to your brain that say, *Hey, this is going to happen, so I need to be ready.* When your brain makes this connection, then doors open where there were none previously.

Use Wise Optimism

When I attract desired states into my life, I utilize what I describe as wise optimism. I usually think: *I'm optimistic; therefore, I can survive the bad times.* I do *not* think: *There's only going to be good times.* There are major differences between these two thoughts.

The first belief leads to actions that prepare you to endure and navigate hardship, while the latter will inevitably prove false and lead to repeated disappointment. Since all actions are based on belief systems, what you accept as true or untrue will ultimately dictate how you act in alignment with those beliefs. Psychological studies on cognitive framing suggest that individuals who develop resilience through realistic optimism are better equipped to handle adversity.[24]

The trick to wise optimism is developing a keen ability to perceive reality as *accurately* as possible. It's about striking a balance—neither catastrophizing nor sugarcoating circumstances. The first half of the thought (*I'm optimistic*) emphasizes an internal condition: your mindset and how you choose to process life's experiences. If you want to see life unfold the way you desire, the first step is to turn your focus inward. Research in cognitive psychology suggests that an optimistic explanatory style contributes to greater emotional resilience and mental well-being.[25]

The second half of the thought (*therefore, I can survive the bad times*) acknowledges *external* conditions. There will be bad times in life—this is guaranteed. However, when you cultivate an optimistic character while enduring those difficult periods, your positive attitude can transform even the harshest experiences into something slightly more bearable. Psychological studies on positive reappraisal suggest that individuals who maintain an optimistic outlook during hardship are more likely to reframe their experiences in a way that fosters growth and emotional stability.[26]

The Serenity Prayer comes to mind when practicing wise optimism:

"God, grant me the serenity
To accept the things I cannot change,
Courage to change the things I can,
And the wisdom to know the difference.
Living one day at a time,
Enjoying one moment at a time;
Accepting hardships as the pathway to peace."

There will always be conditions you can change (*internal*) and circumstances you cannot (*external*). But knowing the difference between the two can mean the difference between progress and stagnation—between peace and distress. Keep your eyes fixed on what you *can* improve, on the person you *can* become, and wisely, peacefully, *ignore* the things beyond your control.

Though You Walk Through The Valley—Fear No Evil

As you enact your desired state and manifest in this world all that you have long put into motion, soberly keep in mind the reality of your success. As I mentioned in *There Are Twice As Many Vices Than Virtues*, most of the world is covered in filth—the very things you do not want. If you plunged your hand into a top hat, the odds of pulling out a rabbit are significantly lower than the chances of plopping out a handful of its feces. Therefore, what lies outside your circle of manifested desire is, in fact, a trail of heartbroken people, all trapped in their unconscious, undesired states. Research in behavioral psychology supports this, showing that people who fail to achieve desired outcomes often experience cognitive dissonance, leading them to reinforce negative thought patterns.[27]

However, even though you may stand as the only light in that pit of darkness, do not fear, for the rod and staff of your unwavering God will guide and protect you. When David declares, "You prepare a table before me in the presence of my enemies; You anoint my head with oil; My cup runs over" (Psalms 23:5), he proudly proclaims the miracles that have unfolded in his desired state. Likewise, I ask the same for you, as my Friend puts it: "I do not pray that You should take them out of the world, but that You should keep them from the evil one" (John 17:15). The goal is not to renounce the world, retreating to the Himalayas with a shaved head, eating a single grain of rice a day until you merge with nirvana. Rather, what the universe requires of us is to shine brightly as a city upon a hill, serving as a beacon of possibility, opportunity, and miracles for all those who are adrift. Studies in positive psychology affirm that individuals who embody purpose and maintain a strong belief in their mission often serve as inspirations, fostering resilience and motivation in those around them.[28]

When you fully live into your desired state, embodying the person who justly deserves what they have manifested, you will be recognized both by yourself and others—anointed with oil—and welcomed into abundance, where your cup runs over. This is not just spiritual rhetoric; psychological research on self-actualization aligns with this idea, demonstrating that those who achieve their highest potential experience fulfillment that radiates outward, impacting their communities.[29]

Therefore, remain steadfast in your desired state by fearlessly focusing on the good life that you live. I love the way Dan Harris expresses it in his compelling book, *10% Happier*: "Your demons may have been ejected from the building, but they're out in the parking lot, doing push-ups." The higher and deeper you go into your desired state, the stronger the temptation to relapse—the urge to sin against your new life. How many people have you seen dive headfirst into their downfall the moment they finally grasp what they had struggled to attain? This phenomenon is well-documented

in psychology, as the fear of success can trigger self-sabotage, causing individuals to revert to old, destructive
habits.[30]

The gate that keeps you on your path, then, becomes
ever narrower as the shadows of your past grow longer.
However, they will not consume you if you remain vigilant
in adherence to your new life. By doing so, you too will
proudly proclaim: "Surely goodness and mercy shall follow me all the days of my life; And I will dwell in the house
of the Lord forever" (Psalms 23:6).

Reject The Devil And He Will Leave—But Not Without Persecution

During my journey of manifesting my desired state,
one of the first things I did was give up my obsession with
weed. I smoked, ate, and absorbed it—you name it—in all
forms throughout my four years of undergrad.

I fucking loved that thing! There was nothing like THC
to start off my morning, glide me through the afternoon,
and levitate me into the night. I was high all the time.
My toker friends were always high. (We self-proclaimed
ourselves as "The Tokers"—we had matching shirts and
everything. Or maybe we didn't. The details are all fuzzy.
I forget. Did I mention we were high?) Looking back now, I
can see how it truly brought us together, and I'm grateful
for experiencing what that was like. But let me be clear:
the gratitude I feel is more like a sense of triumph over
my Goliath than any fondness.

THE BITTER END

When I first received notice that I was about to start my time as a volunteer at Fairfield Prep, the school I currently teach full-time in, all my values became clear. I still remember my conversion experience so vividly. It was Easter, and I was back home. I didn't go to my dad's church (he is a pastor) and stayed home instead. Still being the festive and spiritual creature I am, I decided to celebrate my Friend's victory over life, death, and the world by meditating and praying in the woods. So, I drove to the place where I often walked and smoked—only this time, I was sober, absolutely clearheaded. I then found the tree I had befriended, sat lotus-style, and closed my eyes, pondering Jesus, my life up until then, and my projected desired state. After what felt like an eternity, I, unprovoked, found myself meshed into the unconditional love of God. Tears flowed from my closed eyes, overwhelming and pure.

The world was made anew when I awakened. The light that penetrated my pupils was blinding, and in the time it took for them to dilate, I heard deep within myself my own voice proclaiming: *stop smoking weed*.[31] I blinked, my vision restored, and laughed and laughed like I hadn't laughed before. I was free. I felt so intoxicated—higher than I'd ever been (and I'd greened out on some real good edibles and Kush). I practically—no, quite literally—danced my way out of the woods. Just recalling the story now spreads a smile across my face.

You don't need a life-altering, God-seeing, epiphanic intervention to decide when enough is enough. All you need, my beloved reader, is a deep enough reason to root you in your conviction. Because the truth is that awe-inspiring feeling will fade, but if you have that deeply rooted reason to pursue your goals, then you will push through and reject the Devil like a clingy ex-girlfriend.[32]

Despite never getting high since then—and recently giving up alcohol too—I have been offered many, many opportunities to intoxicate myself. I always view those temptations for what they are: solicitations from the Devil.[33] Since then, I've been in the passenger seat of a past lover who still smokes weed, holding the blunt in my hand yet simply unwilling to lift it to my lips. Can you imagine that old familiar damp, rolled-up piece of earth resting so seductively between your fingers? You know all the next steps—heck, I could literally do this unconsciously (I have).

When you reject the Devil's advances, you send a signal to your brain that you can be trusted.[34] When I say no to these drugs and drinks that somehow find their way over to me, I am not saying no for the first time. My stockpile of *I'd love to hit that dab pen till it's blinking and the cart's so hot it threatens to shatter the glass and melt the whole battery, but no thank you* have fueled me and given me the habit of remaining in my desired state. Where I once mindlessly got faded on autopilot, I now mindlessly say no on autopilot. Not only do I not want to get high anymore, but I also no longer crave it. My body is so used to thriving sober and strong that it now craves my new lifestyle.[35]

To wrap up, I want to warn you: just because you reject the Devil and all your urges go away does not mean that the Devil will not tempt you again. You may have obtained your desired state, but that will not mean anything if you don't constantly improve yourself and become the master of your desired state. The Devil persecutes saints right as they are about to walk through the gates of heaven. So hurry up and slip through that narrow gate, then slam the door behind you. Reside in the peace and bliss that comes with knowing that you live the life you want, do the things you say, and feel in harmony with it all.

Focus On The Process—Not The Outcome

If you're thinking, *Here he goes again, claiming something contradictory to what he's been yapping about,* then bear with me—this is some real secret sauce. Just like a chef may advise his cooks on what *not* to throw into a dish, I am about to guide you down a path that will save you from countless disappointments.

I'll let the esteemed C. S. Lewis describe what I could only hope to replicate from his treasure, *Surprised by Joy*:

> "For by that complaint I smuggled in the assumption that what I wanted was a 'thrill,' a state of my own mind. And there lies the deadly error. Only when your whole attention and desire are fixed on something else—whether a distant mountain, or the past, or the gods of Asgard—does the thrill arise. It is a by-product. Its very existence presupposes that you desire not it but something other and outer. If by any perverse askesis of the use of any drug it could be produced from within, it would at once be seen to be of no value. For take away the object,

and what, after all, would be left?—a whirl of images, a fluttering sensation in the diaphragm, a momentary abstraction. And who could want that? ... Instead, I concluded that it was a mood or state within myself which might turn up in any context. To 'get it again' became my constant endeavour; while reading every poem, hearing every piece of music, going for every walk, I stood anxious sentinel at my own mind to watch whether the blessed moment was beginning and to endeavour to retain it if it did. Because I was still young and the whole world of beauty was opening before me, my own officious obstructions were often swept aside and, startled into self-forgetfulness, I again tasted Joy. But far more often I frightened it away by my greedy impatience to snare it, and, even when it came, instantly destroyed it by introspection, and at all times vulgarised it by my false assumption about its nature ... This discovery flashed a new light back on my whole life. I saw that all my waitings and watchings for Joy, all my vain hopes to find some mental content on which I could, so to speak, lay my finger and say, 'This is it,' had been a futile attempt to contemplate the enjoyed. All that such watching and waiting ever could find would be either an image (Asgard, the western garden, or what not) or a quiver in the diaphragm. I should never have to bother again about these images or sensations. I knew now that they were merely the mental track left by the passage of Joy—not the wave but the wave's imprint on the sand. The inherent dialectic of desire itself had in a way already shown me this; for all images and sensations, if idolatrously mistaken for Joy itself, soon honestly confessed themselves inadequate. All said, in the last resort, 'It is not I. I am only a reminder. Look! Look! What do I remind you of?'"[36]

C. S. Lewis

Lewis' insight reveals a profound truth—joy, or in this case, your *desired state*, is a byproduct. Of course, you must focus on your desired state, but don't become obsessed with it. Life is richer than the vision you have of your future. Instead, lose yourself in the *process*. Hone it, improve it, refine it, and the results will take care of themselves. Research supports this principle—individuals who focus on mastering their craft rather than fixating on success tend to achieve greater long-term satisfaction and sustained excellence.[37]

The concept is reinforced by psychological studies on *flow state*, a term coined by Mihaly Csikszentmihalyi.[38] Flow is the state of full immersion in an activity, where self-consciousness fades, and peak performance emerges. Those who cultivate a strong process—rather than obsessing over outcomes—are more likely to experience flow and, consequently, long-term success. Athletes, musicians, and high-performing professionals often achieve greatness not by fixating on winning but by refining their daily habits.[39]

DONNEL DELVA

To put it simply, do the right things better, and better things will come to you.

THE BITTER END

Immediate Action Steps

1. Clarify Your Desired State: Visualize your ideal life, not just as a distant dream but as a reality that you are actively moving toward. Write down this vision in specific detail—where you live, who you're with, what you're doing, and how it feels. Revisit and refine this vision every day to keep it alive in your mind.

2. Embody Your Desired State: Start living as if your desired state is already true. If you want success, act like a successful person today—dress the part, adopt their mindset, and make decisions as they would. If you desire love, practice self-love and kindness towards others. Walk in the shoes of your future self now.

3. Limit Your Focus to the Present and Desired Future: Let go of past failures and mistakes. If memories or regrets from the past resurface, acknowledge them briefly and refocus on the present moment and the future you are creating. Remind yourself that focusing on what didn't work only strengthens the barriers to what you want.

4. Use Wise Optimism: Embrace optimism, but don't ignore reality. Cultivate an inner belief that things will work out, even when faced with difficulties. In moments of hardship, remind yourself of the bigger picture and trust that the obstacles you face are lead-

241

ing you to greater growth.

5. Do Delayed Gratification: Recognize that transformation is a process. Allow your desired state to unfold naturally, without impatience or pressure. Practice a small example of delayed gratification, even if it's watching TV an hour later in exchange for something productive or meaningful.

6. Assume and Expect What You Desire: Begin each day expecting your desires to manifest. Just as a couple prepares for a child's arrival with anticipation, prepare for your success with the same expectation.

7. Reaffirm Your Vision Daily: Revisit your vision and desired state every day. As soon as you wake up, affirm to yourself that the life you desire is already unfolding. Use positive affirmations to remind yourself that your desired state is not just possible, but inevitable.

8. Take Consistent, Inspired Action: Every day, take actions that move you closer to your desired state. These actions don't have to be grand, but they should be consistent and aligned with your vision. Trust your intuition to guide you toward the next steps.

9. Embrace the Pain of Transformation: Understand that transformation requires shedding your old identity. Be prepared to face discomfort as you transition into your desired state.

THE BITTER END

10. Be the Light in the Darkness: When you encounter obstacles or negativity, remember that you are a beacon of possibility. Shine brightly, even in difficult circumstances, and let your journey be a source of inspiration. For example, publicly oppose something harmful or mean.

12

FLOURISH BUT DON'T FLAUNT

"Let your light so shine before men, that they may see
your good works and glo-
rify your Father in heaven."
—Matthew 5:16

***

Whose approval are you desperately seeking, yearning to impress? Would your success hold any meaning if it went unnoticed by them? Do you truly desire what you possess, or is it merely a performance for another's gaze?

DONNEL DELVA

Go With The Flow

I would like to take this moment to congratulate you. You're on fire. By this point in your journey, you are truly flourishing. The goal of this chapter, then, is to flourish in a self-gratifying way—one that does not flex at the expense of others. I am not naive enough to assume that everyone who reaches this point has taken action. Some of you may have merely read through the book or even skipped ahead to this section. That's fine. But to those few who have been serious enough to implement what I have shared—my heart, you got this!

Now, as you improve and root yourself deeper into your new desired state, remember to go with the flow. The most surefire way to fall from your position of grace is by resisting the natural current, believing that because you are brighter than those around you, you no longer need them. That is a grave mistake.

The truth is, you have no clue—absolutely no real conception—of the grandeur of God's plans. No one does. Psychological research suggests that humans tend to overestimate their control over events, a phenomenon known as the illusion of control.[1] You couldn't swim against the current even if you wanted to, let alone guarantee the success of a plan you believe you created entirely on your own. In fact, by clinging too tightly to your sense of control, you will not only hinder yourself but also risk hurting those who care about you. Studies on emotional intelligence indicate that excessive self-reliance can weaken social bonds and limit

246

long-term success.[2] You've already conquered the scariest part—the leap of faith into the unknown—so why hold onto the illusion of predictability?

Instead, ride the wave that you are on and let it carry you forward. Remember when I was still learning to swim in *There Are Infinite Paradoxical Truths?* I discovered that struggling against the water—flailing and resisting—only causes you to sink, and eventually, drown. Neuroscientific studies on anxiety confirm that excessive resistance to change often leads to mental and emotional distress, reinforcing the very fears we seek to avoid.[3] The same principle applies to your desired state. If you resist the flow out of fear that you will lose what you have worked so hard to build, you will only bring about your own downfall.

The key now is to humbly continue the good work. Resist the urge to become bored with your success and take it for granted. Equally important, resist the temptation to change what is already working. As Niccolò Machiavelli wisely observed, "Men desire novelty to such an extent that those who are doing well wish for a change as much as those who are doing badly."[4] Please, please don't let that be you.

Trust Yourself

The purpose of obtaining your desired state was to flourish. You did not work so hard to effortlessly attract your ideal life into existence only to live in a state of anxiety and self-doubt. The key to flourishing, then, is trusting yourself in the new world you have created.

247

Many people self-sabotage their desired states because they do not trust themselves to cherish and honor such a life—it feels overwhelming. As a result of this fear, they destroy what they love most before it can be taken from them. Psychological research supports this tendency, as studies on self-sabotage indicate that individuals often undermine their own success due to deeply ingrained fears of inadequacy or loss.[5] However, this fear is unfounded because your desired state was never something external that could be given or taken away—it is you. You cannot perceive the light to be too bright when you are the light. You cannot extinguish the light when you are the light. Any attempts to diminish your desired state ultimately reflect a lack of trust in yourself to embody that light.

To learn how to trust yourself with the life you've always wanted, you first need to define what it means to trust yourself. My definition stems from Walt Whitman's glorious (dare I call it any less) poem, *Song of Myself.* In it, he writes a line so profound that his poem managed to surpass Poe's *The Raven* on my list of favorites. He declares, "I exist as I am, that is enough, / If no other in the world be aware I sit content, / And if each and all be aware I sit content."[6] These lines capture the essence of self-trust—being secure in who you are, regardless of external validation.

When you trust yourself, you believe in who you are even when no one is watching. Research in behavioral psychology suggests that true self-discipline is not driven by external consequences but by an internalized sense of identity.[7] If you set a goal to be a disciplined and healthy person, you go to the gym every day because that's who you are—not because your personal trainer will berate you if you don't. Furthermore, you won't secretly binge on Crumbl and Wingstop in your den, far from the judgmental gaze of your trainer. Trusting yourself means upholding your values even in private.

If everyone knows, that's great. And if no one knows, that's great. At the end of the night, you know. You always know.

Go Beyond Plus Ultra +1

I'm not going to lie to you—this is one area where I do not always thrive. Nonetheless, it is one of my favorite X-factors. Those who successfully adopt this practice will always outperform those who never do.

I stole this concept from *My Hero Academia*. I won't spoil the tear-jerking thrill that is *My Hero Academia*, but I will say that going "beyond plus ultra" essentially means pushing past your limits—doing one more. I love this concept because it amplifies the fact that we can always do more than we give ourselves credit for. Psychological research supports this idea, demonstrating that individuals often underestimate their physical and mental endurance due to cognitive biases and self-imposed limitations.[8]

As I work to preserve my desired state, I have decided that the best way to adopt a *plus ultra* disposition is by consistently pushing past my limits and attempting one more. This concept is most obviously present during my time at the gym. When I complete a set until failure, I truly pull and lift until the weight falls out of my hand or until I go numb. Once the pain exceeds what I believe I can endure, I attempt one more. The goal isn't necessarily to achieve one more—just to make the attempt. Studies in sports psychology show that this type of effort, known as *grit training*, enhances mental resilience and physical performance.[9]

By making the attempt to push beyond my limits, I train my brain to understand that just because I am exhausted does not mean I am finished. This strategy has led to greater productivity, achievement, and overall life satisfaction. Research on neuroplasticity suggests that consistently challenging oneself in this way strengthens neural pathways associated with persistence and motivation, ultimately increasing mental toughness.[10]

Imagine this: you wake up at five in the morning, go to the gym, teach English to high schoolers, and then tackle graduate-level studies. If you allow yourself to call it quits early, eventually, you will begin to fall short in some area of your life. To prevent that, at the end of the day, I always attempt—just attempt—to do something challenging. Sometimes it's a set of push-ups until failure; other times, it's simply reading a little more. In any case, I try. And I fail. But in that failure, I show myself that there is always more I can do—even if I don't actually accomplish anything tangible. Psychological studies link this mindset to increased well-being, as individuals who embrace small daily challenges tend to report greater overall life satisfaction and improved sleep quality.[11]

To Thine Own Self Be True

THE BITTER END

This line comes from Polonius in Shakespeare's *Hamlet*, spoken as fatherly advice to his son, Laertes. At the end of his moving speech, he concludes, "This above all: to thine own self be true" (I.iii.78).

Polonius could not have said it better. The art and essence of preserving your desired state lie in your ability to remain true to yourself. You arrived at this point by being honest with yourself. But more importantly, you got here by being true.

What is true to you? Your desired state is more than just external gratification. It stems from an internal truth—one that makes you beam when you look at yourself in the mirror. You are the person you must sleep with every night. That can be a great, empowering thing. Or it can be a sorry, pathetic joke. The goal is to fall asleep proud of the former.

Being true to yourself often requires rejecting what the world believes is true. What the world deems true is not always truth. If you have the choice between living a life that externally resembles your desired state (money, status, recognition) and feeling internally aligned with your desired state despite not yet seeing it manifest physically (joy, peace, love), always choose the latter.[12] Studies on intrinsic motivation suggest that internal fulfillment leads to greater long-term well-being than external rewards.[13]

As human beings, we need to believe that we are good people in order to live meaningful lives. Just think of the externally successful individuals who have committed suicide because they lacked internal joy and fulfillment.[14] It seems like such a paradox—a waste. But in reality, this aligns with human nature. No matter how much you chase, catch, and devour external success, it will not make you feel whole.[15] Research in positive psychology confirms that sustainable happiness is built on internal states of gratitude and purpose rather than material accumulation.[16]

This is precisely why I approach success the way I do: by laying the foundation first—acknowledging your desire and its true cost from a values-and-character standpoint. This slow, intentional approach leads to the most meaningful outcome—the most serene and lasting desired state.

Therefore, always do what feels true to yourself, even if it ruffles a few feathers. You wouldn't believe how many times I have flat-out ignored toxic relationships and so-called "opportunities" disguised as benefits. The greatest asset we have is our peace. It far exceeds even the rarity of time because time can be agonizing when spent in misery. But even a fleeting moment of peace far outweighs the trials and tribulations it took to obtain it.[17]

Keep Holy Your Highest Hope

I first heard this passage read aloud to me by a philosophy professor on the last day of school. I'll place it here and let it speak for itself—she sure knew how to send students aflight.

> "'Alas, I have known noble men who lost their highest hope. And henceforth they slandered all high hopes. Henceforth they lived impudently in brief pleasures, and they had hardly an aim beyond the day. 'Spirit is also sensual pleasure,'

thus they spoke. Then the wings of their spirit broke: now it creeps around and makes dirty what it feeds on. Once they thought of becoming heroes: now they are sensualists. The hero is to them an affliction and a terror. But, by my love and hope I entreat you: do not reject the hero in your soul! Keep holy your highest hope!' Thus spoke Zarathustra."[18]

Friedrich Nietzsche

There is nothing more heartbreaking than listening to defeated heroes. Their pessimism often stems from a single moment of failure in their lives. Instead of viewing it as just that—a moment—they allow it to define the entirety of their existence. As I mentioned before, sometimes the most tangible thing in a person's life is negativity, and for many defeated heroes, that negativity becomes their reality.[19] This leads to a state of perpetual sulking, where they wallow in regret rather than rise to reclaim their purpose.

The truth is, a hero is someone who never lets go of their ideals, values, character, or hopes. They remain steadfast despite opposition and adversity. This resilience is not an accident—it's a defining characteristic of heroism.[20] Heroes serve as pillars of strength, embodying something greater than themselves for those who believe in them. The moment they choose to give up—I shudder at the thought—they not only let themselves down in that instant, but they also betray countless others who looked to them for inspiration, as well as the vast opportunities they once had to flourish.[21]

Attaining something as rare as your desired state carries an inherent responsibility: to thrive, so others may witness that achieving everything you've ever truly wanted *is* possible. Your desired state is precious. Even if your greatest ambition in life is as simple as squeezing someone's boobies like Denji from *Chainsaw Man*, it still holds value—because it is *your* dream, your fulfillment, your catharsis at the end of the hero's journey.[22] And if it is truly what you want, then you deserve to have it.

Dramatic Before Disingenuous

Since you are now doing your thing, you may find it easy to detect people who aren't as ablaze as you. When two coals meet—one lit and the other out—either the lit coal will ignite the unlit one, or the lit coal will be extinguished by the unlit one. The person whose state is more abundantly present will determine whose domain expands. A potent antidote to another's drabness is the commitment to being dramatic before being disingenuous.

Let's face it—we're in the game of obtaining our desired states. That pursuit comes with attention and, at times, standing in the spotlight. The goal is never to seek the spotlight for vanity's sake. However, when you inevitably find yourself right there in the middle of things, thinking *dramatic before disingenuous* can help you overcome all sorts of embarrassment or even guilt. Research suggests that self-expression, even when perceived as theatrical, fosters authenticity and personal fulfillment, reinforcing one's id entity.[23]

THE BITTER END

People will call you "weird," "extra," "too much," "over the top"—the list goes on. What you most accurately are is *dramatic*. Not in a delusional, attention-seeking way, but in the sense that this world is your reflective stage, and you are fully embodying your genuine self. The way you feel in all moments is authentic. You are not the antithesis: disingenuous. Studies in social psychology show that individuals who embrace their natural expressive tendencies, rather than suppressing them for fear of social judgment, tend to experience higher levels of well-being and self-e steem.[24]

If the choice arises between the two, always choose to be dramatic—risking a chance of embarrassment or un-professionalism—rather than disingenuous, which risks reinforcing the very state you desperately don't want to be in. Psychological research indicates that suppressing one's true self can lead to cognitive dissonance, which creates internal stress and diminishes overall happiness.[25]

Many people are stuck in their undesired states and want someone to wallow in their misery with them. As mentioned in the previous section, they are defeated heroes. When they see that someone has accomplished what they fear to attempt, they become jealous and deeply uncomfortable—their failure reflected back at them like an unwelcome mirror. Psychological studies confirm that envy often stems from a threatened self-concept, particularly when one sees another achieving what they themselves have struggled to attain.[26]

Let me be your lover, big bro, or friend and tell you: YOU ARE WORTHY! You are allowed to flourish, even if those around you feel inadequate because of it. How they feel is not your fault. What matters is what *you* think of them.

If you want to flaunt and rub it in their faces, then close this book—I'd be ashamed to have taught you to show off and gloat. But if you want to flourish because it is your birthright, because you are *convicted* to show others what a hero truly is, then please—by all means—show me, sister. Show all of us.

You're Perfectly Normal—You're Normally Perfect

At this point in your journey, it is important to remember that, at baseline, you are typically just chilling. This thing you just accomplished—obtaining, I mean really living out the life you want—is here, is yours. And most importantly, it's your *lifestyle*, not just something you do when you have time. Therefore, it is a true blessing to wake up every morning knowing and feeling like you got this.

All the striving you've done—and still do—has led you to a reality where your *average* result is pretty good. That's the goal: to live your life in a way that yields pretty good results *on average*. I would refrain from thinking that you have to get excellent results every single time—you simply do not. Not only is that impossible, but it's also one of the main excuses people use for why they don't even *try* in the first place.[27] They say, *Since it's not going to be perfect, I won't even begin*—and so they do nothing at all. But not you. Everyone else? Y'all stay safe out there.

Your new normal is now perfect *for you*. Not perfect, full stop. But perfect for the lifestyle you live. Take me, for example: I accidentally slept in this morning and didn't go to the gym at six like I typically do. What does this blunder mean in the context of my desired state? Well, very little. Why? Because that mistake *normally* does not happen. That's the beauty of an average.

Psychological research on habit formation supports this: consistency over time is what truly shapes behavior, not perfection in execution.[28] Normally, I go to the gym at six in the morning five days a week and a bit later on Saturdays (because my gym opens later). I can guarantee you that I'll be there early tomorrow morning—because that's what I *usually* do. That trust in yourself, that confidence in your habits, is what you *earn* with your desired state.[29]

I may have blundered today, but that is an *outlier*, not a *trend*. And you know what? You better believe I'll just be working out at five in the afternoon when I finish teaching. Simple. No self-degradation, no guilt—just going later. The ability to adapt without spiraling into negative self-talk is a hallmark of self-efficacy, a key psychological trait linked to long-term success.[30]

Never Negotiate Or Tolerate Terrorism

Remember, my beloved reader, people will oppose the fact that you flourish simply for the sake of opposition. There is still an equal and opposite force for everything—an antithesis to your claim on life.[31] But you know what? That just means your thesis on life, your desired state, will be tested and ultimately proven to be the life you truly deserve to live.

My issue with lifestyle terrorism (as I have coined it) is that the terrorist, in this case, isn't fighting to win but rather fighting to make you lose. The terrorist is already a loser—they long ago abandoned their desire to obtain the lifestyle they once believed was possible for themselves.[32] As I mentioned before, these are the defeated heroes of society. Having given up, they now seek to fit the only role that gives their life meaning: lifestyle terrorist. Their new mission in life? To bring about the downfall of anyone heading toward greatness.

Therefore, never negotiate with or tolerate a lifestyle terrorist. *Who is a lifestyle terrorist, and how can I stay the fuck away from them?* you ask. Well, I'll tell you: anyone whose energy and presence negatively impact you in any way is a lifestyle terrorist.[33] I'm talking about complainers, victims, cynics, people who always seem to squander their goals, perpetual losers, haters, doubters, villains, and anyone who supports them. Steer clear of these archetypes at all costs! Do not budget time or energy for them! That is what I mean by negotiating.

If they ask you to *"just hear me out," "suppose this or that," "think about it"*—bah humbug—please, do not. Where you are now, your energy and mental state, need to be protected like the Secret Service protects the president: with your life.[34] Please, and I struggle with this myself, so hear me when I say this: it is not worth it! Tolerating a late night, taking just one shot of vodka, driving that hour to the airport—none of it is worth sacrificing your peace for. Why? Because they don't actually want your company—just *any* company in their misery.[35]

258

What draws them to you is the fact that you flourish. They want to reduce that in any way to feel better about not flourishing themselves. I beg you—resist.

I Hope I Just Look Crazy

I wrote that simple phrase while completely high, faded off that good ol' zah (which I used to toke in college). I found that line in my notes, and it still resonates with me deeply—even though I haven't been high off weed in years. The way I go about living out my desired state boils down to that: I just hope that when it is all said and done, people will look back on what I've accomplished and, at worst, say: *Man, that Mr. Donnel Delva was one crazy guy.*

Most people will think you're crazy when they see you flourishing. Your habits and character dispositions will startle them and make them uncomfortable. The reason is that you represent their insecurities, doubts, and fears—overcome. When they look at you, their excuses go out the window; they lose all credibility and rationale. Psychologists have found that cognitive dissonance, the tension between conflicting beliefs and realities, causes discomfort, leading people to rationalize their own limitations when faced with someone who defies them.[36]

Their external world—you, in your desired state—does not match the story they tell themselves internally: *I can't do this. No one can. People are mostly like me. You have to be born a certain way to have what you want.* Your very existence challenges that narrative. Neuroscience research suggests that the brain naturally resists uncertainty, preferring patterns that reinforce its pre-existing beliefs.[37] Because you introduce nuance and unpredictability, their discomfort leads them to assume that if anyone is crazy between the two of you, it must be you. The irony!

But that perception is the worst I hope people say about me. I know people love and respect me—I experience their fondness every day. At the same time, I also know there are those who hate my guts simply because I flourish in the desired state I have worked so hard to attract. Studies in social psychology reveal that individuals who achieve success often become targets of resentment, particularly from those who feel left behind or inadequate by comparison.[38] However they feel, my hope is that, since I refuse to flaunt, they will come to terms with the discrepancy between what they believe and what they experience when they encounter me—and chalk it all up to my craziness.

If I ever got to sit down at a table prepared for me, with them as attendants, I know that is what they would say—if they were being honest. This experience is something you should hope to feel deep within yourself, too: that sense of integrity and inner peace, knowing you have done the right things to attract the life you want. And as a result, no one can validly call you names that do not accurately describe you. The one label they could slap on you that would make any sense is *crazy*.

Don't Judge

I'm going to share something with you that has saved me countless words and an even greater amount of peace: do not judge others for not flourishing or reaching their desired state—especially once you've attracted yours and can now clearly see their mistakes.

This principle has come easily to me because I dislike being judged and, in turn, dislike judging others. However, that doesn't mean it's always easy. I can empathize. As a high school English teacher, I often see students making the same mistakes I once made in different areas of my life, and it's tempting to judge them for it. That would be the easy way out—to say that I am better than them simply because I have overcome my bad habits. But the more difficult choice, the one you should make, is to lead by example and offer mentorship. Research suggests that mentorship fosters resilience and personal growth, helping individuals navigate challenges more effectively.[39]

But not everyone will listen to you. Some people are set on continuing their undesired state simply because it is familiar to them. As family therapist Virginia Satir observed, "People prefer the certainty of misery to the misery of uncertainty."[40] If you find it necessary to confront people stuck in their misery, then you must also take responsibility for helping them back up afterward. Psychological studies on cognitive dissonance suggest that individuals are more receptive to change when guided by those they trust, rather than those who merely criticize them.[41]

Become a mentor to those who need the wisdom you have gained from the mistakes you both share. Coach them. Teach them. Advise them earnestly. Lead them fearlessly. I have realized that the reason I am most tempted to judge others for not being in their desired state is fear—believe it or not. I'm afraid that if I see them unable to attract what they desire, then my worldview—the entire premise of this book, my life's work—will be invalid. They embody my own doubts: *can everyone truly attract what they desire most?* Research on self-fulfilling prophecies indicates that our beliefs about others can shape their outcomes, reinforcing either success or failure depending on our expectations.[42] As a result of this realization, I no longer take the easy way out. Instead, I confront my fear by leading through example. I choose to represent those who can attract their desired states. It is possible, and I refuse to judge those who believe otherwise.

Rather than judging, ask yourself: *what is being valued here?* You will not have a tendency to judge others in the first place if you do not judge yourself. You simply won't. Always ask yourself what you are valuing in different circumstances. You are always valuing *something*. Identify what it is and determine whether it aligns with your desired state. If it does, by all means, continue. If it does not, stop.

If the actions of others do not align with your desired state, do not judge them. Instead, mentor them—if they want your help. If they do not, then leave them alone and protect your energy. Studies in behavioral psychology suggest that maintaining strong personal boundaries is essential for emotional well-being and sustained success.[43]

Impress Only Yourself

Impressing others is not only beyond your jurisdiction but also of little true substance, as all glory ultimately belongs to God. I'll admit it—heck, I'll profess it—you're irresistible! You're absolutely magnetic, captivating, and undeniably attractive. People can't get enough of you; you leave them wanting more. Good. That's great for you.

But here's the thing: you didn't embark on the journey of attracting your desired state for attention or praise. You became someone worthy of the life you live through internal discipline, paying the price, and humbly sacrificing what needed to be removed from your life to maintain what truly matters. Research suggests that true fulfillment comes from intrinsic motivation—doing things for personal growth rather than external validation.[44] That life, your God-given birthright, has always belonged to Him. Therefore, return it all back to Him by impressing yourself daily and instilling within yourself the desire to see your own greatness unfold.

Impressing yourself happens through small, consistent actions that remind you of your highest self. Studies show that developing daily habits of self-discipline strengthens self-efficacy and reinforces a positive self-image.[45] For instance, I impress myself every time I wake up at five in the morning and get to the gym by six o'clock to train hard. Right now, as I type in my classroom, fall is settling in; people have already begun hibernating for winter. No one—besides that gloriously fine and sleek girl I call my gym crush and a couple of old ladies—is at the gym. When I step into that gym, creatine in my system, my bags packed with my dress shirt and pants, Venus and her celestial companions are still out, and Mr. Sun is just being announced by Dawn's opening mouth.

But I'm there. Every. Single. Time.

And that, in itself, is impressive. Research in psychology suggests that maintaining consistent routines fosters discipline, which is directly linked to long-term success and well-being.[46] Does this make me a confident and attractive man? My goodness—duh! But, most importantly, this routine redirects my focus back to God.

The first words on my tongue, the first breath from my lungs every time my alarm calls me from the dream world, are: THANK YOU, GOD! And let me tell you, that is also very impressive. Studies indicate that expressing gratitude daily significantly improves mental health and overall life satisfaction.[47] I have impressed upon myself the truth that the only person I need to improve for is me.

Do not compete with others in your self-improvement journey; do not compare yourself to others to measure your progress. Instead, take stock of yourself from yesterday. Did you improve? Did you stay consistent with a life-improving habit? If you can answer yes to those questions, then say with all your might and luster: THANK YOU, GOD!

Show Not Tell

I'm an English teacher, so this one resonates with me quite harmoniously. Since you're now flourishing, you may want to yap, yap, yap about all you do. Please refrain. Remember how far you've come. Remember what got you here: paying the true internal price for what you want and becoming a person who attracts those things. Nowhere in that journey did you have to yap, yap, yap to anyone—in fact, I specifically warned you against it in *Don't Share A Plan You're*

THE BITTER END

Uncomfortable Revealing, in case of energy vampires. Instead, here's what you should do: model what it is you would say. Show it to the world through your actions, not your words.

Few things get under my skin more than people announcing who they *believe* themselves to be rather than showing us who they *truly* are. Research suggests that people form impressions based on consistent behavioral cues rather than verbal self-descriptions.[48] So, don't *say* you're blessed—manifest it. Don't *say* you're happy—just smile. Psychological studies confirm that genuine smiles activate mirror neurons in others, making your happiness contagious.[49] We've all heard the person who says, *That's funny* after a joke. They don't actually think it's funny. They may recognize something comical about the joke, but unless their belly bursts into laughter, my beloved reader, they're only saving you from embarrassment.[50]

So, don't *say* you're rich—just pull up in a Tesla or donate generously to Fairfield Prep. Trust me, we will *know*. Research on social signaling supports that true wealth, success, and competence are more convincingly displayed through behaviors rather than self-proclamations.[51] Don't yap, yap, yap about how lOcKeD iN you are—just meet me in the gym. Then, I'll get to see for myself.

And let me leave you with this to soothe your vanity. Trust me: I love to toot my own horn as much as the next so-called sigma male. But what keeps me humble is, ironically, the praise I inevitably receive from those who recognize greatness. The *real ones*—those flourishing in their desired states too—will find you and let you know. And oh God, there is no sweeter sound. Studies show that external validation from respected peers carries significantly more psychological weight than self-promotion.[52] The only price you have to pay for that? Zipping it. Stay silent and let your actions speak for you until someone inevitably, profoundly, *glazes* you. Please believe me when I say, it brings you to tears and keeps you going much farther than your own yap, yap, yapping.

How I Flourished By Skipping Rocks

When it comes to synthesizing all the principles laid out in this chapter, I find that everything I have said comes together when I skip rocks. I first attempted to skip a rock across Lake Mohegan in Fairfield, CT, about seven years ago. The first thing I realized is that there is a small process involved in skipping rocks. First, you select a good rock; then, you flick it across the water. That's it. The results are immediate, clear, and even measurable if you want to analyze your technique. Since my first rock-skipping session, I have followed one rule: always skip the rock I pick up.

In life, you inherit an external circumstance that you may or may not have chosen for yourself. Research suggests that while external conditions shape our experiences, our internal responses determine how we navigate them.[53] All you can do is control your internal condition to attract what you'd like in this three-dimensional reality. That exact lesson is what I feel during the rhythmic experience of skipping rocks. If you also skip rocks as much as I do, then you know that it feels almost fraudulent to pick up a rock you intended to skip, only to throw it back down upon inspection. It gives me chills just typing it out. Try! At least try. Fling that thing across the water, even if you don't foresee success. That is what flourishing looks like—you commit, believing completely in yourself.[54]

There is no one to blame but yourself when you skip rocks. You pick the rock. You decide to throw it. You choose. Whether it immediately plunges into the depths or whizzes across the water, it is all on you. You take full responsibility, but you do not have full control. Studies show that people who take personal responsibility for their actions tend to experience higher levels of resilience and personal growth.[55] I wish I could have all the perfect conditions lined up for me to make every throw effortlessly glide. You don't know how much pleasure I'd get from calming every sea right before I throw. But, believe it or not, I don't control any of that. I skip rocks regardless of the external circumstances because I know I've got this.

At this point in my life, I've skipped thousands of rocks across dozens of bodies of water. I've sent rocks flying across Walden Pond, every beach I've visited, and any stream I've come across—you name it. I promise you: there is nothing more impressive or attractive than flinging a rock with your glistening body on the shore, sending it deep into the ocean. And you know what? I don't judge others who struggle to get their rocks to skip. In fact, studies suggest that teaching others a skill reinforces our own learning and deepens our understanding.[56] (I once taught a boyfriend of a couple who observed me skipping rocks how to do it, and let me tell you—easily one of the top ten hottest things I've ever done.)

DONNEL DELVA

Not every rock flashes across the water, and some—even though rare—bounce back toward me. But every rock that I choose to interact with gets something: my best effort. I put my best foot forward, wind up my best arm, give it an honest chance, and flick. Every time I get a result, I am proud because I know the character, disposition, and dedication it took to commit to an action and see it through. That simple, fun hobby I engage in whenever I see a body of water is the embodiment of flourishing. So go—let those fine chips fly, like yourself, either soaring across this ocean of life or sinking under its weight.

Immediate Action Steps

1. Go with the Flow: Embrace the current of your growth. Avoid resisting or over-controlling your journey, as this will only cause unnecessary stress and setbacks. Instead, trust the process, stay humble, and allow your progress to unfold naturally.

2. Trust Yourself: Acknowledge your achievements without sabotaging them. Practice affirmations or daily self-reflection to build confidence and celebrate your growth.

3. Go Beyond Plus Ultra +1: Push past your limits, even when you're exhausted. Next time you're faced with a challenge—whether at the gym, at work, or in life—go beyond what you think is your limit and try just one more.

4. Be True to Yourself: Identify what feels authentic to you and stick with it, even if it goes against societal norms. Take time each day to reflect on your values and ensure your actions align with them.

5. Embrace Dramatic Self-Expression: Express yourself authentically, even if it feels a little extra. Let your individuality shine and resist the urge to suppress your natural tendencies for fear of judgment. Embrace being "dramatic" in the sense of being unapologetically you, by taking some action that allows your

genuine self to lead you to greater fulfillment and peace.

6. Embody Your "New Normal": Recognize that your new desired state is not just a momentary achievement, but a permanent lifestyle change. Focus on consistency rather than perfection. Reflect on how far you've come and acknowledge that living authentically with peace and joy is the most important thing you can continue to cultivate.

7. Never Negotiate with Terrorism: Set clear boundaries with negative influences and protect your peace. Don't tolerate anything that disrupts your flourishing—whether it's external criticism or self-doubt. Stand firm in your desired state and let go of any person or situation that tries to drag you down.

13

PRACTICE UNINTENTIONAL ASCETICISM

"Therefore whoever hears
these sayings of Mine, and
does them, I will liken him
to a wise man who built
his house on the rock:"
—Matthew 7:24

***

Do you believe you can have it all, the bad with the good? What are you holding onto that keeps you from getting what you truly need? What are things you've already had to let go of in the past to move forward and grow? What are you attached to that no longer serves you?

When You Create—You Destroy

Congratulations! You have made it to the final chapter of the book. I am prouder than the finest peacock to see that someone has appreciated my book enough to keep reading (or you've just skipped here—still, I'm not mad at you at all). Not many people are like you; most people don't read,[1] and even fewer will ever apply what they learn to their lives.[2] So, good job. Without further (and much-deserved) admiration, let's dive right into the end.

Now that you're flourishing in the desired state you worked so hard for, you may notice that certain habits and behaviors have fallen by the wayside. This phenomenon is what I call *unintentional asceticism*—the inadvertent renunciation of certain actions that naturally occurs when pursuing a particular goal.

For example, if you are training for a marathon, your focus on endurance and discipline will inevitably prevent you from smoking. You didn't start training with the explicit goal of avoiding cigarettes, but the demands of your regimen made smoking incompatible with your pursuit. Research suggests that behavioral change often works this way; instead of making direct resolutions, people are more likely to maintain habits that align with their broader goals.[3] Similarly, when you strive toward a higher state of being, you will unknowingly shed behaviors and distractions that do not serve you.

When you create the world around you, you simultaneously destroy other potential realities. You are always engaged in this intricate dance of creation and destruction. As economist Thomas Sowell writes in *A Conflict of Visions: Ideological Origins of Political Struggles*, "There are no solutions, only trade-offs."[4] This concept is evident in many aspects of life, including sports.

I coach the freshman defensive line at Fairfield Prep, and one thing I've learned is that there is no one-size-fits-all miracle defensive play. If such a play existed, I'd already have an NFL contract. Instead, every strategy is a trade-off—certain plays are more effective in specific situations, but none work perfectly in all cases. This reality mirrors life: you cannot have a "miracle life" where you smoke a pack a day and run marathons. The choices you make define the opportunities available to you.

For every decision you make, there are infinite decisions you didn't make. I see this principle at work even in video games, particularly in *NBA 2K25*. The game rewards players for actions taken on the court with a "Teammate Grade," a feature that fairly evaluates how well you perform. However, one flaw in the system is that it only grades what you *do*—not what you *refrain* from doing. I've always thought the game should also reward players for the smart, disciplined choices they don't make.

While it may be impossible for an algorithm to evaluate non-actions, real life certainly does. Studies show that self-discipline and the ability to delay gratification lead to greater long-term success.[5] The actions you choose *not* to take—the temptations you resist, the distractions you avoid—yield rewards in ways you may not immediately recognize. When you cross the finish line of your marathon, you'll realize, *Thank God I didn't start smoking.*

So, let your spirit be energized by the decisions you knew would not serve you and deliberately refrained from. Since there are infinite non-actions, there are infinite sources of strength and momentum propelling you forward. Thanking God for what you didn't do is just as powerful as thanking Him for what you have accomplished. By reinforcing your desired state with both affirmations of action and restraint, you remind your mind, body, and spirit that success is not only about what you *do* but also about what you *refuse* to do.

Law Of Equivalent Exchange

I first learned of the Law of Equivalent Exchange while watching *FullMetal Alchemist.* The law states, "In order to obtain or create something, something of equal value must be lost or given." My favorite word in that law is *value.* Research suggests that when individuals engage in self-discipline, they do not randomly sacrifice activities but instead give up those of comparable significance to their goals.[6] For example, marathon training would not suddenly lead you to stop driving or chewing gum—those activities are either excessive or irrelevant. However, if your goal is to own a Tesla, you may begin to allocate a portion of your income toward that purchase, sacrificing unnecessary spending to reach your objective. Studies show that this type of trade-off—deliberately exchanging one behavior for another—reinforces goal-directed behavior.[7] The exchange, what you give or lose, will always be of equal value to what you receive and earn.

It is essential to understand that the value of your desired state is determined by *you*. Having a million dollars in the bank might overwhelm a homeless person but would not faze a billionaire. The universe operates within this dimension of exchange, granting what you put forth the effort to achieve.[8] Therefore, it is your responsibility to assess both the value of your desired state—what that lifestyle means to you—and who you must become internally to fully realize it. This transformation is often referred to as *identity-based change*, where individuals must align their habits and mindset with the person they wish to become.[9] If you think you can enjoy even one smoke a month while training for a marathon, then you have not yet become the person you need to be to reach that goal. In that case, you are still a smoker who would like to run. But you can become a runner—period. And runners do not smoke, ever. *Why is it like that?* you ask. Simply because *that's the law*.

Everywhere in nature, the Law of Equivalent Exchange is at work. Research in ecology highlights how life is sustained through constant trade-offs, with each organism adapting to ensure survival.[10] An apple tree, for instance, may yield hundreds of apples, but not without an equivalent exchange of energy. It absorbs water, draws nutrients from the soil, and harnesses sunlight to sustain itself. These exchanges shape not only the natural world but also human lives. They do not *change* who you are but instead *reveal* who you have always been. It is an elegant and beautiful system—because if it walks and talks like a duck, then it *is* a duck. What makes a

275

person any different? We are products of nature, just like any other life form. So, if someone walks and talks like a winner, then they *are* a winner, flourishing in their desired state. They have paid the true internal cost and now deserve precisely what they have earned.

You're Already Doing It

As I close this chapter and finish this book, I want to remind you that when it comes to practicing unintentional asceticism to attract your desired state, you are always making a decision. Whether through inactivity or activity, you are choosing. Research suggests that even in moments of perceived inaction, the brain is actively processing and reinforcing behavioral patterns, making non-action just as consequential as action itself.[11]

I cannot tell you how many times I've stared at my phone or paced back and forth, wondering how to respond to a lover of mine. One day, after an hour of this, a realization struck me: *What have I already been doing for the past hour?* Not saying anything. That was my decision. I might as well feel good about it. And so, this time, I didn't text her—and I felt great about it. Psychological studies show that self-perception plays a crucial role in decision-making; when we frame our choices as intentional rather than passive, we experience a greater sense of control and emotional stability.[12]

Before I make a decision (unless I'm already in a flow state), I ask myself two essential questions: *What do I want to do right now?* and *What do I value most?* These two questions have saved me years of pain, regret, and exhaustion from decision fatigue. Studies suggest that minimizing decision fatigue by aligning choices with deeply held values can enhance overall well-being and mental clarity.[13] I don't debate myself as much anymore because I understand that whatever I am doing, I have already decided. You cannot sip wine while debating whether to go sober—the irony is completely lost on those who try. Research indicates that cognitive dissonance—the mental discomfort from holding conflicting beliefs—can lead to emotional stress, which is why consistency between values and actions is critical for long-term fulfillment.[14]

My beloved reader, please, save yourself. Spare yourself the sadistic hardship of indecision. Take ownership of the life you are already bringing into existence so that you can change it. You can't ride into the sunset in the passenger seat, because you were never in the passenger seat to begin with. You are the one who drove yourself to the dumps—and the one who can change course, one degree at a time. Neuroscientific research affirms that small, consistent changes in behavior, known as micro-shifts, can rewire neural pathways over time, making transformation a gradual yet powerful process.[15]

When asking yourself those two aforementioned questions, the easiest way to commit to what you're doing is by feeling your emotions. Research suggests that emotional awareness is key to making values-based decisions; emotions serve as internal compasses, guiding us toward alignment or dissonance.[16] What you do is what you want right now—admitting that truth is step one. What you value most should remain consistent (though it may evolve over years).

If your current actions align with your deepest values, you will likely feel good. However, if they are misaligned, discomfort will follow. The goal, then, is to align your actions with your values and feel good about doing what matters most to you.

That being said, sometimes you will feel bad even after acting in alignment with your values, and that's okay. Research indicates that delayed gratification and value-driven actions often result in short-term discomfort but long-term fulfillment.[17] Feeling good about doing the right thing can be cultivated with time and positive feedback loops. When you reflect on your growth and the benefits of making aligned choices, it becomes easier to trust that you made the right decision. My beloved reader, I know there is so much more love and light for you—right here and in the days to come.

Immediate Action Steps

1. Define Your Trade-offs: Reflect on the goals you're currently pursuing. Write down the habits or behaviors that no longer serve you in the pursuit of these goals. What can you let go of to make space for your desired reality?

2. Create a Behavior Contract with Yourself: Write a brief contract where you list specific actions you will commit to and the ones you expect to unintentionally avoid to align with your bigger goals.

3. Identify Your Values: At the start of each day, ask yourself, *What do I want to do today?* and *What do I value most?* Write down your answers, and use them as your guiding principles throughout the day.

4. Observe Your Micro-shifts: Throughout the day, note any small decisions where you either consciously chose a positive action or passively allowed an old behavior to continue. Reflect on how these micro-shifts, over time, are rewiring your habits and pushing you closer to your ideal state.

5. Evaluate Your Decisions: At the end of each week, look back at the decisions you made and the habits you practiced. Were there any habits you unintentionally shed? Celebrate progress and identify actions to eliminate for continued growth.

Epilogue

"Again, the kingdom of
heaven is like treasure hidden in a field, which a man
found and hid; and for joy
over it he goes and sells all
that he has and buys that
field." —Matthew 13:44

Do you think you will actually put what we've discussed into
practice, or did this conversation merely reaffirm what you
already believed? After everything we explored, do you feel
as though you've uncovered something profound, or do you
find yourself still at square one, struggling just to break
even? What would need to happen for you to know, without
a doubt, that you have escaped the cycles that once held you
back? And perhaps most importantly, how can you use what
you've learned to help others avoid the same pitfalls?

My Kingdom Of Heaven

My Friend and Teacher, our Lord Jesus Christ, speaks often of the kingdom of heaven in the Gospel, and His words have led me to envision my own version of the kingdom. So, if I may, allow me to humbly add my perspective on its foundation, transformation, and preservation.

My kingdom of heaven is a world where people do not wait until they hit rock bottom to ask for help. They do not wait until desperation forces them to change. Instead, they seek growth before suffering necessitates it. They understand that the greatest gift is not the fish but the knowledge of how to fish. Research suggests that individuals who proactively seek personal development experience greater long-term fulfillment and resilience, rather than merely reacting to hardship when it arises.[1]

And that is why this journey has mattered. Because even if someone could hand you your desired state, it would not bring you lasting happiness. Fulfillment does not come from simply receiving something new—it comes from becoming someone new. That is why we laid the foundation. That is why you have changed. Your inner state has shifted, and in doing so, your outer world now flourishes. And because you now know how to fish, you are no longer bound to a single outcome. You can claim new states, new heights, endlessly. Even more, you can teach others to do the same.

Everything we have explored comes down to this one truth: you can improve. No matter where you are—whether rebuilding from nothing or reaching for greater heights—there is always room to grow. Studies show that adopting a growth mindset leads to higher achievement, greater well-being, and a stronger sense of purpose.[2] But the real power of self-improvement does not end with you.

When you believe in your ability to grow, you begin to see that same potential in others. And that is where true transformation happens—not just within yourself, but in the world around you. Self-improvement is not just for you; it is for the least and the greatest of us. It is for the struggling and the thriving, for those at their lowest and those already soaring. And as you grow, you will learn to walk the delicate balance between striving for the next horizon and feeling deep contentment with where you are.

Imagine a world where this belief is common, where growth is not just a personal pursuit but a shared value. A world where people take responsibility for their lives, not out of fear, but out of hope. Where even the smallest adjustments in daily habits ripple outward, elevating not just the individual, but the entire community. Each improvement raises the baseline for what is considered normal, and in doing so, the whole kingdom is lifted higher.

And in this world, people do not merely force themselves to improve—they *desire* to. They feel the pull, the excitement of rising, not just for their own sake, but for their lovers, their families, their friends. They want to be role models. They want to be lighthouses. They want to be heroes.

How different would life be if more people embraced this way of being? How many tragedies, crimes, and conflicts could have been prevented if more people had felt that they had enough—that they *were* enough? Studies in positive psychology indicate that when individuals feel a sense of purpose and self-worth, they are significantly less likely to engage in harmful behaviors or fall into despair.[3] The stronger we become, the less we take from the world, and the more we are able to give.

So *believe in yourself.* Believe in the power that resides within you. Trust that your efforts will bear fruit.

And do not wait. Start right now. Go for it. Take action—any action—to prove to yourself that you are the person who deserves everything you have ever desired. Do not wait until you have lost it all to begin. Do not wait for someone else to validate you. Every moment is an opportunity to learn, to grow, to strengthen. It should not be an obsession, but a way of life—a lifestyle you give to yourself and to others.

Because whether you realize it or not, someone is watching you. Someone is learning from you. You are the example they have been waiting for.

It has been you this whole time.

I can see my kingdom of heaven. And it is beautiful.

Not just beautiful—*abundant*. Overflowing with life, with joy, with possibility. So full of goodness that in certain lights, it almost looks like the greatest version of earth—our common home, but refined, uplifted, made whole.

In this world, everyone has enough within themselves to reach their highest potential. Everyone gives generously, not just from their excess, but from their wisdom, their strength, their journey. The widow with the two mites gives two today, but two and a half tomorrow. The Good Samaritan does not simply help the wounded—he creates a world where fewer people are wounded in the first place. Gyms are full, not just with bodies, but with minds committed to discipline and vitality. The world is clean. Teeming with life. A place where people get better, where laughter echoes, where new beginnings are always welcome.

A home.

And in my kingdom of heaven, teachers are *rich*.

My Post-Anime Dilemma

I have watched about thirty anime, and each time I finish a new one, I reencounter the same dilemma: *Do I start another?*

This question mirrors exactly how I feel about self-improvement and attaining my desired states.

I hesitate and ponder because the conflict lies in the possibility that the new anime—or the new desired state—might be a letdown. *What if it doesn't live up to the last one?* Research suggests that humans instinctively resist new challenges, often fearing that the next endeavor won't measure up to a previous high.[4] We are wired to avoid discomfort, to cling to what feels familiar and safe.

After reaching a higher level of living, it stings to start from zero again—to be a rookie, to struggle anew. The climb is always daunting, and the fall from expectation can be painful. The higher we've soared, the harder it can be to accept the humility of beginning again.

But after thirty anime and several desired states fulfilled, let me tell you: it is *always* worth going the distance again.

Everything worth having demands an inner cost—discipline, patience, and endurance.[5] The uncertainty of the new is always outweighed by the richness of the journey.

And so, I will always risk the possibility of spoilers rather than never experience the story at all. Because the truth is, the journey *is* the reward. The same is true for chasing the next level of my life.

Like former President Theodore Roosevelt once blessed us with:

> "It is not the critic who counts; not the man who points out how the strong man stumbles, or where the doer of deeds could have done them better. The credit belongs to the man who is actually in the arena, whose face is marred by dust and sweat and blood; who strives valiantly; who errs, who comes short again and again, because there is no effort without error and shortcoming; but who does actually strive to do the deeds; who knows great enthusiasms, the great devotions; who spends himself in a worthy cause; who at the best knows in the end the triumph of high achievement, and who at the worst, if he fails, at least fails while daring greatly, so that his place shall never be with those cold and timid souls who neither know victory nor defeat."

When I wrestle with whether to get back into the arena and grind it out again, I remind myself: the newest grind is being faced by the *newer me*. Each time I stand at the base of a new challenge, I am not the same person who stood here before. I am stronger, wiser, more capable.

Research on resilience shows that each successful challenge rewires the brain, making future challenges easier to tackle.[6] Every battle won is a lesson learned, a skill honed, a belief in oneself strengthened. Each time we achieve a desired state, we don't just reach a goal—we expand our capacity to reach even greater ones.

This creates a positive feedback loop: the more you overcome, the more you become capable of overcoming. Studies in neuroplasticity reveal that repeated victories reinforce our neural pathways, strengthening our belief in ourselves and making future success more automatic.[7] Confidence isn't just a feeling—it's a structure built through action.

And over time, you don't just obtain the inner states and materials you desire in life—you *attract* a higher level of existence. Again and again, with each pursuit, you ascend.

And when you reach that level, the universe itself bends in your favor. Call it faith, energy, or divine alignment, but time and again, those who persist see life open doors where none seemed to exist before.[8] It's not magic; it's the compounded effect of self-belief and action.

So, embrace the process. Let the improvement wash over you. Let it sharpen you. If you have that urge to watch a new anime, even though you've already seen so many—watch it. Because that desire has a realization. Every single one of your desires has a corresponding fulfillment—it exists.

So quench the burning within yourself.

The Bitter End

The bitter end. We've finally made it. The bitter, bitter end. I'm in tears as I type these words. This has truly been a journey. I have learned so much about myself—how my sense of humor shapes the way I teach, why I think and behave in ways that may not always align with my emotions, and how the feelings that seem to arise without reason still hold deep influences over my state of being.

I have come to understand my perception of faith in God in ways I never had before.

And none of this would have happened without a single moment of inspiration—one that struck three years ago as I walked to Walnut Beach, skipping rocks and unknowingly planting the first seed of what would become this book. That moment led me here, to this conversation, to this shared experience between you and me. My sincerest hope is that these pages in your hands have been as impactful for you as the last three years of writing have been for me.

But now, you ask: *What is the bitter end?*

The bitter end is this: you may do nothing with the knowledge you have just gained.

Research suggests that for every hundred people who embark on a self-transformation journey, ninety-nine will ultimately return to their undesired way of life, unchanged, untransformed.[9] The spark of motivation fades, and old habits creep back in. Studies show that while motivation and inspiration can spark change, true, sustained transformation requires deep behavioral shifts—something most people struggle to commit to.[10]

THE BITTER END

Maybe you felt that surge of motivation while reading. Maybe, for a fleeting moment, you saw a glimpse of a new reality—one that made your spirit feel alive. But now, as you near the back cover, you glance beyond the pages and find yourself confronted with the same surroundings, the same patterns, the same circumstances that have long defined your world. And the temptation will be strong—to let this book become just another fleeting inspiration, another ghost of potential lost to time.

But for those who take action—for those who don't just hear my words but *live* them—the bitter end means something else entirely.

It marks the final chapter of your undesired caterpillar existence. The time spent reading, reflecting, and absorbing in your chrysalis has prepared you for this moment. And now, you emerge—transformed.

The research is clear: those who commit to deliberate action, to restructuring their habits, to immersing themselves in a new reality, are the ones who achieve lasting change.[11]

And so, with your monk mode behind you, you spread your wings. You leave behind the life you never wanted and step into the life you were always meant to live.

Someday, you and I will meet again—not in some distant afterlife, but *here.* In the world we create, in the reality we choose. A world of love, peace, happiness, abundance, and generosity.

So let us not meet only in some deathless dimension. Let us meet here, in this third-dimensional world—as the highest versions of ourselves.

DONNEL DELVA

The Music Never Ends

To close this lifework of mine, this precious conversation we've shared, allow this young musician to leave you with these final words: *The music never ends.*

One thing I've learned from sitting at the beautiful keys is that while I may have stopped playing, the music itself never stops. You and the piano—your soul and your instrument—may be at rest, but the melody continues. If the music of your life were written on a staff, it would stretch endlessly, filled with measures of whole rests and soaring crescendos. People and events come and go, weaving in and out like instruments in a grand symphony, but the song itself never ceases. Research suggests that the way we experience life—our highs and lows, our moments of harmony and discord—is much like the ebb and flow of a composition, with each phase contributing to the masterpiece of our existence.[12]

At times, you may fall out of tune. Other times, you may find yourself resonating perfectly with the universe, your spirit vibrating in sync with something greater than yourself. The revelation that *the music never ends* is not just poetic—it is a reflection of a higher truth, a glimpse into the greater glory of God.

And that, my beloved reader, is where I wish to direct your gaze: *Ad Majorem Dei Gloriam*—for the greater glory of God! Every note of your existence, every beat, every rhythm, exists to magnify His glory, not your own.[13] Studies show that individuals who find purpose beyond themselves, who align their actions with a higher calling, experience greater fulfillment and resilience.[14] Your symphony—your trials, your triumphs, your moments of silence and crescendo—is relative to you, but to the Almighty, it is everything it already *is.* You expressing your joys and enduring your hardships is itself an act of glorification, a testament to the divine order of creation.[15]

God is vibration. God is light. God is every force that makes music possible. Your role is not to play alone but to co-create, to compose alongside the Divine. You will never see the entire score—*Heaven*—you will never see all the parts layered upon one another, every movement from beginning to end. That's how vast, how intricate the composition is.

But *God does.*

God hears. God knows. God conducts. And above all, God wants you to strike the right chord, to find your key, to attune yourself to the Most High. Trust the Conductor, the Maestro, the One who holds the baton. My faith has carried me this far, and it is the sweetest sound my humble ears have ever known.

I love you, God.

And I love *you*, my dear reader, my friend.

Goodbye.

Now—can I get a ***THANK YOU, GOD?!***

Immediate Action Steps

1. Proactively Seek Growth: Identify one area of your life where you feel stagnant or reactive (e.g., emotional health, relationships, career). Take proactive steps today to learn something new in that area—whether it's reading a book, taking an online course, or seeking guidance from a mentor.

2. Develop a Growth Mindset: Reflect on a recent setback or failure and reframe it. Instead of seeing it as a roadblock, identify how it's an opportunity for growth. Commit to adopting a mindset that views challenges as stepping stones to greater achievements.

3. Elevate Your Community: Commit to one act of service this week. Whether it's offering support to a colleague, helping a friend, or giving back to a cause, aim to elevate not just yourself but the community around you through intentional acts of kindness and growth.

4. Take Responsibility for Your Life: Identify one habit or behavior you currently blame on external circumstances (e.g., lack of time, stress). Shift your perspective and take full responsibility for changing it. Start by taking small, manageable steps that put you in control.

5. Visualize Your Kingdom of Heaven: Take five minutes each day to visualize your ideal world—your "kingdom of heaven." Imagine how you'd act, how others would treat each other, and how your environment would look. Reflect on how you can start making that vision a reality today, even in small ways.

6. Face the New Challenges with Courage: The next time you're faced with a daunting new challenge, remind yourself of the value of growth. Instead of hesitating or fearing failure, embrace the process. Begin by taking the first step, no matter how small it seems.

7. Commit to Ongoing Transformation: Start today by committing to one area of your life where you can make continuous improvements (e.g., physical fitness, learning, relationships). Set a daily goal to improve just a little each day, building momentum over time.

8. Replace Motivation with Consistent Action: Set one goal that requires you to take daily, measurable action over the next 30 days. Track your progress, and when you succeed, raise your standards for the next 30 days.

9. Cultivate Resilience: When faced with adversity, pause and ask yourself: *How have I grown from past challenges?* Recognize how past failures or setbacks have shaped you into a stronger version of yourself, and let that fuel your resilience moving forward.

10. Seek the Divine Symphony: Take a moment each day to align your actions with a higher purpose. Whether through prayer, meditation, or reflection, connect with the belief that your life is part of a greater symphony, and your role is to contribute to it through your unique talents and actions.

AFTERWORD

Well, here we are—the end of *The Bitter End*. But really, this is just the beginning.

You've made it through, page by page, principle by principle, and now it's time for the most important part: putting it all into action.

Whether this was your first self-help book (which, by the way, is an absolute honor), or you've devoured hundreds like I have, what matters most is what happens next.

I don't want this to be one of those books you finish, set down, and forget about. No way. I want to hear from you. I want to know how this book helped, what clicked for you, what still needs clarification, and—most importantly—how you're now living the life you truly want.

So Here's Your Call To Action:

- Follow me on **TikTok (@mr..donnel.delva)**—I post motivational and instructional content all the time. My **YouTube (Mr. Donnel Delva)** is also linked there, so check it out!

- Spam my inbox if you want. Seriously. If you have

thoughts, questions, breakthroughs, or just want to tell me how your journey is going, please email me at __mrdonneldelva@gmail.com__. I read everything.

- Leave a review. If this book helped you, even just a little, please let me and the world know. Reviews help more people find this book and start their own transformation.

Further Reading

If you're ready to take your transformation even further, here are some books that deeply influenced me and that I referenced throughout *The Bitter End*. These are must-reads for continuing your journey:

For mastering mindset shifts and rewiring your habits:

- *Atomic Habits* by James Clear – Small, consistent habits lead to massive transformations. This book is like a roadmap for behavior change.

- *The Subtle Art of Not Giving a Fck** by Mark Manson – A blunt but insightful book about focusing on what truly matters and letting go of what doesn't.

For building self-discipline and resilience:

- *The 7 Habits of Highly Effective People* by Stephen R. Covey – The foundation of personal effectiveness. If you want to level up your discipline and decision-making, start here.

- *The War of Art* by Steven Pressfield – Perfect for anyone battling procrastination, fear, or self-doubt—this book will make you take action.

For understanding purpose and long-term fulfillment:
- *The Power of Now* by Eckhart Tolle – If aligning with your deepest purpose is a goal of yours, this book will help you stay present and intentional.

- *Essentialism: The Disciplined Pursuit of Less* by Greg McKeown – A book about cutting out the noise, focusing on what truly matters, and designing a life that aligns with your purpose.

For financial and lifestyle freedom:
- *The Millionaire Next Door* by Thomas J. Stanley & William D. Danko – If you want financial independence, this book will reframe how you think about money.

- *The Psychology of Money* by Morgan Housel – A brilliant look at how our behavior impacts wealth-building.

This isn't goodbye; it's just the next step. I cannot wait to hear how you're flourishing, how you've navigated your own *bitter end*, and how you've stepped into the life you've always wanted. If you ever see me out in the world, please tell me your story—nothing would make me happier.

Until then, go live the life you deserve.

Peace,
Donnel

ACKNOWLEDGEMENTS

First and foremost, I want to thank God. None of this would be possible without His divine guidance, boundless grace, and unrelenting love. Every word I write, every step I take, every breath I breathe is a testament to His mercy and favor. He has carried me through every trial, lifted me in every triumph, and blessed me beyond measure. This book, like my entire existence, is and forever will be dedicated to His greater glory—**Ad Majorem Dei Gloriam**—for the greater glory of God. My life is His, my purpose is His, and I pray that this work serves as a reflection of His goodness and love.

To my parents, **Lemane and Erla Delva**, the two most selfless and extraordinary people I have ever known. You have given me everything—your love, your wisdom, your sacrifices, your very lives. You have provided for me not just financially but spiritually, emotionally, and habitually, shaping me into the man I am today. Every opportunity I've had, every door that has opened, every bit of strength I've carried is because of you. You placed books in my hands, dreams in my heart, and faith in my soul. You have worked tirelessly, endlessly, and unconditionally to ensure my success and happiness. To be your son is my greatest blessing, and I will spend my life making you proud. From the depths of my soul, thank you.

To my younger brother, **Carl Delva**, my constant confidant, my best friend, and one of my greatest inspirations. Without you, I wouldn't be who I am. You don't just push me to be better—you *pull* me toward greatness in a way that makes success feel natural, like a force I'm meant to follow. There is no pressure, no force—just an undeniable pull toward abundance, hope, and possibility because of who we are together. From the moment you were born, I have been there, and I will always be here. Our bond is unshakable, and I am endlessly grateful for the light you bring into my life.

To my professors, teachers, and mentors—at **Fairfield Prep, College of the Holy Cross, and Fairfield University**—you have been architects of my mind. You have challenged me, expanded my understanding, and ignited a fire within me for English, writing, and self-improvement. Because of you, I am not just educated; I am evolved. Your dedication to your craft has inspired me beyond words, and I carry your lessons with me daily.

To my **colleagues and administrators**, who remind me that teaching is not just a job but a mission. Every day, we step into classrooms not just to educate but to empower. You inspire me to serve with integrity and passion, and together, we are shaping futures.

A special thank you to **Maurice Chiyumba**, my brother in all but blood. You are the glue, the spark, the *motion* in our lives. You bring energy, joy, and an unstoppable ambition that keeps me fired up. People don't always see the serious businessman behind your charisma, but I do. I have the privilege of witnessing your drive, your strategy, your hustle—and it fuels me. Your social media agency, **High Rize**, has been instrumental in bringing this book to the world, but beyond that, your faith in me has been invaluable. I refuse to let you leave me in the dust—we're *UP* together.

And finally, to **you**, the reader. Thank you for taking this step with me. I do not take your time, trust, or attention lightly. May this book serve as a guide, an inspiration, and a reminder that the life you desire is within reach. You have the power to transform, to preserve, and to thrive. May your journey be blessed, and may you always move forward for the greater glory of God.

With love, gratitude, and endless hope,
Donnel Delva

Notes

Believe In Your Unwavering Imagination

1. Taylor, Marjorie. *Imaginary Companions and the Children Who Create Them.* Oxford University Press, 1999.

2. Heisenberg, Werner. *Physics and Philosophy: The Revolution in Modern Science.* Harper & Brothers, 1958.

3. Lillard, Angeline. *The Science of Imagination: How Pretend Play Develops the Mind.* Oxford University Press, 2017.

4. Hoffman, Donald D. *The Case Against Reality: Why Evolution Hid the Truth from Our Eyes.* W. W. Norton & Company, 2019.

5. Noë, Alva. *Action in Perception.* MIT Press, 2004.

6. Jung, Carl. *The Archetypes and the Collective Unconscious.* Princeton University Press, 1959.

7. Damasio, Antonio. *The Strange Order of Things: Life, Feeling, and the Making of Cultures.* Pantheon Books, 2018.

8. Dispenza, Joe. *Breaking the Habit of Being Yourself.* Hay House, 2012.

9. Jung, Carl. *The Undiscovered Self.* Princeton University Press, 1958.

10. James, William. *The Will to Believe.* Longmans, Green & Co., 1897.

11. Lipton, Bruce. *The Biology of Belief.* Hay House, 2005.

12. Goddard, Neville. *The Power of Awareness.* DeVorss & Company, 1952.

13. Byrne, Rhonda. *The Secret.* Atria Books, 2006.

14. Neville, G. *Feeling is the Secret.* DeVorss & Company, 1941.

15. James, William. *The Varieties of Religious Experience: A Study in Human Nature.* Longmans, Green & Co., 1902.

16. Frankl, Viktor E. *Man's Search for Meaning.* Beacon Press, 1946.

17. Wang, Z., Busemeyer, J. R., Atmanspacher, H., & Pothos, E. M. "The Potential of Quantum Probability Theory in Cognitive Modeling." *Topics in Cognitive Science*, vol. 5, no. 4, 2013, pp. 672–688.

18. Pascual-Leone, A., Amedi, A., Fregni, F., & Merabet, L. B. "The Plastic Human Brain Cortex." *Annual Review of Neuroscience*, vol. 28, 2005, pp. 377–401.

19. Jung, C. G. *The Archetypes and the Collective Unconscious.* Princeton University Press, 1969.

20. Dweck, Carol S. *Mindset: The New Psychology of Success.* Random House, 2006.

You Must Be Disciplined

1. Dalio, Ray. *Principles: Life and Work.* Simon & Schuster, 2017.

2. Covey, Stephen R. *The 7 Habits of Highly Effective People: Powerful Lessons in Personal Change.* Free Press, 1989.

3. Duckworth, Angela. *Grit: The Power of Passion and Perseverance.* Scribner, 2016.

4. Dweck, Carol S. *Mindset: The New Psychology of Success.* Random House, 2006.

5. Peterson, Jordan B. *12 Rules for Life: An Antidote to Chaos.* Random House Canada, 2018.

6. Sinek, Simon. *Start with Why: How Great Leaders Inspire Everyone to Take Action.* Portfolio, 2009.

7. Clear, James. *Atomic Habits: An Easy & Proven Way to Build Good Habits & Break Bad Ones.* Avery, 2018.

8. Marks, Howard. *The Most Important Thing: Uncommon Sense for the Thoughtful Investor.* Columbia University Press, 2011.

9. Einstein, Albert. *Quoted in Various Sources, including* Einstein: His Life and Universe *by Walter Isaacson.* Simon & Schuster, 2007.

10. Forleo, Marie. *Everything is Figureoutable.* Portfolio, 2020.

11. Mischel, Walter. *The Marshmallow Test: Understanding Self-Control and How to Master It.* Little, Brown and Company, 2014.

12. Buffett, Warren. *Berkshire Hathaway Annual Shareholder Letter.* Berkshire Hathaway Inc., 2004.

13. Newport, Cal. *Digital Minimalism: Choosing a Focused Life in a Noisy World*. Portfolio, 2019.

14. Dweck, Carol S. *Mindset: The New Psychology of Success*. Random House, 2006.

15. Gladwell, Malcolm. *Outliers: The Story of Success*. Little, Brown and Company, 2008.

16. Kahneman, Daniel. *Thinking, Fast and Slow*. Farrar, Straus and Giroux, 2011.

17. Thoreau, Henry David. *Walden; or, Life in the Woods*. Ticknor and Fields, 1854.

18. Ericsson, K. Anders, and Robert Pool. *Peak: Secrets from the New Science of Expertise*. Houghton Mifflin Harcourt, 2016.

19. Gardner, Howard. *Frames of Mind: The Theory of Multiple Intelligences*. Basic Books, 2011.

20. Csikszentmihalyi, Mihaly. *Flow: The Psychology of Optimal Experience*. Harper & Row, 1990.

21. Newport, Cal. *Deep Work: Rules for Focused Success in a Distracted World*. Grand Central Publishing, 2016.

22. James, William. *Pragmatism: A New Name for Some Old Ways of Thinking*. Harvard University Press, 1907.

23. Dweck, Carol S. *Mindset: The New Psychology of Success*. Ballantine Books, 2006.

24. Duckworth, Angela. *Grit: The Power of Passion and Perseverance*. Scribner, 2016.

25. Frankl, Viktor E. *Man's Search for Meaning*. Beacon Press, 1946.

26. Goleman, Daniel. *Emotional Intelligence: Why It Can Matter More Than IQ*. Bantam Books, 1995.

27. Peterson, Jordan B. *12 Rules for Life: An Antidote to Chaos*. Random House Canada, 2018.

28. Seligman, Martin E. P. *Learned Optimism: How to Change Your Mind and Your Life*. Vintage, 1991.

29. Covey, Stephen R. *The 7 Habits of Highly Effective People: Powerful Lessons in Personal Change*. Free Press, 1989.

30. Evslin, Bernard. *Orpheus and Other Greek Myths*. Scholastic Inc., 2001.

1. Dalio, Ray. *Principles: Life and Work.* Simon & Schuster, 2017.

2. Pianka, Eric R. *Evolutionary Ecology.* Harper & Row, 1983.

3. Lipton, Bruce. *The Biology of Belief: Unleashing the Power of Consciousness, Matter & Miracles.* Hay House, 2005.

4. Mengzi. *The Essential Mengzi: Selected Passages with Traditional Commentary.* Hackett Publishing, 2009.

5. Mengzi (Mencius). *The Works of Mencius.* 4th century BCE.

6. Dispenza, Joe. *Becoming Supernatural.* Hay House, 2017.

7. Dweck, Carol S. *Mindset: The New Psychology of Success.* Random House, 2006.

8. Kahneman, Daniel. *Thinking, Fast and Slow.* Farrar, Straus and Giroux, 2011.

9. Bandura, Albert. *Self-Efficacy: The Exercise of Control.* W. H. Freeman, 1997.

10. *The Kybalion – A Study of The Hermetic Philosophy of Ancient Egypt and Greece.* The Three Initiates, 1908.

11. Lipton, Bruce. *The Biology of Belief.* Hay House, 2005.

12. *The Kybalion – A Study of The Hermetic Philosophy of Ancient Egypt and Greece.* The Three Initiates, 1908.

13. Jung, Carl. *The Archetypes and the Collective Unconscious.* Princeton University Press, 1959.

14. Heisenberg, Werner. *Physics and Philosophy: The Revolution in Modern Science.* Harper & Row, 1958.

15. Goddard, Neville. *The Power of Awareness.* 1952.

16. Dispenza, Joe. *Breaking the Habit of Being Yourself.* Hay House, 2012.

17. Trismegistus, Hermes. *Corpus Hermeticum.* 2nd–3rd century CE.

18. *The Kybalion – A Study of The Hermetic Philosophy of Ancient Egypt and Greece.* The Three Initiates, 1908.

19. Barsalou, L. W. "Grounded Cognition." *Annual Review of Psychology*, vol. 59, 2008, pp. 617–645.

20. Damasio, Antonio. *Descartes' Error: Emotion, Reason, and the Human Brain.* Penguin Books, 1994.

21. Doidge, Norman. *The Brain That Changes Itself.* Viking Press, 2007.

22. Benedetti, Fabrizio. *Placebo Effects: Understanding the Mechanisms in Health and Disease.* Oxford University Press, 2009.

23. Beck, Aaron T. *Cognitive Therapy and the Emotional Disorders.* International Universities Press, 1979.

24. *The Kybalion – A Study of The Hermetic Philosophy of Ancient Egypt and Greece.* The Three Initiates, 1908.

25. Bohm, David. *Wholeness and the Implicate Order.* Routledge, 1980.

26. Dweck, Carol S. *Mindset: The New Psychology of Success.* Random House, 2006.

27. Braden, Gregg. *The Divine Matrix.* Hay House, 2007.

28. Lipton, Bruce. *The Biology of Belief.* Hay House, 2005.

29. Dispenza, Joe. *Becoming Supernatural.* Hay House, 2017.

30. Davidson, Richard J., and Sharon Begley. *The Emotional Life of Your Brain.* Hudson Street Press, 2012.

31. Goddard, Neville. *Feeling is the Secret.* 1944.

32. *The Kybalion – A Study of The Hermetic Philosophy of Ancient Egypt and Greece.* The Three Initiates, 1908.

33. Goddard, Neville. *The Power of Awareness.* 1952.

34. Heisenberg, Werner. *Physics and Philosophy: The Revolution in Modern Science.* Harper & Row, 1958.

35. Beck, Aaron T. *Cognitive Therapy and the Emotional Disorders.* International Universities Press, 1979.

36. *The Kybalion – A Study of The Hermetic Philosophy of Ancient Egypt and Greece.* The Three Initiates, 1908.

37. Camus, Albert. *The Myth of Sisyphus.* Gallimard, 1942.

38. David, Susan. *Emotional Agility.* Avery, 2016.

39. Lyubomirsky, Sonja. *The How of Happiness.* Penguin, 2007.

40. *The Kybalion – A Study of The Hermetic Philosophy of Ancient Egypt and Greece.* The Three Initiates, 1908.

41. Hawking, Stephen. *The Grand Design.* Bantam Books, 2010.

42. Mischel, Walter. *The Marshmallow Test: Mastering Self-Control.* Little, Brown and Company, 2014.

43. Kahneman, Daniel. *Thinking, Fast and Slow.* Farrar, Straus and Giroux, 2011.

44. Hume, David. *A Treatise of Human Nature.* Oxford University Press, 1739.

45. Kant, Immanuel. *Critique of Pure Reason.* Cambridge University Press, 1781.

46. *The Kybalion – A Study of The Hermetic Philosophy of Ancient Egypt and Greece.* The Three Initiates, 1908.

47. Butler, Judith. *Gender Trouble.* Routledge, 1990.

48. Moore, Robert, and Douglas Gillette. *King, Warrior, Magician, Lover.* HarperOne, 1990.

49. Jung, Carl. *Aion: Researches into the Phenomenology of the Self.* Princeton University Press, 1951.

50. Laozi. *Tao Te Ching.* 4th century BCE.

51. Lipton, Bruce. *The Biology of Belief.* Hay House, 2005.

52. Kahneman, Daniel. *Thinking, Fast and Slow.* Farrar, Straus and Giroux, 2011.

53. Damasio, Antonio. *Descartes' Error: Emotion, Reason, and the Human Brain.* Putnam Publishing, 1994.

54. Ekman, Paul. *Emotions Revealed: Recognizing Faces and Feelings to Improve Communication and Emotional Life.* Holt Paperbacks, 2003.

55. Haidt, Jonathan. *The Righteous Mind: Why Good People Are Divided by Politics and Religion.* Pantheon, 2012.

56. Goddard, Neville. *Feeling Is the Secret*. Martino Publishing, 2015.

Expand Your Realm Of Consciousness

1. Goddard, Neville. *The Power of Awareness*. 1952.

2. Dispenza, Joe. *Breaking the Habit of Being Yourself*. Hay House, 2012.

3. Frankl, Viktor. *Man's Search for Meaning*. Beacon Press, 1946.

4. Jung, Carl. *Modern Man in Search of a Soul*. Harcourt, 1933.

5. Allen, James. *As a Man Thinketh*. 1903.

6. Lipton, Bruce. *The Biology of Belief*. Hay House, 2005.

7. Byrne, Rhonda. *The Secret*. Atria Books, 2006.

8. Goddard, Neville. *Infinite Potential*. DeVorss & Company, 1947.

9. Campbell, Joseph. *The Hero with a Thousand Faces*. Princeton University Press, 1949.

10. Jung, Carl. *Man and His Symbols*. Doubleday, 1964.

11. Lipton, Bruce. *The Biology of Belief*. Hay House, 2005.

12. Mengzi. *The Essential Mengzi: Selected Passages – The Parable of the Ox and the Sheep*. Hackett Publishing, 2009.

13. Dispenza, Joe. *Breaking the Habit of Being Yourself*. Hay House, 2012.

14. James, William. *The Varieties of Religious Experience*. Longmans, Green & Co., 1902.

15. Daalman, K., Boks, M. P., Diederen, K. M., de Weijer, A. D., Blom, J. D., Kahn, R. S., & Sommer, I. E. (2011). "The same or different? Auditory verbal hallucinations in healthy and psychotic individuals." *Journal of Clinical Psychiatry*, 72(3), 320-325.

16. Heider, F., & Simmel, M. (1944). "An experimental study of apparent behavior." *American Journal of Psychology*, 57(2), 243-259.

17. Dalio, Ray. *Principles: Life and Work*. Simon & Schuster, 2017.

18. Gross, J. J. (2002). "Emotion regulation: Affective, cognitive, and social consequences." *Psychophysiology*, 39(3), 281-291.

19. Seligman, Martin E. *Learned Optimism: How to Change Your Mind and Your Life.* Knopf Doubleday Publishing Group, 1991.

20. Langer, Ellen. *Mindfulness.* Addison-Wesley, 1989.

21. Sapolsky, Robert. *Why Zebras Don't Get Ulcers.* Holt Paperbacks, 1994.

22. Kahneman, Daniel. *Thinking, Fast and Slow.* Farrar, Straus and Giroux, 2011.

23. Csikszentmihalyi, Mihaly. *Flow: The Psychology of Optimal Experience.* Harper & Row, 1990.

Words Are Charmed

1. Dispenza, Joe. *Breaking the Habit of Being Yourself.* Hay House, 2012.

2. Emoto, Masaru. *The Hidden Messages in Water.* Atria Books, 2004.

3. Tesla, Nikola. *The Secrets of the Universe.*

4. Braden, Gregg. *The Divine Matrix.* Hay House, 2007.

5. Goswami, Amit. *The Self-Aware Universe.* TarcherPerigee, 1993.

6. Doidge, Norman. *The Brain That Changes Itself.* Viking Press, 2007.

7. Sheldrake, Rupert. *The Presence of the Past.* Harper & Row, 1988.

8. Boroditsky, Lera. *How Language Shapes the Way We Think.* TED, 2017.

9. Steele, Claude. *Self-Affirmation: How the Power of the Mind Shapes Reality.*

10. Newberg, Andrew, & Waldman, Mark Robert. *Words Can Change Your Brain.* Avery, 2012.

11. Lipton, Bruce. *The Biology of Belief.* Hay House, 2005.

12. Gollwitzer, P. M. (1999). "Implementation intentions: Strong effects of simple plans." *American Psychologist,* 54(7), 493-503.

13. Gollwitzer, P. M., & Sheeran, P. (2006). "Implementation Intentions and Goal Achievement: A Meta-Analysis of Effects and Processes." *Advances in Experimental Social Psychology,* 38, 69-119.

14. Hegel, G. W. F. *The Phenomenology of Spirit.* 1807. (Trans. A. V. Miller, Oxford University Press, 1977).

15. Oyserman, D., & James, L. (2011). "Possible Selves: From Content to Process." In M. Alicke & C. Sedikides (Eds.), *The Handbook of Self-Enhancement and Self-Protection* (pp. 373-394). Guilford Press.

16. Goddard, Neville. *Feeling Is the Secret.* DeVorss & Company, 1944.

17. Coué, Émile. *Self Mastery Through Conscious Autosuggestion.* American Library Service, 1922.

18. Newberg, Andrew, & Waldman, Mark Robert. *Words Can Change Your Brain.* Avery, 2012.

19. Beck, Aaron T. *Cognitive Therapy and the Emotional Disorders.* International Universities Press, 1979.

20. Seligman, Martin E. *Flourish.* Atria Books, 2011.

21. Pennebaker, James. *The Secret Life of Pronouns: What Our Words Say About Us.* Bloomsbury Press, 2011.

22. Emoto, Masaru. *The Hidden Messages in Water.* Atria Books, 2004.

23. Newberg, Andrew, & Waldman, Mark Robert. *Words Can Change Your Brain.* Avery, 2012.

24. Helmstetter, Shad. *What to Say When You Talk to Yourself.* Gallery Books, 1986.

25. Burns, David D. *Feeling Good: The New Mood Therapy.* William Morrow, 1980.

26. Bem, D. J. (1972). "Self-Perception Theory." *Advances in Experimental Social Psychology*, 6, 1-62.

27. Critcher, C. R., & Dunning, D. (2015). "Self-Affirmations Provide a Broader Perspective on Self-Threat." *Personality and Social Psychology Bulletin*, 41(1), 3-18.

28. Byrne, Rhonda. *The Secret.* Atria Books, 2006.

29. Rozin, P., & Royzman, E. B. (2001). "Negativity Bias, Negativity Dominance, and Contagion." *Personality and Social Psychology Review*, 5(4), 296-320.

30. Lupyan, G., & Bergen, B. (2016). "How Language Shapes Thought: The Role of Linguistic Structure in Shaping Neural Representations." *Topics in Cognitive Science*, 8(2), 408-424.

Solitude Builds Strength That Becomes Power

1. Leary, M. R., & Kowalski, R. M. (1990). "Impression management: A literature review and two-component model." *Psychological Bulletin*, 107(1), 34–47.

2. Cacioppo, J. T., & Patrick, W. (2008). *Loneliness: Human Nature and the Need for Social Connection*. W. W. Norton & Company.

3. Deci, E. L., & Ryan, R. M. (2000). "The 'what' and 'why' of goal pursuits: Human needs and the self-determination of behavior." *Psychological Inquiry*, 11(4), 227–268.

4. Thoreau, H. D. (1854). *Walden; or, Life in the Woods*. Ticknor and Fields.

5. Goleman, D. (1995). *Emotional Intelligence: Why It Can Matter More Than IQ*. Bantam Books.

6. Rogers, Carl. *On Becoming a Person*. Houghton Mifflin, 1961.

7. Baumeister, R. F., & Leary, M. R. (1995). "The need to belong: Desire for interpersonal attachments as a fundamental human motivation." *Psychological Bulletin*, 117(3), 497–529.

8. Goleman, D., Boyatzis, R., & McKee, A. (2013). *Primal Leadership: Unleashing the Power of Emotional Intelligence*. Harvard Business Review Press.

9. Csikszentmihalyi, Mihaly. *Flow: The Psychology of Optimal Experience*. Harper Perennial, 1990.

10. Nakamura, J., & Csikszentmihalyi, M. (2009). "The concept of flow" in *Oxford Handbook of Positive Psychology*.

11. Ryan, R. M., & Deci, E. L. (2000). "Self-determination theory and the facilitation of intrinsic motivation, social development, and well-being." *American Psychologist*, 55(1), 68–78.

12. Maslow, A. H. (1943). "A theory of human motivation." *Psychological Review*, 50(4), 370-396.

13. Bass, B. M. (1990). "From transactional to transformational leadership: Learning to share the vision." *Organizational Dynamics*, 18(3), 19–31.

14. Cacioppo, John T., and William Patrick. *Loneliness: Human Nature and the Need for Social Connection*. W. W. Norton & Company, 2008.

15. Bandura, Albert. *Self-Efficacy: The Exercise of Control*. W. H. Freeman, 1997.

16. Festinger, Leon. *A Theory of Cognitive Dissonance*. Stanford University Press, 1957.

17. Christakis, Nicholas A., and James H. Fowler. *Connected: The Surprising Power of Our Social Networks and How They Shape Our Lives*. Little, Brown and Company, 2009.

18. Pascal, Blaise. *Pensées*. 1670.

19. Frankl, Viktor E. *Man's Search for Meaning*. Beacon Press, 1946.

20. Thoreau, Henry David. *Walden*. 1854.

21. Jung, Carl. *Modern Man in Search of a Soul*. Harcourt, Brace & World, 1933.

22. Kahneman, Daniel. *Thinking, Fast and Slow*. Farrar, Straus, and Giroux, 2011.

23. Holiday, Ryan. *The Daily Stoic*. Penguin Publishing Group, 2016.

24. Goddard, Neville. *The Power of Awareness*. DeVorss & Company, 1952.

25. Dispenza, Dr. Joe. *Breaking the Habit of Being Yourself*. Hay House, 2012.

26. Jung, Carl. *The Undiscovered Self*. Princeton University Press, 1957.

27. James, William. *The Will to Believe*. Longmans, Green & Co., 1897.

28. Lipton, Dr. Bruce. *The Biology of Belief*. Hay House, 2005.

29. Smart, Ralph. *Infinite Waters: Diving Deep*. YouTube Channel, various videos on mindfulness and self-improvement.

30. Sweller, John. "Cognitive Load Theory in Educational Psychology." *Educational Psychology Review*, 1988.

31. Duhigg, Charles. *The Power of Habit: Why We Do What We Do in Life and Business*. Random House, 2012.

32. Valliant, George E. *Adaptation to Life*. Harvard University Press, 1977.

33. Clance, Pauline R., and Suzanne A. Imes. "The Impostor Phenomenon in High Achieving Women: Dynamics and Therapeutic Intervention." *Psychotherapy: Theory, Research & Practice*, 1978.

34. Maslow, Abraham H. *Motivation and Personality*. Harper & Row, 1954.

35. Aristotle. *Nicomachean Ethics*. Translated by W. D. Ross, 350 BCE.

36. James, William. *The Principles of Psychology*. Henry Holt and Company, 1890.

37. Zimbardo, Philip. *The Lucifer Effect*. Random House, 2007.

38. Dhammapada, verses 183-185.

39. Ignatius of Loyola. *Autobiography*. 1553.

40. Ellison, Ralph. *Invisible Man*. Random House, 1952.

41. Plato. *Republic*, Book VII.

42. Dispenza, Dr. Joe. *Breaking the Habit of Being Yourself*. Hay House, 2012.

43. Goddard, Neville. *The Power of Awareness*. DeVorss & Company, 1952.

Think For Yourself

1. Davis, Angela. *Women, Race, & Class*. Vintage Books, 1981.

2. McKenna, Terence. *Food of the Gods*. Bantam Books, 1992.

3. Loewen, James W. *Lies My Teacher Told Me*. The New Press, 1995.

4. Alexander, Michelle. *The New Jim Crow*. The New Press, 2010.

5. Asch, Solomon E. "Opinions and Social Pressure." *Scientific American*, 1955.

6. Turner, John C., & Oakes, Penelope J. "The significance of the social identity concept for social psychology with reference to individualism, interactionism, and social influence." *British Journal of Social Psychology*, 1986.

7. Staub, Ervin. *The Roots of Evil: The Origins of Genocide and Other Group Violence*. Cambridge University Press, 1989.

8. Dawkins, Richard. *The Selfish Gene*. Oxford University Press, 1976.

9. Merriam-Webster. "Memetics Definition & Meaning." Merriam-Webster, 2023.

10. Christakis, D. A., & Moreno, M. A. (2009). "Trapped in the Net: Will Social Media Change Our Brains?" *Pediatrics*, 124(4), 1232-1234.

11. Montag, C., Lachmann, B., Herrlich, M., & Zweig, K. (2019). "Addictive Potential of Social Media: The Dopamine Reward Pathway." *Trends in Cognitive Sciences*, 23(8), 610-612.

12. Haferkamp, N., & Krämer, N. C. (2011). "Social Comparison 2.0: Examining the Effects of Online Profiles on Social-Networking Sites." *Cyberpsychology, Behavior, and Social Networking*, 14(5), 309-314.

13. Carr, N. (2010). *The Shallows: What the Internet Is Doing to Our Brains*. W.W. Norton & Company.

14. Twenge, J. M., Joiner, T. E., Rogers, M. L., & Martin, G. N. (2018). "Increases in Depressive Symptoms, Suicide-Related Outcomes, and Suicide Rates Among U.S. Adolescents After 2010 and Links to Increased Social Media Use." *Clinical Psychological Science*, 6(1), 3-17.

15. Chou, H. T. G., & Edge, N. (2012). "'They Are Happier and Having Better Lives Than I Am': The Impact of Using Facebook on Perceptions of Others' Lives." *Cyberpsychology, Behavior, and Social Networking*, 15(2), 117-121.

16. Alter, A. (2017). *Irresistible: The Rise of Addictive Technology and the Business of Keeping Us Hooked*. Penguin Press.

17. Kahneman, Daniel. *Thinking, Fast and Slow*. Farrar, Straus, and Giroux, 2011.

18. Oliver, Dr. Mary Beth & Raney, Dr. Arthur. *Media Effects: Advances in Theory and Research*. Routledge, 2011.

19. Twenge, Dr. Jean. *iGen: Why Today's Super-Connected Kids Are Growing Up Less Rebellious, More Tolerant, Less Happy*. Atria Books, 2017.

20. Davidson, Dr. Richard. *The Emotional Life of Your Brain*. Hudson Street Press, 2012.

21. Siegel, Daniel J. *Mindsight: The New Science of Personal Transformation*. Bantam Books, 2010.

22. Schwartz, Jeffrey M., & Begley, Sharon. *The Mind and the Brain: Neuroplasticity and the Power of Mental Force*. HarperCollins, 2002.

23. Dispenza, Dr. Joe. *Becoming Supernatural*. Hay House, 2017.

24. Davidson, Richard J., & Goleman, Daniel. *Altered Traits: Science Reveals How Meditation Changes Your Mind, Brain, and Body*. Avery, 2017.

25. Maslow, Abraham. *Toward a Psychology of Being*. Van Nostrand, 1962.

26. Fredrickson, B. L. (2001). "The role of positive emotions in positive psychology: The broaden-and-build theory of positive emotions." *American Psychologist*, 56(3), 218-226.

27. Nickerson, R. S. (1998). "Confirmation bias: A ubiquitous phenomenon in many guises." *Review of General Psychology*, 2(2), 175-220.

28. Doidge, Norman. *The Brain That Changes Itself: Stories of Personal Triumph from the Frontiers of Brain Science*. Viking Press, 2007.

29. Bandura, Albert. *Self-efficacy: The exercise of control*. W. H. Freeman, 1997.

30. Maslow, A. H. (1943). "A theory of human motivation." *Psychological Review*, 50(4), 370-396.

31. Durkheim, Emile. *The Elementary Forms of Religious Life*. Free Press, 1912.

32. Foucault, Michel. *Discipline and Punish*. Pantheon Books, 1977.

33. Jung, Carl. *Modern Man in Search of a Soul*. Harcourt, Brace & World, 1933.

34. Asch, Solomon E. "Opinions and Social Pressure." *Scientific American*, 1955.

35. Dweck, Dr. Carol. *Mindset: The New Psychology of Success*. Random House, 2006.

36. Seligman, Martin E. P. *Learned Helplessness: A Theory for the Age of Personal Control*. W. H. Freeman, 1975.

37. Kahneman, Daniel. *Thinking, Fast and Slow*. Farrar, Straus, and Giroux, 2011.

38. McRaney, David. *You Are Not So Smart*. Perigee, 2011.

39. Dweck, Carol S. *Mindset: The New Psychology of Success*. Random House, 2006.

40. Csikszentmihalyi, Mihaly. *Flow: The Psychology of Optimal Experience*. HarperPerennial, 1990.

41. Beck, Aaron T. *Cognitive Therapy and the Emotional Disorders*. International Universities Press, 1976.

42. Deci, Edward L. & Ryan, Richard M. *Self-Determination Theory: Basic Psychological Needs in Motivation, Development, and Wellness*. The Guilford Press, 2017.

43. Jung, Carl. *The Archetypes and the Collective Unconscious*. Princeton University Press, 1959.

44. McKee, Robert. *Story: Substance, Structure, Style, and the Principles of Screenwriting*. HarperCollins, 1997.

45. Jung, Carl. *Aion: Researches into the Phenomenology of the Self*. Princeton University Press, 1951.

46. James, William. *Pragmatism*. Longmans, Green, and Co., 1907.

47. Watts, Alan. *The Wisdom of Insecurity*. Pantheon Books, 1951.

48. Campbell, Joseph. *The Hero with a Thousand Faces*. Princeton University Press, 1949.

49. Goddard, Neville. *Awakened Imagination*. DeVorss & Company, 1954.

50. Deci, Edward L., & Ryan, Richard M. (2000). "The 'what' and 'why' of goal pursuits: Human needs and the self-determination of behavior." *Psychological Inquiry*, 11(4), 227-268.

51. Diamond, Adele. (2013). "Executive functions." *Annual Review of Psychology*, 64, 135-168.

52. Roychoudhuri, Onnesha. "Michael Pollan Debunks Food Myths." Interview with Michael Pollan, 2017.

53. Tversky, Amos, and Daniel Kahneman. *Judgment Under Uncertainty: Heuristics and Biases*. Cambridge University Press, 1974.

54. Nickerson, Raymond S. "Confirmation Bias: A Ubiquitous Phenomenon in Many Guises." *Review of General Psychology*, 2(2), 175-220, 1998.

55. Doidge, Norman. *The Brain That Changes Itself: Stories of Personal Triumph from the Frontiers of Brain Science*. Penguin, 2007.

56. Bohm, David. *Wholeness and the Implicate Order*. Routledge, 1980.

57. Beck, Aaron T. *Cognitive Therapy and the Emotional Disorders*. International Universities Press, 1976.

58. Bandura, Albert. *Self-Efficacy: The Exercise of Control*. W. H. Freeman, 1997.

59. Kolb, David A. *Experiential Learning: Experience as the Source of Learning and Development*. Prentice Hall, 1984.

60. Barsalou, Lawrence W. "Grounded Cognition." *Annual Review of Psychology*, 59, 2008, 617-645.

61. Dweck, Carol S. (2006). *Mindset: The New Psychology of Success*. Random House.

62. Beck, Aaron T. *Cognitive Therapy and the Emotional Disorders*. International Universities Press, 1976.

63. Seligman, Martin E. P. (1991). *Learned Optimism: How to Change Your Mind and Your Life*. Vintage.

64. Bandura, Albert. *Self-Efficacy: The Exercise of Control*. W. H. Freeman and Company, 1997.

65. Graziosi, D., & Shelton, T. (2021). "The Power of Perception: Seeing Things Through Your Own Lens." *YouTube*.

66. Various. "Graziosi, D., & Shelton, T. (2021). *The Power of Perception: Seeing Things Through Your Own Lens.*" *YouTube*.

Overcome Negative Emotions

1. Dweck, C. S. (2006). *Mindset: The new psychology of success*. Random House.

2. Seligman, M. E. P. (1991). *Learned optimism: How to change your mind and your life*. Vintage.

3. Bandura, A. (1997). *Self-efficacy: The exercise of control*. W. H. Freeman and Company.

4. Peterson, C., & Seligman, M. E. P. (2004). *Character strengths and virtues: A handbook and classification*. Oxford University Press.

5. Fagerström, K.-O. (2012). The epidemiology of smoking: Health consequences and the role of nicotine. *American Journal of Public Health*, 102(3), 443–453.

6. Tversky, A., & Kahneman, D. (1974). Judgment under uncertainty: Heuristics and biases. *Science*, 185(4157), 1124–1131.

7. Lally, P., van Jaarsveld, C. H. M., Potts, H. W. W., & Wardle, J. (2010). How are habits formed: Modelling habit formation in the real world. *European Journal of Social Psychology*, 40(6), 998–1009.

8. Neff, K. D. (2011). *Self-compassion: The proven power of being kind to yourself*. William Morrow.

9. LeDoux, J. E. (1996). *The emotional brain: The mysterious underpinnings of emotional life.* Simon & Schuster.

10. Mikulincer, M., & Shaver, P. R. (2007). *Attachment in adulthood: Structure, dynamics, and change.* The Guilford Press.

11. Doidge, N. (2007). *The brain that changes itself: Stories of personal triumph from the frontiers of brain science.* Viking Penguin.

12. Kolb, B., & Whishaw, I. Q. (1998). *An introduction to brain and behavior.* Worth Publishers.

13. Goleman, D. (1995). *Emotional intelligence: Why it can matter more than IQ.* Bantam Books.

14. Siegel, D. J. (2010). *The mindful therapist: A clinician's guide to mindsight and neural integration.* Norton & Company.

15. Dalio, R. (2017). *Principles: Life and work.* Simon & Schuster.

16. Brown, B. (2012). *Daring greatly: How the courage to be vulnerable transforms the way we live, love, parent, and lead.* Gotham Books.

17. Gross, J. J., & Levenson, R. W. (1997). Hiding feelings: The acute effects of inhibiting negative and positive emotion. *Journal of Abnormal Psychology*, 106(1), 95-103.

18. Pennebaker, J. W. (1997). Writing about emotional experiences as a therapeutic process. *Psychological Science*, 8(3), 162-166.

19. Kernis, M. H. (2003). Toward a conceptualization of optimal self-esteem. *Psychological Inquiry*, 14(1), 1-26.

20. Tugade, M. M., & Fredrickson, B. L. (2004). Resilient individuals use positive emotions to bounce back from negative emotional experiences. *Journal of Personality and Social Psychology*, 86(2), 320-333.

21. Reis, H. T., & Shaver, P. (1988). Intimacy as an interpersonal process. In S. Duck (Ed.), *Handbook of personal relationships* (pp. 367-389). John Wiley & Sons.

22. Lipton, B. (n.d.). *The biology of belief.*

23. Ekman, P. (2003). *Emotions revealed: Recognizing faces and feelings to improve communication and emotional life.* Henry Holt and Company.

24. LeDoux, J. E. (1996). *The emotional brain: The mysterious underpinnings of emotional life.* Simon & Schuster.

25. Doidge, N. (2007). *The brain that changes itself: Stories of personal triumph from the frontiers of brain science.* Viking Penguin.

26. van der Kolk, B. (2014). *The body keeps the score: Brain, mind, and body in the healing of trauma.* Viking.

27. Investopedia. (n.d.). Understanding higher lows in trading. Retrieved from https://www.investopedia.com/

28. Duckworth, A. (2016). *Grit: The power of passion and perseverance.* Scribner.

29. Dispenza, J. (2017). *Becoming supernatural: How common people are doing the uncommon.* Hay House.

The Universe Is An Aiding Force

1. Seligman, M. (1975). *Learned helplessness: A theory for the age of personal control.* W. H. Freeman.

2. Plato. (1992). *The Republic* (B. Jowett, Trans.). Dover Publications. (Original work published ca. 380 BCE)

3. Heisenberg, W. (2000). *Physics and philosophy: The revolution in modern science.* Harper Perennial.

4. Lipton, B. (2005). *The biology of belief.* Mountain of Love/Elite Books.

5. National Park Service. (n.d.). *Fire ecology.* Retrieved from https://www.nps.gov/subjects/fire/fire-ecology.htm

6. Darwin, C. (1998). *On the origin of species* (6th ed.). Penguin Classics. (Original work published 1859)

7. Dispenza, J. (2014). *You are the placebo: Making your mind matter.* Hay House.

8. Tedeschi, R. G., & Calhoun, L. G. (2004). Posttraumatic growth: Positive changes in the aftermath of crisis. *Psychological Inquiry*, 15(1), 1-18.

9. Goddard, N. (2006). *The power of awareness.* Martino Fine Books.

10. Dispenza, J. (2012). *Breaking the habit of being yourself: How to lose your mind and create a new one.* Hay House.

11. Lipton, B. (2005). *The biology of belief*. Mountain of Love/Elite Books.

12. Seligman, M. (2011). *Flourish: A visionary new understanding of happiness and well-being*. Atria Books.

13. Prigogine, I. (1984). *Order out of chaos: Man's new dialogue with nature*. Bantam Books.

14. Wattles, W. D. (1910). *The science of getting rich*. The Science of Getting Rich.

15. Wilson, E. O. (1992). *The diversity of life*. Belknap Press.

16.

17. Dispenza, J. (2017). *Becoming supernatural: How common people are doing the uncommon*. Hay House.

18. Jung, C. G. (1960). *Synchronicity: An acausal connecting principle*. Princeton University Press.

19. Einstein, A. (1922). *The meaning of relativity*. H. Holt and Company.

20. Einstein, A. (1954). *Ideas and opinions*. Crown Publishers.

21. Dispenza, J. (2017). *Becoming supernatural: How common people are doing the uncommon*. Hay House.

22. Byrne, R. (2006). *The secret*. Atria Books.

23. Goddard, N. (2006). *Feeling is the secret*. Martino Fine Books.

24. Doidge, N. (2007). *The brain that changes itself: Stories of personal triumph from the frontiers of brain science*. Viking Penguin.

25. Jung, C. G. (1964). *Man and his symbols*. Doubleday.

26. Lipton, B. (2005). *The biology of belief*. Mountain of Love/Elite Books.

27. Covey, S. R. (1989). *The 7 habits of highly effective people*. Free Press.

28. Attenborough, D. (1995). *The secret life of plants*. BBC Worldwide.

29. Levitin, D. J. (2006). *This is your brain on music: The science of a human obsession*. Dutton.

30. Galpin, A. (2020). *Unplugged: Evolve from technology to upgrade your fitness, performance & consciousness*. Lioncrest Publishing.

31. Lipton, B. (2005). *The biology of belief.* Mountain of Love/Elite Books.

32. Chopra, D. (2003). *The spontaneous fulfillment of desire: Harnessing the infinite power of the universe to create miracles.* Three Rivers Press.

33. Festinger, L. (1957). *A theory of cognitive dissonance.* Stanford University Press.

34. Aronson, E. (2011). *The social animal* (11th ed.). Worth Publishers.

35. Baumeister, R. F. (2008). *Willpower: Rediscovering the greatest human strength.* Penguin Press.

36. Kolb, D. A. (1984). *Experiential learning: Experience as the source of learning and development.* Prentice Hall.

37. Dewey, J. (1916). *Democracy and education: An introduction to the philosophy of education.* Macmillan.

38. Jensen, E. (2005). *Brain-based learning: The new science of teaching and training.* Corwin Press.

39. Wolpe, J. (1958). *Psychotherapy by reciprocal inhibition.* Stanford University Press.

40. Bandura, A. (1997). *Self-efficacy: The exercise of control.* W. H. Freeman and Company.

41. Emerson, R. W. (1841). *Essays: First series.* James Munroe and Company.

42. Davey, G. C. L. (1992). *The nature of anxiety and fear.* Wiley.

43. Newton, I. (1687). *Philosophiæ naturalis principia mathematica.* Royal Society.

44. Ouellette, J. A., & Wood, W. (1998). Habit and intention in everyday life: The multiple processes by which past behavior predicts future behavior. *Psychological Bulletin,* 124(1), 54-74.

45. Hebb, D. O. (1949). *The organization of behavior: A neuropsychological theory.* Wiley.

46. Baumeister, R. F., & Tierney, J. (2011). *Willpower: Rediscovering the greatest human strength.* Penguin Press.

47. Chopra, D. (2005). *The seven spiritual laws of success: A practical guide to the fulfillment of your dreams.* Amber-Allen Publishing.

48. Goleman, D. (1995). *Emotional intelligence: Why it can matter more than IQ.* Bantam Books.

49. Hicks, E., & Hicks, J. (2004). *Ask and it is given: Learning to manifest your desires*. Hay House.

50. Einstein, A. (1921). *Relativity: The special and general theory*. H. Holt and Company.

Don't Believe In Excuses

1. Duckworth, A. (2016). *Grit: The Power of Passion and Perseverance*. Scribner.

2. Goleman, D. (1995). *Emotional Intelligence: Why It Can Matter More Than IQ*. Bantam Books.

3. Festinger, L. (1957). *A Theory of Cognitive Dissonance*. Stanford University Press.

4. Duckworth, A. (2016). *Grit: The Power of Passion and Perseverance*. Scribner.

5. Bandura, A. (1997). *Self-Efficacy: The Exercise of Control*. W. H. Freeman and Company.

6. Byrne, R. (2006). *The Secret*. Atria Books.

7. Kosslyn, S. M. (1994). *Image and Brain: The Resolution of the Imagery Debate*. MIT Press.

8. Clear, J. (2018). *Atomic Habits: An Easy & Proven Way to Build Good Habits & Break Bad Ones*. Avery.

9. Seligman, M. (2011). *Flourish: A Visionary New Understanding of Happiness and Well-Being*. Atria Books.

10. Lyubomirsky, S. (2007). *The How of Happiness: A New Approach to Getting the Life You Want*. Penguin Press.

11. Meadows, D. H. (2008). *Thinking in Systems: A Primer*. Chelsea Green Publishing.

12. Dweck, C. S. (2006). *Mindset: The New Psychology of Success*. Random House.

13. Duckworth, A. (2016). *Grit: The Power of Passion and Perseverance*. Scribner.

14. Clear, J. (2018). *Atomic Habits: An Easy & Proven Way to Build Good Habits & Break Bad Ones*. Avery.

15. Dispenza, J. (2012). *Breaking the Habit of Being Yourself: How to Lose Your Mind and Create a New One*. Hay House.

16. Iyengar, S. (2010). *The Art of Choosing*. Twelve.

17. Duhigg, C. (2012). *The Power of Habit: Why We Do What We Do in Life and Business.* Random House.

18. Locke, E. A., & Latham, G. P. (2002). *A Theory of Goal Setting & Task Performance.* Prentice Hall.

19. Goddard, N. (2006). *The Power of Awareness.* Martino Fine Books.

20. Dweck, C. S. (2006). *Mindset: The New Psychology of Success.* Random House.

21. Dispenza, J. (2012). *Breaking the Habit of Being Yourself: How to Lose Your Mind and Create a New One.* Hay House.

22. Kahneman, D. (2011). *Thinking, Fast and Slow.* Farrar, Straus and Giroux.

23. Brown, B. (2010). *The Gifts of Imperfection: Let Go of Who You Think You're Supposed to Be and Embrace Who You Are.* Hazelden.

24. Cialdini, R. B. (2007). *Influence: The Psychology of Persuasion.* Harper Business.

25. Dweck, C. S. (2006). *Mindset: The New Psychology of Success.* Random House.

26. Seligman, M. (1975). *Learned Helplessness: A Theory for the Age of Personal Control.* W. H. Freeman.

27. Doidge, N. (2007). *The Brain That Changes Itself: Stories of Personal Triumph from the Frontiers of Brain Science.* Viking Penguin.

28. Emmons, R. A. (2007). *Thanks!: How Practicing Gratitude Can Make You Happier.* Houghton Mifflin Harcourt.

29. Duckworth, A. (2016). *Grit: The Power of Passion and Perseverance.* Scribner.

30. Seligman, M. (1991). *Learned Optimism: How to Change Your Mind and Your Life.* Vintage Books.

31. Dweck, C. S. (2006). *Mindset: The New Psychology of Success.* Random House.

32. van der Kolk, B. (2014). *The Body Keeps the Score: Brain, Mind, and Body in the Healing of Trauma.* Viking.

33. Kahneman, D. (2011). *Thinking, Fast and Slow.* Farrar, Straus and Giroux.

34. Goleman, D. (1995). *Emotional Intelligence: Why It Can Matter More Than IQ.* Bantam Books.

35. Tannen, D. (1998). *The Argument Culture: Stopping America's War of Words*. Random House.

36. Rosenberg, M. (2003). *Nonviolent Communication: A Language of Life*. Puddle Dancer Press.

37. Cloud, H., & Townsend, J. (1992). *Boundaries: When to Say Yes, How to Say No to Take Control of Your Life*. Zondervan.

38. Latané, B., & Darley, J. M. (1970). *The Unresponsive Bystander: Why Doesn't He Help?* Appleton-Century-Crofts.

39. Karau, S. J., & Williams, K. D. (1993). *Social Loafing: A Meta-Analytic Review and Theoretical Integration*. Journal of Personality and Social Psychology, 65(4), 681-703.

40. Bandura, A. (1977). *Social Learning Theory*. Prentice Hall.

41. Sen, A. (1981). *Poverty and Famines: An Essay on Entitlement and Deprivation*. Oxford University Press.

42. Klein, N. (2014). *This Changes Everything: Capitalism vs. The Climate*. Simon & Schuster.

43. The Bhagavad Gita. (2008). *Bhagavad Gita: As It Is* (A.C. Bhaktivedanta Swami Prabhupada, Trans.). Bhaktivedanta Book Trust.

44. Jung, C. G. (1957). *The Undiscovered Self*. Princeton University Press.

45. Clear, J. (2018). *Atomic Habits: An Easy & Proven Way to Build Good Habits & Break Bad Ones*. Avery.

46. Kimmerer, R. W. (2013). *Braiding Sweetgrass: Indigenous Wisdom, Scientific Knowledge, and the Teachings of Plants*. Milkweed Editions.

47. Hayes, S. C., Strosahl, K. D., & Wilson, K. G. (2011). *Acceptance and Commitment Therapy: The Process and Practice of Mindful Change*. Guilford Press.

48. Goddard, N. (2006). *Your Faith is Your Fortune*. Martino Fine Books.

49. Emmons, R. A., & McCullough, M. E. (2003). "Counting blessings versus burdens: An experimental investigation of gratitude and subjective well-being in daily life." *Journal of Personality and Social Psychology*, 84(2), 377-389.

50. Helson, H. (1964). *Adaptation-Level Theory: An Experimental and Systematic Approach to Behavior*. Harper & Row.

51. Frankl, V. E. (1959). *Man's Search for Meaning*. Beacon Press.

52. Fredrickson, B. L. (2001). "The Role of Positive Emotions in Positive Psychology: The Broaden-and-Build Theory of Positive Emotions." *American Psychologist*, 56(3), 218-226.

53. Seligman, M. E. P. (1972). *Learned Helplessness: The Psychology of Failure and Success*. W. H. Freeman.

54. Ericsson, K. A., Krampe, R. T., & Tesch-Römer, C. (1993). "The Role of Deliberate Practice in the Acquisition of Expert Performance." *Psychological Review*, 100(3), 363-406.

55. Beck, A. T. (1976). *Cognitive Therapy and the Emotional Disorders*. International Universities Press.

Focus Only On The Desired State

1. Lewis, C. S. (1952). *Mere Christianity*.

2. Maslow, A. H. (1954). *Motivation and Personality*.

3. Dispenza, J. (2012). *Breaking the Habit of Being Yourself*.

4. Huberman, A. (2021). *Neuroscience of Visualization and Performance*.

5. Busemeyer, J., & Bruza, P. (2012). *Quantum Models of Cognition and Decision*.

6. Clear, J. (2018). *Atomic Habits*.

7. Nolen-Hoeksema, S. (2000). The Role of Rumination in Depressive Disorders and Mixed Anxiety/Depressive Symptoms. *Journal of Abnormal Psychology, 109*(3), 504-511.

8. Lyubomirsky, S., & Tkach, C. (2004). The Consequences of Dysphoric Rumination. *Journal of Personality and Social Psychology, 85*(4), 722-739.

9. Carr, N. (2010). *The Shallows: What the Internet Is Doing to Our Brains*.

10. Schacter, D. L. (2001). *The Seven Sins of Memory: How the Mind Forgets and Remembers*.

11. Bonilla-Silva, E. (2018). *Racism Without Racists: Color-Blind Racism and the Persistence of Racial Inequality in America*.

12. Phelps, E. A. (2004). Human Emotion and Memory: Interactions of the Amygdala and Hippocampus in Memory Consolidation. *Psychological Science, 13*(5), 213-218.

13. Jung, C. (1968). *Psychology and Alchemy.*

14. Goddard, N. (1952). *The Power of Awareness.*

15. Dispenza, J. (2012). *Breaking the Habit of Being Yourself.*

16. James, W. (1897). *The Will to Believe.*

17. Lipton, B. (2005). *The Biology of Belief.*

18. Byrne, R. (2006). *The Secret.*

19. Kosslyn, S. M. (1994). *Image and Brain: The Resolution of the Imagery Debate.*

20. Benedetti, F. (2008). *Placebo Effects: Understanding the Mechanisms in Health and Disease.*

21. Duhigg, C. (2012). *The Power of Habit.*

22. Byrne, R. (2006). *The Secret.*

23. Hebb, D. O. (1949). *The Organization of Behavior: A Neuropsychological Theory.*

24. Seligman, M. E. P. (1991). *Learned Optimism: How to Change Your Mind and Your Life.*

25. Carver, C. S., & Scheier, M. F. (2002). Optimism, Pessimism, and Self-Regulation. *American Psychologist.*

26. Folkman, S., & Lazarus, R. S. (1980). An Analysis of Coping in a Middle-Aged Community Sample. *Journal of Health and Social Behavior.*

27. Festinger, L. (1957). *A Theory of Cognitive Dissonance.*

28. Seligman, M. E. P. (2002). *Authentic Happiness: Using the New Positive Psychology to Realize Your Potential for Lasting Fulfillment.*

29. Maslow, A. H. (1968). *Toward a Psychology of Being.*

30. Hendrick, C. (2013). *Self-Sabotage in Personal and Professional Success: Psychological Patterns and Strategies for Change.*

31. Volkow, N. D., et al. (2014). The Role of THC in Neurological and Behavioral Reinforcement. *New England Journal of Medicine, 370*(23), 2219–2227.

32. Miller, W. R., & Thoresen, J. E. (2003). Religious and Spiritual Transformations and Their Impact on Addiction Recovery. *American Psychologist, 58*(1), 24–35.

33. Draganski, B., et al. (2004). Neuroplasticity and Behavioral Change. *Nature, 427*(6972), 311–312.

34. Wood, W., & Neal, D. T. (2007). Habit Formation and Self-Control Mechanisms. *Psychological Review, 114*(4), 843–863.

35. Baumeister, R. F., & Tierney, J. (2011). *Willpower: Rediscovering the Greatest Human Strength*.

36. Lewis, C. S. (1955). *Surprised by Joy: The Shape of My Early Life*.

37. Dweck, C. (2006). *Mindset: The New Psychology of Success*.

38. Csikszentmihalyi, M. (1990). *Flow: The Psychology of Optimal Experience*.

39. Ericsson, K. A., et al. (2006). *The Cambridge Handbook of Expertise and Expert Performance*.

Flourish But Don't Flaunt

1. Langer, E. J. (1975). The illusion of control. *Journal of Personality and Social Psychology, 32*(2), 311–328.

2. Goleman, D. (1995). *Emotional Intelligence: Why It Can Matter More Than IQ*. Bantam Books.

3. Carleton, R. N. (2016). Fear of the unknown: One fear to rule them all? *Journal of Anxiety Disorders, 41*, 5-21.

4. Machiavelli, N. (1532). *The Prince*.

5. Baumeister, R. F., & Scher, S. J. (1988). Self-defeating behavior patterns among normal individuals: Review and analysis of common self-destructive tendencies. *Psychological Bulletin, 104*(1), 3–22.

6. Whitman, W. (1855). *Song of Myself*. In *Leaves of Grass*.

7. Deci, E. L., & Ryan, R. M. (1985). *Intrinsic Motivation and Self-Determination in Human Behavior*. Springer Science & Business Media.

8. Baumeister, R. F., & Tierney, J. (2011). *Willpower: Rediscovering the Greatest Human Strength*. Penguin Books.

9. Duckworth, A. L., & Eskreis-Winkler, L. (2013). Grit and perseverance: The psychology of effort. *Journal of Personality and Social Psychology, 104*(1), 129-140.

10. Dweck, C. S. (2006). *Mindset: The New Psychology of Success*. Random House.

11. Seligman, M. E. P. (2011). *Flourish: A Visionary New Understanding of Happiness and Well-Being*. Free Press.

12. Ryan, R. M., & Deci, E. L. (2000). Self-determination theory and the facilitation of intrinsic motivation, social development, and well-being. *American Psychologist, 55*(1), 68-78.

13. Sheldon, K. M., & Kasser, T. (1998). Pursuing personal goals: Skills enable progress, but not all progress is beneficial. *Personality and Social Psychology Bulletin, 24*(12), 1319-1331.

14. Baumeister, R. F. (1991). *Meanings of Life*. Guilford Press.

15. Diener, E., & Seligman, M. E. P. (2004). Beyond money: Toward an economy of well-being. *Psychological Science in the Public Interest, 5*(1), 1-31.

16. Lyubomirsky, S. (2007). *The How of Happiness: A New Approach to Getting the Life You Want*. Penguin.

17. Frankl, V. E. (1984). *Man's Search for Meaning*. Beacon Press.

18. Nietzsche, F. (2005). *Thus Spoke Zarathustra*. Penguin Classics.

19. Beck, A. T. (1999). *Prisoners of Hate: The Cognitive Basis of Anger, Hostility, and Violence*. HarperCollins.

20. Peterson, J. B. (2018). *12 Rules for Life: An Antidote to Chaos*. Random House.

21. Duckworth, A. (2016). *Grit: The Power of Passion and Perseverance*. Scribner.

22. Maslow, A. H. (1954). *Motivation and Personality*. Harper.

23. Brown, B. (2017). *Braving the Wilderness: The Quest for True Belonging and the Courage to Stand Alone*. Random House.

24. Ryan, R. M., & Deci, E. L. (2000). Self-determination theory and the facilitation of intrinsic motivation, social development, and well-being. *American Psychologist, 55*(1), 68-78.

25. Festinger, L. (1957). *A Theory of Cognitive Dissonance*. Stanford University Press.

26. Smith, R. H., & Kim, S. H. (2007). Comprehending envy. *Psychological Bulletin, 133*(1), 46-64.

27. Dweck, C. S. (2006). *Mindset: The New Psychology of Success*. Random House.

28. Clear, J. (2018). *Atomic Habits: An Easy & Proven Way to Build Good Habits & Break Bad Ones*. Avery.

29. Wood, W., & Phillips, J. L. (2012). Habit persistence and change: Conditions for habit formation and its role in self-regulation. *European Review of Social Psychology, 23*(1), 288-327.

30. Bandura, A. (1977). Self-efficacy: Toward a unifying theory of behavioral change. *Psychological Review, 84*(2), 191-215.

31. Newton, I. (1687). *Philosophiæ Naturalis Principia Mathematica*.

32. Baumeister, R. F. (1991). *Meanings of Life*. Guilford Press.

33. Festinger, L. (1957). *A Theory of Cognitive Dissonance*. Stanford University Press.

34. Kahneman, D. (2011). *Thinking, Fast and Slow*. Farrar, Straus and Giroux.

35. Schopenhauer, A. (1851). *Parerga and Paralipomena*.

36. Festinger, L. (1957). *A Theory of Cognitive Dissonance*. Stanford University Press.

37. Hohwy, J. (2013). *The Predictive Mind*. Oxford University Press.

38. Alicke, M. D., & Zell, E. (2008). Social comparison and envy. In R. M. Ryan & E. L. Deci (Eds.), *The Oxford Handbook of Human Motivation*. Oxford University Press.

39. Allen, T. D., & Eby, L. T. (2011). *The Blackwell Handbook of Mentoring: A Multiple Perspectives Approach*. Blackwell Publishing.

40. Satir, V. (1988). *The New Peoplemaking*. Science and Behavior Books.

41. Festinger, L. (1957). *A Theory of Cognitive Dissonance*. Stanford University Press.

42. Rosenthal, R., & Jacobson, L. (1968). *Pygmalion in the Classroom: Teacher Expectation and Pupils' Intellectual Development*. Holt, Rinehart & Winston.

43. Cloud, H., & Townsend, J. (1992). *Boundaries: When to Say Yes, How to Say No to Take Control of Your Life*. Zondervan.

44. Deci, E. L., & Ryan, R. M. (1985). *Intrinsic Motivation and Self-Determination in Human Behavior*. Springer.

45. Duckworth, A. L. (2016). *Grit: The Power of Passion and Perseverance*. Scribner.

46. Baumeister, R. F., & Tierney, J. (2011). *Willpower: Rediscovering the Greatest Human Strength*. Penguin Press.

47. Emmons, R. A., & McCullough, M. E. (2003). Counting blessings versus burdens: An experimental investigation of gratitude and subjective well-being in daily life. *Journal of Personality and Social Psychology, 84*(2), 377-389.

48. Goffman, E. (1959). *The Presentation of Self in Everyday Life*. Anchor Books.

49. Niedenthal, P. M. (2007). Embodying emotion. *Science, 316*(5827), 1002-1005.

50. Kahneman, D. (2011). *Thinking, Fast and Slow*. Farrar, Straus and Giroux.

51. Bourdieu, P. (1984). *Distinction: A Social Critique of the Judgment of Taste*. Harvard University Press.

52. Baumeister, R. F., & Leary, M. R. (1995). The need to belong: Desire for interpersonal attachments as a fundamental human motivation. *Psychological Bulletin, 117*(3), 497-529.

53. Dweck, C. S. (2006). *Mindset: The New Psychology of Success*. Random House.

54. Seligman, M. E. P. (2011). *Flourish: A Visionary New Understanding of Happiness and Well-Being*. Free Press.

55. Bandura, A. (1997). *Self-Efficacy: The Exercise of Control*. W. H. Freeman and Company.

56. Ericsson, K. A., & Pool, R. (2016). *Peak: Secrets from the New Science of Expertise*. Houghton Mifflin Harcourt.

Practice Unintentional Asceticism

1. National Endowment for the Arts. (2007). *To Read or Not to Read: A Question of National Consequence* (Research Report #47).

2. Brown, P. C., Roediger, H. L., & McDaniel, M. A. (2014). *Make It Stick: The Science of Successful Learning*. Belknap Press.

3. Wood, W., & Neal, D. T. (2007). A new look at habits and the habit-goal interface. *Psychological Review, 114*(4), 843–863.

4. Sowell, T. (2007). *A Conflict of Visions: Ideological Origins of Political Struggles*. Basic Books.

5. Mischel, W., Shoda, Y., & Rodriguez, M. L. (1989). Delay of gratification in children. *Science, 244*(4907), 933–938.

6. Baumeister, R. F., & Tierney, J. (2011). *Willpower: Rediscovering the Greatest Human Strength*. Penguin Press.

7. Duckworth, A. (2016). *Grit: The Power of Passion and Perseverance*. Scribner.

8. Murphy, J. (2001). *The Power of Your Subconscious Mind*. Bantam.

9. Clear, J. (2018). *Atomic Habits: An Easy & Proven Way to Build Good Habits & Break Bad Ones*. Avery.

10. Odum, E. P., & Barrett, G. W. (2004). *Fundamentals of Ecology*. Brooks Cole.

11. Baumeister, R. F., & Tierney, J. (2011). *Willpower: Rediscovering the Greatest Human Strength*. Penguin Press.

12. Deci, E. L., & Ryan, R. M. (2000). "The 'What' and 'Why' of Goal Pursuits: Human Needs and the Self-Determination of Behavior." *Psychological Inquiry, 11*(4), 227-268.

13. Schwartz, B. (2004). *The Paradox of Choice: Why More Is Less*. Harper Perennial.

14. Festinger, L. (1957). *A Theory of Cognitive Dissonance*. Stanford University Press.

15. Duhigg, C. (2012). *The Power of Habit: Why We Do What We Do in Life and Business*. Random House.

16. Barrett, L. F. (2017). *How Emotions Are Made: The Secret Life of the Brain*. Houghton Mifflin Harcourt.

17. Mischel, W. (2014). *The Marshmallow Test: Mastering Self-Control*. Little, Brown and Company.

Epilogue

1. Duckworth, A. (2016). *Grit: The Power of Passion and Perseverance*. Scribner.

2. Dweck, C. S. (2006). *Mindset: The New Psychology of Success*. Random House.

3. Seligman, M. E. P. (2011). *Flourish: A Visionary New Understanding of Happiness and Well-Being*. Atria Books.

4. Kahneman, D. (2011). *Thinking, Fast and Slow*. Farrar, Straus and Giroux.

5. Duckworth, A. (2016). *Grit: The Power of Passion and Perseverance*. Scribner.

6. Dweck, C. S. (2006). *Mindset: The New Psychology of Success*. Random House.

7. Doidge, N. (2007). *The Brain That Changes Itself: Stories of Personal Triumph from the Frontiers of Brain Science*. Viking.

8. Seligman, M. E. P. (2011). *Flourish: A Visionary New Understanding of Happiness and Well-Being*. Atria Books.

9. Prochaska, J. O., Norcross, J. C., & DiClemente, C. C. (1994). *Changing for Good: A Revolutionary Six-Stage Program for Overcoming Bad Habits and Moving Your Life Positively Forward*. HarperCollins.

10. Deci, E. L., & Ryan, R. M. (2000). The "what" and "why" of goal pursuits: Human needs and the self-determination of behavior. *Psychological Inquiry*, *11*(4), 227-268.

11. Clear, J. (2018). *Atomic Habits: An Easy & Proven Way to Build Good Habits & Break Bad Ones*. Avery.

12. Csikszentmihalyi, M. (1990). *Flow: The Psychology of Optimal Experience*. Harper & Row.

13. Lewis, C. S. (1947). *The Abolition of Man*. Oxford University Press.

14. Frankl, V. E. (1984). *Man's Search for Meaning*. Beacon Press.

15. Haidt, J. (2006). *The Happiness Hypothesis: Finding Modern Truth in Ancient Wisdom*. Basic Books.

www.ingramcontent.com/pod-product-compliance
Lightning Source LLC
Chambersburg PA
CBHW021213130626
46554CB00004B/1200